DOC CHILDRE & SARA PADDISON

EDITED BY HOWARD MARTIN

HEARTMATH®

Discovery

PROGRAM

LEVEL ONE

Daily Readings and
Self-Discovery Exercises
for Creating a More Rewarding Life

PLANETARY

Publishers of the HeartMath® System

P.O. BOX 66, 14700 WEST PARK AVENUE, BOULDER CREEK CA 95006

Publisher: Planetary Publications
              P.O. Box 66
              Boulder Creek, California   95006
              (800)372-3100 (408)338-2161 Fax (408)338-9861

Cover Design by Sandy Royall

Library of Congress Cataloging-in-Publication Data
Childre, Doc Lew, 1945-
    HeartMath discovery program : daily readings and self-discovery exercises for creating a more rewarding life / Doc Childre, Sara Paddison ; edited by Howard Martin
        p.   cm.
    "Level one."
    ISBN 1-879052-28-8 (pbk.)
    1. Conduct of life--Problems, exercises, etc. I. Paddison, Sara, 1953-
II. Martin, Howard, 1949-   . III. Title.
BF637.C5C48 1998
158.1--dc21   98-5774
                                                        CIP

10 9 8 7 6 5 4 3 2 1

Table of Contents

Welcome to the HeartMath Discovery Program

Congratulations on your decision to participate in the HeartMath Discovery Program. You are about to begin your experience of the HeartMath system. More than just new thinking, HeartMath offers a new way of living in a complex and often challenging world. It introduces a new psychology, a new view of physiology and practical, common-sense tools that when applied with sincerity, open the door to new intelligence, increased fulfillment and a higher quality life.

The HeartMath system was created by Doc Lew Childre. Doc spent over twenty years developing HeartMath and proved its effectiveness before officially releasing it to the public in 1991 when he founded and launched the Institute of HeartMath. Tens of thousands of people and hundreds of organizations have now been trained in HeartMath. In addition, the Institute has conducted groundbreaking scientific research which is profoundly impacting medicine and science. HeartMath training programs and materials are making a sustainable difference in the quality of companies, government agencies, schools, communities and in the hearts of people all over the world. Through this program you will have the opportunity to benefit personally from the many years of work put into developing and implementing the HeartMath system.

The HeartMath Discovery Program was created so individuals and small groups could learn and practice HeartMath on their own in an organized and systematic manner. Your guidebook presents six months of specific and sequential study material. Each month is divided into four weeks that consist of five daily lessons per week which include reading material and self-discovery exercises. Each month covers a specific theme and each week within the month will give you an education and experience of a different HeartMath concept and/or tool.

The accompanying audio portion of this program (optional) provides tapes covering each month's material and a cassette copy of *Heart Zones*, scientifically-designed music, which you will use throughout this course. A CD of *Heart Zones* is also included with your study guide, giving you the convenience of access to both formats. Although the program can be easily conducted with just the study guide, it is highly recommended that you obtain the HeartMath Discovery Program audio tapes from Planetary—Publishers of the HeartMath System. The audio tapes are designed to provide an overview of what you will be studying each month, additional information about the subjects you will cover and motivation to energize your practice of the material. Through the HeartMath Discovery Program, you will attain a practical, useful and transformative understanding of the first level of the HeartMath system.

How the HeartMath Discovery Program was Developed

First let me express my gratitude for the time, energy and care that has gone into creating the HeartMath Discovery Program. This program was created by Doc Lew Childre, founder of the Institute of HeartMath (IHM) and president of HeartMath LLC and Sara Paddison, president of IHM. Their desire was to provide a home study resource that anyone could use to learn and apply HeartMath. The design called for materials both written and audio that would lead people through a progression of subjects designed to develop the intelligence of the heart. Doc and Sara intended the program to be applicable to both the individual and small groups.

Mimi Hersh, a long-time member of the Los Angeles HeartMath Hub Group who has spent many years studying the HeartMath system, was given the task of organizing all of Doc and Sara's material for the program to help create the daily lessons. These lessons were drawn from the HeartMath Hub materials, information presented in HeartMath training programs and information from three HeartMath Series books—*Self Empowerment: The Heart Approach to Stress Management* and *FREEZE-FRAME®* by Doc Lew Childre and *The Hidden Power of the Heart* by Sara Paddison. Mimi's own experience and participation in a HeartMath Hub provided a knowledgeable, working understanding of the material.

Next, several key HeartMath staff members and trainers were given assignments to review a particular month/months and informally record a tape describing the essence of what would be studied while adding their own experiences and insights about the material. The purpose of doing this was to include perspectives from experienced HeartMath trainers so the user of the program could benefit from the wealth of experience these people have gained from teaching and applying the tools and concepts presented.

My job and gift was to edit Mimi's work, write scripts from the tapes created by the HeartMath people, produce the finished audio tapes which have been narrated by noted professional reader, Craige Flater, and to act as the creative director on the project. Having spent over twenty five years working with Doc Lew Childre and the development of HeartMath, I found this to be a project I could really put my "heart" into.

The result of these efforts is, I believe, a program that will make a sustainable change in the quality of life for anyone who completes the course. Learning and applying these key HeartMath concepts and tools will not necessarily make all of your problems go away. They will however make it easier to adapt to whatever comes your way and open the door to new, exciting and hopeful possibilities for your present and future realities.

> All the best to you,
> Howard Martin, Editor
> President, Planetary LLC

How to Use the HeartMath Discovery Program

Learning anything new requires a little discipline. If you were learning to play golf or exploring a new software program for your computer, regular practice would be essential for you to master these new skills. The same would be true in using the HeartMath Discovery Program. This program is easy to use. It will however take a commitment from you to find time to listen to your tapes and do the reading and self-discovery exercises that are presented in your guidebook. Completing the daily lesson, five days a week for twenty four weeks, with consistency, will be the key to gaining maximum benefit from this program. Here's how to do it.

1. **Listen:** If you have the audio portion of this program (optional), start each month by listening to the audio tape that corresponds to the month you are working on. Listen to your tape as often as you like. Repeated listening during the month will reinforce your practice of the study material.

2. **Read:** Your guidebook provides daily lessons. Each day you have a short reading assignment titled "Today's Reading."

3. **Write:** After you have completed "Today's Reading," you do a short journaling exercise about what you have just read. Next, you move to the "Exercise" section. Follow the instructions and do written exercises around the subject/tool covered that day.

4. **Practice:** You will have the opportunity to do the "Follow-up Exercise— Bonus Insights" section. This section will give you direction on how to practice what you have learned throughout your day.

5. **Evaluate:** The "Follow-up Exercise—Bonus Insights" section is often accompanied by a journaling exercise where you can record your impressions about the day's practice.

The entire process should take between 20 and 30 minutes each day. It may be preferable to start your daily lesson in the morning so that you can practice what you learned throughout the day. With today's hectic lifestyles this may not always be possible. If this is the case, just try to find times that suit your schedule—perhaps in the evening when you can relax—that still allow you to fully experience each daily lesson.

Once you get started and begin to routinely make time to enjoy your daily lesson, doing the program five days a week will get easier. It will become a regular part of your life—valuable for your growth and well-being and something to look forward to. If for any reason you get off track, that's okay. Just pick up right where you left off and keep at it.

Upon completion of the program, we'd like you to fill out the questionnaire in the back of the guidebook and mail it to us. This will certify your completion of the HeartMath Discovery Program, Level 1. Upon receipt, you will be issued a certificate of completion and you will be entitled to a discount on any HeartMath seminar held at the Institute of HeartMath's training and research center (details are provided on page 380).

If you have access to the internet, we would also like to invite you to participate in the HeartMath Discovery Program discussion group. This on-line discussion group gives people who are using the program an opportunity to share ideas about the subjects covered, ask questions about how the tools are being used, share success stories and so on. You can find the discussion group at http://www.planetarypub.com/HMDchat.html. Just log on and explore HeartMath with your fellow participants in the program.

The HeartMath Discovery program will be enlightening and challenging. You will discover and develop your heart intelligence, which will lead you to new levels of self-management, fulfillment and expanded perception. Enjoy!

HeartMath Hub Groups

The HeartMath Discovery Program was designed for individual and group study. This program will work quite well for individuals studying on their own but just as with most learning, doing it with others can be an advantage.

The Institute of HeartMath has created a study group program which has now produced dozens of HeartMath Hub Groups around the country. HeartMath Hub Groups meet weekly to study materials provided by the Institute of HeartMath which include this program. The Hubs are provided with guidelines for meetings and receive regular communication from the Institute. These groups have been very successful and are an important part of the expansion of the HeartMath system.

If you are interested in starting or joining a HeartMath Hub, please contact Katherine Floriano at:

Institute of HeartMath
14700 West Park Ave.
P.O. Box 1463
Boulder Creek, CA 95006
408-338-8500

MONTH 1
The Science of the Heart

And now here is my secret, a very simple secret; it is only with the heart
that one can see rightly; what is essential is invisible to the eye.

— *Antoine de Saint-Exupery*

DAY 1

Today's Reading

Today, let's get to the heart of the matter. In her book *The Hidden Power of the Heart*, Chapter 2, Sara Paddison shares her discoveries of the profound powers of the heart.

> Scientific research has proven that there is an electrical energy field surrounding the physical heart. What IHM has discovered is that this electrical field of the heart is also a source of higher intelligence providing valuable information for making efficient choices in life. You can access this information by listening to your intuitive feelings or the still, small voice that gives you a sense of inner knowingness. Through learning the difference between the head and the heart, you can utilize the wisdom of what you perceive from the heart to experience more peace and understanding. The heart can bring in the highest intelligence—called heart intelligence or heart power—a power that illuminates understanding.

> As I focused attentively on the core of my heart, I began to experience the heart as a pump for the life force, supplying me with vitality and contact with the energy of my spirit. ...I realized that there is a heart mainframe, a main computer into which every person's heart computer is networked. I saw, too, that love is the power flowing through the global network. At last, I understood how everything in life could really be connected. Love is the electromagnetic core frequency...

Have there been times in your life when you felt especially vibrant and alive, really connected with someone, or everyone, and everything seemed just right? Feelings like this happen when people are in rapport with their heart and you can consistently create more of those fulfilling moments by learning how to access the power of your heart. Remember a time when you felt the power of your heart and write down a few sentences about your experience.

_____

_____

_____

_____

_____

_____

_____

_____

Exercise

Let's begin discovering and experiencing some of the core feelings of the heart: love, care, compassion, tolerance, patience, forgiveness, appreciation and kindness. These feelings are called "core heart frequencies." They are not just "soft" or "mushy" feelings. They are powerful heart-based qualities that regenerate us mentally, emotionally and physically.

Take a few moments now and try to access or feel any of these core heart frequencies. You might want to begin with the feelings of appreciation or care. To help you experience these heart qualities, think about someone or something you appreciate or care about—a person, pet or even a favorite place. As you do this, focus your attention in the area around your heart as if you are breathing in and out through your heart. Relax and enjoy the feeling.

List the heart feelings you accessed and describe the textures or qualities you experienced.

Feelings	*Textures or Qualities*
(e.g. love)	(e.g. peace, contentment)

1. _____
2. _____
3. _____
4. _____
5. _____

Follow Up Exercise—Bonus Insights

Observe yourself throughout the day. Ask yourself from time to time, "Am I experiencing a measure of peace and satisfaction or am I experiencing stress?" If you're like most people caught up in the busy workday, chances are you might be experiencing stress. Take time periodically during the day to try and access a core heart feeling. This will provide regeneration for your system and will help to neutralize stressful feelings.

At the end of your day, jot down your observations from doing this exercise. What insights did you gain from being conscious of your heart and making a conscious effort to generate a core heart feeling? What did you learn from this that will be helpful to you tomorrow?

_____

_____

_____

_____

_____

> Where the heart lies, let the brain lie also.
>
> — *Robert Browning*

DAY ②

Today's Reading

Continuing in Chapter 2, Sara explains how you can improve the quality of life by following your heart directives, guidance and wisdom from within.

> The heart has an electrical system which is forty times stronger than the brain's electrical system. HeartMath research has proven that feelings of love, care, compassion and appreciation produce a measurable, qualitative change in the heart's electrical field and have profound effects on our physical, mental and emotional well-being. Learning to activate and sustain these positive feelings from the heart increases intuition. As you listen to your heart directives and act on what they tell you, you start to reprogram and harmonize your entire mental and emotional nature to bring balance and fulfillment.

Sara's own explorations into her heart led her to further insights and she uses the analogy of a computer to illustrate.

> As time went by I saw more clearly how the heart computer brings in higher intelligence to the human system. The mind becomes illuminated and functions at its fullest potential when it serves as a subterminal for intelligence programs directed by the heart. I practiced and practiced focusing my energies in my heart core to gain even more understandings. I was able to go deeper by radiating out love while I asked questions about the heart, including the physical heart. Love and care are access codes to the deeper heart wisdom, to your higher intelligence programs. Heart understanding is a major shift past ordinary thinking.

Can you recall times when your day flowed smoothly, you had all the answers and didn't let anything disturb you? As you practice going to your heart, you can create more of these days. Recall how you felt during those times when you were in the flow—in your heart—and write down a few sentences about what you remember.

_____

_____

_____

_____

Exercise

You draw more heart intelligence into your awareness as you relax the mind and listen to your heart. Heart intelligence is intuitive knowingness that comes from heart contact and it is experienced as a sense of well being and clarity that feels right. This inner information is called a "heart directive." To begin learning how to recognize and listen to your heart directives, take a few moments now to relax the mind, focus your attention around the area of your heart as if you are breathing through your heart, and listen for your heart directives—a still, small voice inside—a sense of clarity or a positive feeling. Don't try too hard. Just relax, focus on the heart and let your heart be your guide. Write any insights you gained from this experience.

_____

_____

_____

You learn to access heart directives by making an effort to quiet your mind and allow the intuitive intelligence of the heart to unfold. Sometimes it takes a little time before you get a read-out of intuitive intelligence, especially while you're just learning. You are learning to become more sensitive to the intuitive intelligence of the heart. Heart intelligence, combined with the logical, linear processes of the mind, is a powerful combination essential for living a quality life.

You've experienced heart directives before—perhaps many times. Can you remember a personal or professional situation where you chose to act from the heart? In other words, you knew what was best, what to do or not do, and that knowingness was accompanied by a solid, balanced feeling. You just knew. Recall the outcome of this event and write it down.

_____

_____

_____

_____

_____

Follow Up Exercise—Bonus Insights

Living life from the heart creates more efficiency. Observe yourself throughout the day to see if your thoughts and actions feel efficient or inefficient. Are they bringing you more peace and fulfillment or more stress? How you use your time and energy during the course of a day determines the quality of your life experience. It takes remembering and practice to go to the heart and use heart intelligence to guide your actions and decisions, but it's worth the energy investment because it pays big dividends in how you feel in the moment and at the end of the day. Write down any observations you have about your day from observing efficient or inefficient thoughts, feelings and actions.

_____

_____

_____

_____

> The mind in its own place, and of itself,
> can make a heaven of hell, a hell of heaven.
>
> — *John Milton*

DAY ③

 *Today's Reading*

In *The Hidden Power of the Heart,* Chapter 3, "The Head," Sara emphasizes the importance of creating a joint venture between the head and the heart.

The brain/mind/intellect is a fantastic and complicated piece of machinery. For the sake of simplicity, I'll refer to them collectively as the head, since they operate together within a certain frequency range of intelligence called head frequency bands. The principal function of the head is to sort, process and analyze information. The head also assesses, calculates, memorizes and compares. It is a very important and useful part of your system, and you would have a hard time surviving without it.

The head and heart frequencies are designed to work together. When the unmanaged head operates without the wisdom of the heart, it often creates distorted perspectives, resulting in stressful thoughts and emotions. On its own, the head just doesn't have a wide enough range of intelligence to achieve a frequency perspective that creates balance and fulfillment instead of stress.

But again, as wonderful as the head can be, when it's not connected with your heart frequencies and isn't running efficient programs, it creates a lot of stress. Some of the most common stress-producing head frequencies are self-judgments and judgments of others, fear, envy, resentment and worry. These mental attitudes and reactions are by-products of comparison, assessment or analysis without the wider understanding of the heart.

A re there times in your life when you let your head go unmanaged? You may feel like you can't shut off inefficient thoughts or things seem out of control, distorted and unpleasant. Recall how this feels and notice the difference between those feelings and ones generated by making contact with your heart. Jot down your observations.

_____

_____

_____

_____

_____

Exercise

Let's look at your conscious mind. Thoughts can run rampant long after an unpleasant event or experience has ended. As much as you try to shut off your head, the thoughts or memories keep coming back. Negative thought patterns result in stress and wear and tear on your system. This self-defeating mind behavior never brings peace or fulfillment and it accelerates the aging process. Yet we allow these repeating thought patterns to run through our consciousness anyway. This would be an example of a head that is not managed by the heart. If people find themselves in this state, an efficient course of action is to use the power of the heart to bring the mind back into balance, gain new, intuitive perspectives and stop draining ourselves needlessly.

Recall an event or situation that occupies your thoughts. Ask your heart to give you a wider perspective. Remember to focus on the area around your heart and try to feel a core heart feeling instead of thinking about the problem, person, event, etc. This exercise may seem hard at first and you may not be able to stop the thoughts from returning by just making the effort to access your heart. If that's the case, keep trying, and remember to consult your heart regularly during the day. Above all, have patience, and remember that patience is itself a core heart frequency. Over time you can experience a release from the thought patterns. This exercise will help you greatly in bringing your heart and head into alignment as well as stopping an inefficient thought pattern. Write down the insights that you gained from this exercise.

_____

_____

_____

_____

_____

_____

Follow Up Exercise—Bonus Insights

Take the exercise one step further and observe other ways that you are allowing your head to go unmanaged. Then make the effort to make a business deal between your head and heart—a "joint venture"—and synchronize your head and heart to access a more comprehensive intelligence. Observe how much your head and heart are working together. Write down what you observed about yourself before you end your day.

_____

_____

_____

_____

_____

_____

An honest heart being the first blessing, a knowing head is the second.

— Thomas Jefferson

 **DAY 4**

 Today's Reading

Continuing in Chapter 3, "The Head," Sara explains how thoughts can be inefficient expenditures of energy growing in velocity and intensity. As you gain an understanding of the process, you can avoid making mountains out of molehills.

> Take a look at a common scenario: First you feel frustrated with some-one, then you assess their faults, then you feel justified in your feelings, then the anger starts and the negative thought patterns spin, obscuring your view of reality. That's a typical example of a head program running in a loop. Each time the loop goes around, your thoughts increase in speed, intensifying your emotions.
>
> The head magnetically calls up from memory similar experiences you've had, which reinforce that frequency perspective. Then the head pro-gram keeps running that perspective in a loop, adding energy to the loop, building the problem into a mountain, a crisis, instead of just a small bump in life.

> The longer you let negative thought patterns run, the more intensified they become and the harder they are to stop. You don't have to let stress build and accumulate to the point of anguish, tears of despair and numbness.
>
> There is hope! You do have a choice. Your perspective in the moment will influence which direction you take. Your most efficient course of action is to go to your heart and gain the widest possible perspective. Without the heart involved, the head processors often won't shut off, like an old LP record stuck in a groove or a cassette tape in an endless loop.

Think of times when you've been stuck in a mind loop. It's okay. You can gain a wider perspective. Ask your heart for a deeper understanding of the situation. Write a few sentences about when you were caught in a mind loop.

_____

_____

_____

_____

Exercise

Science has long known that thoughts affect physiology and cause undue stress and wear and tear on the system. Try to catch these negative thought patterns and circumvent unnecessary aging of your system. When you find yourself in a loop, it's time to go back to your heart—pronto—and get a new program from the mainframe, the core of your highest intelligence. The heart will bring in more comprehensive intelligence that feels better to your system. Then the head will dutifully formulate that feeling into new thoughts to give you a new perspective of the situation based on heart intelligence. Find a new perspective on an old mind loop. Ask your heart for guidance. Write down your insights.

Mind Loop:

_____

_____

_____

Insights:

_____

_____

_____

As we've discovered, the head has the ability to expand any thought, if we allow it. Is there a possibility that you might have some molehills beginning their upheaval into mountains? If so, now would be a good time to go to your heart and do some major excavating. Write down some of your "mole-hills." Then ask your heart for a better understanding and make a sincere effort to do what it prompts you to do. Write down what your heart says.

Follow Up Exercise—Bonus Insights

Some situations can also create tension and anxiety even before your thoughts about it start to command your attention. These more subtle thoughts or uncomfortable feelings are called "Whisper Worries." You can start to eliminate Whisper Worries by becoming more conscious of them and then intercepting these thoughts with heart intelligence, in the moment, before they evolve into a mind loop. It's really not that hard. Your heart's right there waiting for you to ask it for assistance. By building a solid connection between your head and your heart, you can become more sensitive to your thoughts and can choose to think as you wish. Positive thinking is beneficial but more often than not it takes heart power to sustain it.

Today, observe yourself when you feel tense and anxious. Then consult with your heart to bring these thoughts and feelings into proper perspective. You'll receive answers that give you more understanding and security. Jot down your observations.

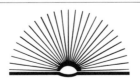

If you look at life one way, there is always cause for alarm.

— *Elizabeth Bowen*

DAY **5**

Today's Reading

In this last section of Chapter 3, "The Head," Sara explains how our thought patterns can hasten the aging process.

> Crystallization is a process that occurs when a thought pattern becomes imprinted in the mind and body. When you become crystallized (or hardened) in your ways, you have no desire to see and understand a wider perspective or improve attitudes within yourself. Crystallizations often form around attachments to "belief structures," your concepts about the way things are.

> The mind decides that it "knows what it knows," and leaves no room for new perspectives. Once people thought the earth was flat. As life variables change, your perspectives and thought patterns have to be able to change too. Don't become stagnant in "knowing what you know." You only hurt yourself when you're not expanding and growing. Many people can't stand the thought of aging, but it's the crystallized thought patterns and inflexible mind-sets that age people before their time.

> If you're attached to certain creature comforts, and believe you must always have them, you lose the flexibility that you had as a child when you were always ready for adventure. Some adults will no longer go to the beach because they don't like getting sand in their clothes. Others will turn down a beautiful hike in the woods because they fear they'll be tired the next morning. New ideas are a bigger challenge when you're crystallized in your ways. Life just can't deliver all the gifts it wants to give you.

C an you think of areas in your life where you have become rigid and inflexible? Write them down.

_____

_____

_____

_____

_____

_____

_____

_____

_____

Exercise

Mind-sets are mind rigidities that say "we know what we know" about people, issues or situations and they keep us from a wider understanding. Sincerely surrendering to your heart intuition gives you access to new intelligence and opens the door for new possibilities. Add heart intelligence to your attitudes and conceptual understandings so the head can operate with less limitation.

Select a situation where you are stuck in a mind-set and ask your heart for another perspective. Write down any new perspectives.

Follow Up Exercise—Bonus Insights

Observe yourself throughout the day. How often do you catch yourself in a mind-set—"knowing what you know"? Are you flexible enough in the moment to go to your heart and get a broader perspective of the situation? Try to be aware of these thoughts sneaking in, in order to maintain the status quo and outsmart them from the heart.

Jot down your observations before you end your day.

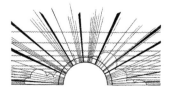

Take a rest, a field that has rested gives a bountiful crop.

— Ovid

DAY ①

Today's Reading

In Chapter 2 of his book, *FREEZE-FRAME®, Fast Action Stress Relief,* Doc Lew Childre explains the purpose of FREEZE-FRAME.

FREEZE-FRAME is a tool whose effectiveness has been scientifically proven in a variety of research studies. This research is proving what many of us already know intuitively—that our mental and emotional attitudes are directly related to the health of our heart, our immune system and our happiness.

FREEZE-FRAME means telling yourself to stop and freeze whatever internal program you are experiencing so that you can evaluate any situation with more clarity. You know what your TV looks like when you press the pause button on the VCR. The picture freezes. When you practice FREEZE-FRAME, you simply become still inside and frame the moment. Then by activating the heart you gain more objectivity and clarity needed for improved decision making. We have all heard the saying, "Be still and know." FREEZE-FRAME shows you how.

FREEZE-FRAME is an important tool that will give you a window of opportunity to make more intuitive decisions rather than mechanical reactions. FREEZE-FRAME means to stop the movie of your life for just a moment and go your heart to gain a wider perspective. When you realize that life is truly a holographic movie which you are co-creating by your choices at every moment, you can begin to re-write the script and change the movie more to your liking.

Think about the times you reacted or made a spur-of-the-moment decision, and later regretted that choice. Then think about the time wasted berating yourself or having to clean up the debris created by that decision. Jot down your insights related to these incidents.

_____

_____

_____

_____

_____

Exercise

You'll start learning the FREEZE-FRAME technique tomorrow. To begin preparing, start by identifying your most common mental and emotional reactions to people and situations. Inefficient responses can drain your energy. Do you experience behavior patterns such as impatience, hurt, disappointment, jealousy, self-doubt, judgment, anger, etc.?

Identify areas in your life where you could use more mental and emotional self-management to become more efficient.

Personal life—relationships, situations, etc.

_____

_____

_____

_____

Business life—relationships, situations, etc.

_____

_____

_____

_____

Follow Up Exercise—Bonus Insights

Continue to observe yourself in any situation—especially the stressful ones, to see if these are patterns you are reacting to from your head or from your heart.

Jot down your observations about the patterns you find.

_____

_____

_____

_____

_____

_____

_____

Inside myself is a place where I live all alone
and that's where you renew your springs that never dry up.
— Pearl S. Buck

DAY ②

Today's Reading

Continuing in his book, Doc shares his insights on the value of FREEZE-FRAME and how it can save tremendous wear and tear on the system.

> Stressful reactions to the events of life drain our vitality and rob us of real quality. Learning how to manage our thoughts and feelings so that we can adapt to challenges is a key step in attaining fulfillment. Many times people have to wait until they are in a quiet place or on a vacation to re-group and unwind from the accumulation of stress. Managing stress after the fact is like closing the barn door after the horses have already gotten out—the damage is already done. Once we experience a stressful episode, we then have to re-accumulate the energy that was lost to bring our system—mental, emotional and physical—back into balance. Efficient living would involve taking care of business in the moment so that we do not have to experience the degenerative effects of our own internal reactiveness. By learning to step back in the moment, FREEZE-FRAME, and use the heart when life is presenting a situation that may lead to a stress-producing perception, we save a tremendous amount of energy. The energy that we save from learning how to become self-managed can, instead, be used creatively, providing us with more fun, improved health and sustained fulfillment. Heart Intelligence is the key and FREEZE-FRAME is a tool that can get you there fast.

❦

Adding heart to any moment changes the quality of your perspectives. Even when life is good it can get better when experienced through the heart. Activating heart energy pays back in a ratio of 1:9. One sincere effort to listen to and follow your heart—one sincere effort to put out love where you would have become insecure or angry—pays back nine times. Your 9's are gifts that come in many wonderful ways—more peace, fun, deeper relationships, surprise events and more. The more you practice, the more the system will work for you.

Can you recall a time when perhaps you reluctantly changed your attitude towards a person or situation and surprisingly things turned out better than you would have ever anticipated? In other words, you did a 1 and got a 9 return. Recall some of those experiences and jot them down.

_____

_____

_____

_____

Exercise

Let's become familiar with the steps of the FREEZE-FRAME technique. Here are the steps:

1. Recognize the stressful feeling and FREEZE-FRAME it. Take a time out.

2. Make a sincere effort to shift your focus to the area around your heart. Pretend you are breathing through the heart to help focus your energy in this area. Keep your focus there for ten seconds or more.

3. Recall a fun, positive feeling or time you've had in life and attempt to re-experience it.

4. Now, using your intuition, common sense, and sincerity, ask your heart—what would be a more efficient response to the situation—one that would minimize future stress?

5. Listen to what your heart says in answer to your question.

It's good to close your eyes while learning how to FREEZE-FRAME. It can also be helpful to put your hand on your heart in step 2 to help focus your attention there. Let's try it and do a written exercise. You can study the example work sheet to gain more clarity on how to do this exercise.

INSTITUTE OF HEARTMATH®

FREEZE-FRAME® WORKSHEET

STEPS:

1. STRESSFUL SITUATION: Write down a few words that describe the situation.
2. HEAD REACTION: write down how you have been mentally or emotionally reacting to this situation.
3. FREEZE-FRAME: Take a time-out!
4. SHIFT TO THE HEART: Focus your attention in the area around the heart for 20 to 30 seconds.
5. ACTIVATE A HEART FEELING: Recall a positive experience or feel care or appreciation for someone or something.
6. ACCESS HEART PERSPECTIVE: Use your intuition, common sense, and sincerity to determine what would be a more efficient response to the situation and write it down.

STRESSFUL SITUATION   I'm in a hurry and the line at the food store is taking too long.

HEAD REACTION   I was supposed to be at the meeting 5 minutes ago, and this checker is taking FOREVER! I can't believe she's talking and joking with the customers ahead of me—doesn't she realize some people have more important things to do than stand here in this line? Her easy-going attitude is really getting on my nerves.

FREEZE-FRAME

HEART PERSPECTIVE   Because I was feeling so stressed and hurried, I was directing my irritation at this checker, who in reality is doing a good job while maintaining her own sense of humor under trying circumstances (a long line of people). The line is going to take however long it takes and I can choose to spend the rest of my time in line appreciating the people who contribute to making the food available at this store, from the farmers to the middle men to the truckers, stockers, managers, checkers and so on. That will be good for me and it will help others.

❖INSTITUTE OF HEARTMATH • P.O. Box 1463 • Boulder Creek, CA 95006 • Tel. 408-338-8700 • fax 408-338-9861

Identify an area in your life that is causing you stress. Don't pick your biggest stressor yet; you are just learning. Write down a few words about the situation. Next, write down how you have been reacting to it under Head Reaction. Now close your eyes and try the steps of FREEZE-FRAME. After doing the technique, write down any new perspectives about how to handle the situation under Heart Intuition Response.

Situation

_____

_____

Head Reaction

_____

_____

_____

Heart Intuition Response

_____

_____

_____

_____

Observe the difference between what you have written down under Head Reaction and Heart Intuition Response to see what shifts in perception have come from doing this simple exercise.

It's important to know that sometimes you may not get an answer right away or the answer you do get can be simple, common sense or something you already knew. Other times you may experience a major shift in perspective. With sincere practice, FREEZE-FRAME can produce these kinds of shifts with consistency.

Follow Up Exercise—Bonus Insights

Try to use the FREEZE-FRAME technique during the day. At least three times during the day, stop and do a short FREEZE-FRAME. You don't necessarily need to write anything down but it can be very helpful if you do while learning the technique. It may be when you are feeling stressed or when you would just like an extra boost of intuitive, heart-based intelligence.

Jot down your insights about doing these three FREEZE-FRAMES today.

_____

_____

_____

_____

_____

Do you know that every moment of your life you're creating
through thought? You create your own inner condition;
you're helping create the conditions around you.

Peace Pilgrim

DAY 3

Today's Reading

In Chapter 4, Doc explains the scientific benefits of FREEZE-FRAME.

There is a two-way communication between the heart and the brain
that regulates heart rate and blood pressure....Our perceptions and
emotional reactions are transmitted between the heart and brain via
the sympathetic and parasympathetic nervous systems and can be seen
in the patterns of our heart rhythms (as measured by heart rate variability—HRV).... For example, when you're frustrated, your nervous
system is out of balance, your blood vessels constrict, blood pressure
rises, and you waste a lot of energy. If this happens consistently, ...you
greatly increase your risk of heart disease.

On the other hand, feelings of sincere appreciation create cardiovascular efficiency. The two nervous systems are "entraining" and working
together at maximum efficiency instead of fighting each other. When
your head and heart, thoughts and feelings, are working harmoniously
together, you have more clarity and inner balance—and you feel better.

———

Heart rate variability is an excellent measure of nervous system balance, and research is showing that our perceptions and reactions affect
our heart rhythms. Therefore, heart rate variability is an important
indication of how well we are balancing our lives. As you become practiced in FREEZE-FRAME, you can balance your nervous systems and
change your heart rhythm patterns in the moment.

Think about the times when you were out of balance and could feel the effects of stress in your body: headache, stiff neck, tightness in your back and shoulders, butterflies in your stomach, etc. Jot down how you feel physically in stressful situations.

_____

_____

_____

_____

Exercise

People spend a lot of time keeping spreadsheets, checkbook ledgers, and balance sheets of their finances in order to be efficient with money. Here is an exercise to keep track of your "energy bank account"—which energy expenditures are adding to your account and which are depleting it. Review your day yesterday. Determine what events, interactions, etc. added energy or quality to your life and write them down under assets. Next, determine what things depleted your energy or decreased the quality of your life and write them down under deficits. Look at what you have written down. This will give you a picture of your day from a new perspective.

Assets	*Deficits*
Efficient and Fulfilling Thoughts and Actions	*Inefficient Thoughts and Actions*

In looking at your deficits, what events, episodes, actions, reactions, etc. could have been handled differently with FREEZE-FRAME? Pick one of them and do a written FREEZE-FRAME exercise to determine what the best course of action would now be. Just write down the situation, then briefly describe how you handled it. Then go through the steps of FREEZE-FRAME and write down your new insights.

Situation

_____

_____

Head Reaction

_____

_____

_____

Heart Intuition Response

_____

_____

_____

_____

Follow Up Exercise—Bonus Insights

Review the steps of FREEZE-FRAME and make an effort to use FREEZE-FRAME as often as you can during the day when you need clarity or want to reduce stress. Try it three times today.

A wiser man changes his mind; a fool never.

— *Unknown*

DAY 4

Today's Reading

Continuing in Chapter 4, Doc explains how unmanaged thoughts and emotions affect health.

IgA (immunoglobulin A) is an immune system antibody and one of the body's first lines of defense against colds, flu and infections of the respiratory and urinary tracts. IgA is found in our saliva, blood, lungs, digestive and urinary systems. In a group study (twenty individuals) comparing the effects of anger versus care and compassion on average IgA levels, it was found that one five-minute episode of mentally and emotionally recalling an experience of anger and frustration caused an immediate but short rise of IgA, followed by a depletion that was so severe it took the body more than six hours to restore normal production of IgA. What this study showed is that even a single episode of recalling an experience of anger and frustration can depress your immune system for almost an entire day.

———

This same IgA study also showed that one five-minute episode of mentally and emotionally experiencing the emotions of care and compassion caused a much larger, immediate rise in IgA—an average of 34%—followed by a return to normal (baseline). However, the IgA levels then gradually climbed above baseline throughout the next six hours. With today's hectic lifestyle, how many of us have more enjoyable experiences, care, fun or passion for life than we do anger or frustration on any given day? Learning to manage the moment and increase the ratio of our positive attitudes and feelings can improve our quality of life and well-being.

Are there times when you were having fun or sincerely helping someone or deeply appreciating an experience? Recall those times. How do they make you feel mentally, emotionally and physically? Do they add quality to your day? Jot down your insights about today's reading.

_____

_____

_____

_____

Exercise

FREEZE-FRAME is also a valuable tool to use to solve communication or relationship issues. FREEZE-FRAME can help give you insights on how to improve the quality of any communication. Are there areas of your life where you feel you would like to improve communication between you and another person? Write down the communication or relationship issue. Do a FREEZE-FRAME exercise to gain more clarity on how to improve this situation.

Situation

_____

_____

Head Reaction

_____

_____

_____

Heart Intuition Response

_____

_____

_____

Remember to FREEZE-FRAME before that important meeting or before you pick up the telephone to make a call. One of the advantages of FREEZE-FRAME is you can do it anywhere, anytime.

Follow Up Exercise—Bonus Insights

Now that you have learned how to FREEZE-FRAME, try doing it casually with your eyes open during the day. See how you can apply it creatively to stay balanced and to have more consistent access to the intelligence of the heart. Jot down your observations about actively applying FREEZE-FRAME today.

If your thoughts are thoughts that draw low-frequency energy current to you, your physical and emotional attitudes will deteriorate, and emotional or physical disease will follow, whereas thoughts that draw high-frequency energy current to you create physical and emotional health.

— *Gary Zukav*

DAY ⑤

📖 *Today's Reading*

Doc concludes Chapter 4 with a detailed explanation of how our perceptions trigger a cascade of physiological events which determine our behavior and in turn affect our next perception and, ultimately, affect our health.

> The FREEZE-FRAME technology focuses your attention in the area around the heart (where people subjectively feel love, care, appreciation, etc.) These feelings have been shown to help balance the nervous systems. When you FREEZE-FRAME, an electrical signal is triggered in the perceptual center in the brain via another set of nerves which lead from the brain to the heart. This helps to give you a more balanced perspective of any situation.

> Your perceptions trigger your mental and emotional responses, which cause electrical changes in the nervous system, heart and brain. Those electrical changes directly affect your heart rate, blood pressure, hormonal and immune response, which in turn influence health and aging. These changes result in physical energy or depletions, mental and emotional clarity or the lack of it, whether you relate well to others or not, and how well you relate to yourself. As you practice FREEZE-FRAME, you will gain a higher ratio of positive to negative effects on your health and well-being.

> FREEZE-FRAME is a technology that gives you the conscious ability to self-manage your reactions, gain clarity and have more quality, fun

and well-being in the moment. You gain the power to make better choices and decisions and not be victimized by your reactions to people, places and situations. Just as the detrimental effects of stress are cumulative, so are the beneficial effects of FREEZE-FRAME. Practice leads to increased mental and emotional buoyancy, cardiovascular efficiency and improved quality of life. Learning to manage the moment can literally change the quality of your life.

Have you noticed any changes in how you feel (mentally, emotionally, physically) after having consistently and sincerely practiced FREEZE-FRAME? Jot down your observations.

_____

_____

_____

_____

Exercise

FREEZE-FRAME can also be used to enhance creativity. It's much more than a stress management tool. It is actually a convenient doorway to intuitive intelligence. Is there a project that you are working on which could use a creative boost or perhaps an idea that could benefit from a more creative approach? FREEZE-FRAME can assist you. Pick a project or idea you would like more creativity on. Go through the steps of FREEZE-FRAME and write down your insights. If you don't get what you need from doing one FREEZE-FRAME exercise, do it again or later on until you feel you have accessed as much creativity as you can.

Project or Idea

_____

_____

_____

_____

Heart Intuition Response

_____

_____

_____

FREEZE-FRAME is a powerful tool to bring more peace, fun and fulfillment into your life. Have you noticed any differences in yourself or in the way others react to you since you have begun to practice FREEZE-FRAME? How has it affected your day-to-day life? Remember, the more you practice, the more the system will work for you. Write down the insights you have gained from practicing FREEZE-FRAME.

_____

_____

_____

_____

Follow Up Exercise—Bonus Insights

Learn to self-correct during the day by practicing your FREEZE-FRAME exercises. Make a fun game out of how fast you can catch yourself in an inefficient reaction or thought pattern and FREEZE-FRAME. See the difference in your heart intelligence perspective compared to the head reaction. Your heart will give you a wider, positive view of the same situation if you let it. And, remember to use FREEZE-FRAME to enhance creativity or when you just want to make contact with your heart. Write down the three most important insights you gained this week.

1. _____

2. _____

3. _____

Peace is a daily, a weekly, a monthly process, gradually changing opinions, slowly eroding old barriers, quietly building new structures.

— John F. Kennedy

DAY (1)

Today's Reading

Stress pervades our society. According to Sara Paddison, in Chapter 4 of her book, *The Hidden Power of the Heart*, stress is "the social disease" with disastrous effects:

> ...prolonged exposure to stress can accelerate the aging of brain cells in the same region of the brain affected by Alzheimer's disease, leading to impairment of learning and memory....people who bottled up their emotions under stress were likely to be more prone to cancer. Stress has been correlated with a higher risk for heart disease and is quickly proving to be the leading cause of death.
>
> It's really not the major crises that create the most stress. It's the constant daily hassles that cause so many to say they experience high levels of stress. A recent Harris poll showed that 89% of all adults—158 million Americans from all walks of life—experience what they call high levels of stress....90% of all adults surveyed said they experience high levels of stress once or twice a week; 25% experience high levels of stress every day. No wonder 75% of all doctors' visits are for stress-related complaints!

> Stress is the mental and physical strain caused by having more to cope with than one can comfortably handle. The missing formula for stress relief is within your heart. It's strong, unmanaged head frequency bands that block one's heart intelligence from being able to prevent and release stress. It is your reaction to each event that determines your level of stress.

Your perceptions and reactions to events affect your level of stress. For example, what is your reaction if you're caught in a traffic jam on the way to work? Since you can't change the situation, all you can change is your perception of the traffic jam. An energy-efficient response would be to use the time to plan your day or perhaps see it as an opportunity to practice FREEZE-FRAME. An inefficient response would be to get upset and angry about a situation over which you have no control. You would arrive at work either ready to go or drained—in the same amount of time. Write down what you consider to be "traffic jams" in your life.

_____

_____

_____

Exercise

Symptoms of stress are like alarm clocks going off—signals of inefficient energy expenditures. They are your system's natural way of giving feedback, of telling you something needs adjusting. Take this stress test to get a read-out on the amount of stress in your life. Check off the areas that apply to you.

❏ feeling you have no time
❏ moodiness; lots of ups and downs
❏ inability to concentrate
❏ bored
❏ quick to get irritated or frustrated
❏ short tempered
❏ feeling unloved or unliked
❏ headaches; too much to cope with
❏ can't shut your mind off and relax
❏ pain in the neck or back
❏ loss of or excessive appetite

❏ other _____

Is there stress in your life that could be alleviated or lessened by changing your perception? Write down a situation that is causing you stress and go through the steps of FREEZE-FRAME to shift your perspective. Write down your new perspectives.

Situation

Head Reaction

Heart Intuition Response

Follow Up Exercise—Bonus Insights

Observe yourself throughout the day. Are you responding to stressful situations from the heart or reacting from the head? Remember to FREEZE-FRAME as these situations arise. Jot down your observations.

What we call "normal" in psychology is really a psychopathology of the average,
so undramatic and so widespread that we don't even notice it.

— *Abraham Maslow*

DAY ②

 Today's Reading

In Chapter 1 of *Self Empowerment: The Heart Approach to Stress Management*,
Doc Lew Childre talks about the importance of self-management so that we
are able to deal with stress.

> External situations (such as traffic jams, job anxieties, problems at home,
> etc.) create inner stress. When you experience stress, then hormones
> and other bio-chemical reactions are released in your system which
> can cause dis-ease and debilitations in your mental, emotional and
> physical nature. Learning how to manage stress develops the ability to
> self-regulate your hormonal patterns—meaning that you become an
> efficient "self-pharmacist" in a sense. Your most productive drugs are
> within your own endocrine system. In other words, you could stay
> younger longer—feel more alive and especially have more energy and
> vitality—depending on your hormonal flow. You influence this flow
> more than you may think by the management or non-management of
> attitudes and thought patterns. Developing a closer relationship with
> your heart intuition efficiently guides you through your own energy-
> management process.

> At the present level of global consciousness, people tend to think that
> living with stress is natural. Well, it's not natural. It's just a result of
> social ignorance, but innocently so until society is educated otherwise.

> Some wait and hope for things to get better, but it's people who have
> to better themselves by learning to manage their energy expenditures.
> It's the lack of self-government in the mental, emotional and physical
> aspects of your nature that leaves you vulnerable to stress overloads.

Are there stressful areas in your life which you have come to accept as "natural"? Jot down your insights in light of the above information.

_____

_____

_____

_____

_____

_____

_____

Exercise

Some people say that stress is actually good. It's important to know the difference between stress and creative resistance energy. Stress dilutes your energy, while creative resistance energy can be a healthy challenge with the right attitude. For example, when you transform resistances into fun creative achievements—such as weightlifting, jogging that extra mile, meeting a deadline, closing a sale, etc.—you're still releasing positive hormones into your system. Working late on a job you do not like and wishing you were out of there would have a very different effect. As you meet resistances, it's your attitude that regulates the amount of stress in the outcome. The balancing and management of attitudes is a key factor in understanding and dissipating stress.

Think of a creative achievement, where you succeeded against resistance. Recall how that felt versus how you feel when you have to work extra hard to accomplish a task "when your heart just wasn't into it."

Are you waiting for a situation to change so that you can reduce your stress and have inner peace? If you wait for the economy to improve or the wars to stop before you have peace, you could have a long wait. Or, if you wait for relationships to change, or for children to meet your idealistic expectations or for harmony in your workplace before you have inner peace, you may never find it. Consult with your heart and ask what you can do or change to alleviate the stress in a particular area in your life. Listen to the intelligent truth in your own heart, find your own peace and write down what it says.

Situation

Heart Response

Follow Up Exercise—Bonus Insights

The power to think yourself into misery is within you and the power to stop it is within you also. Observe yourself throughout the day to see if you are blaming other people and circumstances for your stress. Take responsibility for your reactions by going to your heart for an efficient way to handle these situations. Jot down your observations about any blame of others, situations, etc. you may have experienced today.

Men often bear little grievances with less courage than they do large misfortunes.

—*Aesop*

 **DAY 3**

Today's Reading

Continuing in Chapter 4, *The Hidden Power of the Heart*, Sara explains how so many have come to associate stress with major crises. However, it's really the daily hassles which rob us of our vitality.

> A constant dose of minor irritations and griping will feed back in your system over time, robbing you of your energy and vitality. It's really not the major crises that create the most stress. As I've said before, in a major crises, people do tend to go to their heart. People seek out friendship and receive understanding from others. Just think of all the heart-warming stories of communities banding together after a disaster...It's really the constant daily hassles that cause so many to say they experience high levels of stress.

> Managing your reactions to stressful situations is the key to health and well-being. Stress is not just an effect. Stress accumulated in the system not only causes many major life crises—like divorce, a teenager in trouble, a heart attack, drug or alcohol addiction, and many other chronic, human social problems—but diminishes our ability to deal with them effectively. When you overload your head computer with negative thoughts and feelings, you eventually "CRASH," at which point you cease to function normally, mentally, emotionally or physically.

> Pain is louder stress, a screaming alarm bell warning us that something is not right. Irritation + frustration + anger + judgment + resentment = a guaranteed formula for stress.

C onsider how not dealing with inefficient attitudes and perspectives can eventually deplete your system and keep you from experiencing the quality life you could easily have—a life with more fun and less stress. Write down your insights about what you have read today.

_____

_____

_____

_____

_____

Exercise

Stress is an inharmonious energy or experience that results from inefficient reactions. It leaves you exhausted and unfulfilled by the end of the day. Review your day yesterday to see where you could have been more energy-efficient with your actions and reactions. Remember, it's often the little things that count. At the same time, why not give yourself a pat on the back for those times you were energy-efficient and write them down too?

Inefficient Actions or Reactions	*Efficient Actions or Reactions*

Frustrated reactions to minor, everyday hassles create stress and constrict your flow of energy. Identify a "daily hassle" that you are allowing to create stress for you and use FREEZE-FRAME for deeper understanding and a new direction.

41

Situation

_____

_____

Head Reaction

_____

_____

_____

Heart Intuition Response

_____

_____

_____

Follow Up Exercise—Bonus Insights

Observe yourself throughout the day and take an inventory of how you are dealing with those daily hassles. Are you responding efficiently or inefficiently? Working on the little things accumulates power to deal with larger issues when they come up. Jot down what you observed.

_____

_____

_____

_____

_____

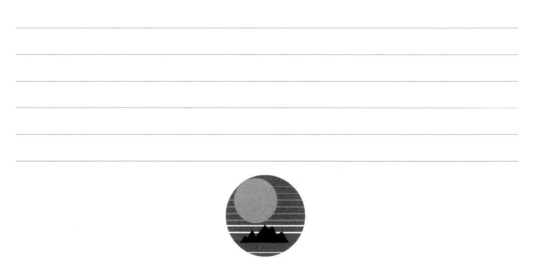

Happy are they that hear their detractions and can put them to mending.
—*Shakespeare*

DAY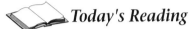

Today's Reading

Continuing in Chapter 4, "Stress: The Social Disease," Sara explains how our stressful reactions to situations can have negative effects on our physiology, as well as exacerbate the situation itself. She suggests that when we can't change the external conditions, perhaps it's time to make internal changes—within ourselves.

Stressors are stimuli that can cause physiological or behavioral changes in people. When people can't handle stressors efficiently, whether on the job or at home, internal stress results. Often we can't change our environment, at least not in the moment. We can, however, change ourselves so that we can handle our environment without creating stress in ourselves. Stress never feels good, nor does it make for a fulfilling lifestyle. Lack of self-management is what can cause a massive stress buildup within a person's system. The mind bounces back and forth with thoughts—about the day, about the future, about the past, about "Where should I be?" "What should I do next?" "Which direction should I go?" and on and on. When the head gets going, it can seize on a thought and make a headstrong decision that is not easily restrained. If that decision doesn't work out as you hoped, you can feel miserable, defeated.

Ironically, many people who want to change the world become so frustrated, angry and resentful, they dilute their power to change the conditions that cause their frustration. You can see this in certain people in the environment, abortion rights, equal opportunity and peace movements. This is not to say that we shouldn't work for social change. But by learning to manage our stress, we can increase our power to implement the positive changes we want to see.

Think of something that you really believe in or want to see change, but it's causing you stress. Is your reaction facilitating the change you desire or impeding its progress? Are your attachments to ideas, expectations, etc. causing you stress and, in the process, diluting your effectiveness? Are your mind-sets blocking you from trying to find another perspective? Jot down your feelings about what you have just read.

Exercise

Identify a situation that you can't possibly change, or change in the immediate future. It could be a social issue that is beyond your control or perhaps a personal situation that will take time to resolve if ever. Look at how this may be affecting you. It may seem difficult, but make the effort and try to see it as untransformed opportunity for empowerment rather than a hinderance. Now, do a FREEZE-FRAME and use the power of your heart to find the wider perspective. See how you can better deal with the situation in ways that save you from stress. Even eliminating some of the stress around the situation can be of great benefit to you physically, mentally and emotionally.

Situation

Heart Intuition Response

_____

_____

_____

Follow Up Exercise—Bonus Insights

The purpose of stress isn't to hurt you, but to let you know it's time to go back to the heart and balance out your system. Observe yourself throughout the day and when situations arise that might be stress-producing, go back to the heart and activate a core heart feeling.

Without inner peace, it is impossible to have world peace.

— *The Dalai Lama*

DAY ⑤

Today's Reading

Continuing in Chapter 4, Sara makes us aware of the insidiousness of stress. However, at the same time, she does give us hope! It is possible to live in peace.

> Global stress is accumulating at a faster rate in the '90s because of constant unmanaged head processors, nervous systems on overload and the pressure to make fast decisions in a time of rapid change. The struggle to make decision after decision has become so confusing and overwhelming that people are frustrated with life.

> As stress sets in and isn't released, it wears and tears on your entire system. It wears and tears on the family, schools, businesses, government—the entire social system. There is great injury happening to individuals in our society today as a result of stress. Much of it occurs silently inside. It occurs inside the mind before it inflicts itself on others or on one's own body. There is a way out. You can start by learning to balance yourself, day-to-day, by using your heart computer—your higher intelligence. As you begin to practice, you will discover that there is a place beyond suffering. You begin to see clearly that you can choose how you react to any situation in life.

> Through the hidden power of the heart, it really is possible to bring the peace of heaven to earth. As you learn to manage your day-to-day stress, you will find your next level of peace. Peace is the opposite of stress. Those two frequencies—peace and stress—cannot live in the same place as they cancel each other out. It is each individual's choice. The game of life is a game with you and you. You can heart empower yourself, once you know how. You can de-stress your life. It starts with de-stressing the simple ordinary day-to-day hassles.

Think of heart-based patterns that you have developed naturally that save you from stress. It could be something like having patience and not minding if you have to stand in lines or you are naturally kind and don't get angry easily when things don't go your way. How could these same qualities be applied to other areas that do cause you stress? Jot down your insights.

_____

_____

_____

_____

Exercise

Observe and identify whether your stress responses come from the heart or from the unmanaged head. See where your head, when not connected to your heart, takes you. Evaluate whether the head, operating on its own, produces efficient or inefficient expenditures of your energy. Notice how operating more from heart intelligence affects your attitudes, your under-standings, your communications with others and your stress levels. With self-management from the heart, you can achieve real peace and inner security in a stressful world. Write down your insights about this self-observation.

_____

_____

_____

_____

_____

_____

_____

Follow Up Exercise—Bonus Insights

Reflect on your week. See how much progress you have made in eliminating stress by using FREEZE-FRAME and the power of your heart. Remember, every time you stop a stressful reaction you gain energy—energy that will add sparkle and quality to your life. Write down the three most important things you have gained from this week's practices.

1. _____

_____

_____

2. _____

_____

_____

3. _____

_____

_____

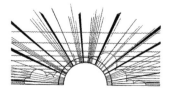

> The heart has such an influence over the understanding
> that it is worth while to engage it in our interest.
>
> — *Lord Chesterfield*

DAY ①

Today's Reading

In *The Hidden Power of the Heart*, Chapter 5, "Higher and Lower Heart Frequencies," Sara gives us some insights on the importance of the heart in managing our emotions.

"E-motion" is energy in motion. It amplifies or adds a charge to your thoughts and feelings. Emotions can be called the affective aspect of your consciousness.... But emotional energy in itself is neutral. It picks up its coloration either from the head or from the heart. Emotional energy can be added either to a disturbance or to a fun excitement....How we manage our emotions determines whether they add quality to our lives or bring us stress....The head alone cannot manage the emotions or heal the mind when it short circuits.

Too much emotion becomes emotionalism, the indulgence in unbalanced emotion. Emotionalism may feel good in the moment, but doesn't solve the basic problem. It can also drain the vitality out of your system. Emotionalism can also be created on the opposite side of the spectrum by over-excitement. While genuinely looking forward to a vacation or a special date, you can overload your emotional nature with anxiety, expectations and an impatient feeling of "can't wait." That overload unbalances your energies, blocking your heart flow.

———— ❦ ————

When your emotions are managed, not suppressed, they can be used to add more fun, texture and quality to life. They are like free fuel for your system; but if left unmanaged they're highly flammable. As you find balance between your heart and your head, your emotions turn into creative passion and become a tremendous asset.

49

Y our heart is your best friend and best ally in managing your emotions so they can work for you. Ask your heart for guidance on how to better manage emotions. Jot down any insights.

_____

_____

_____

_____

Exercise

Expectations are often the result of unmanaged emotions and expectation can become an energy drain. It's not good to build an expectation so huge that if what you're wanting doesn't happen, you will be crushed or deeply disappointed. A good way to approach expectations is to manage your perspectives so you can be excited about an upcoming situation, a fun "can't wait," but in a balanced way. By using your heart to balance emotionalism, you aren't shoveling the emotions under the carpet or repressing them. You're taking control of them so they work for you to keep the fun and adventure in life going your way.

Ask your heart to give you a balanced approach to a situation about which you might be overly expectant.

Situation

_____

_____

Heart Response

_____

_____

_____

Follow Up Exercise—Bonus Insights

Observe yourself throughout the day. Are your emotions draining you or are they adding quality to your life? It could be both. At the end of your day, jot down your observations in answer to this question.

> One ought to hold on to one's heart;
> for if one lets it go, one soon loses control of the head too.
>
> *Nietzsche*

DAY ②

 Today's Reading

In Chapter 5 of his *FREEZE-FRAME* book, Doc helps us to understand the power of emotions and our need for emotional management.

> People know their emotions can be like a dark cloud, making it difficult to see solutions. FREEZE-FRAME will help you calm your emotions so they won't keep rampaging the mind. When the emotions are backed off, your mind has a chance to achieve clear common sense. In talking about the necessity of managing the emotions, I'm not trying to imply that your emotions are the bad guy in the human system, or that FREEZE-FRAME is intended to suppress them. I am saying that you'll save energy when you learn to first neutralize their intent before you engage them. When the heat of the emotions is turned down, the mind can see more options and more solutions. As research has proven, when your unmanaged emotions fuel negative thought patterns, you pay a price in accelerated aging, weakened immune system and impaired cardiovascular function. Letting excessive negative emotions blow through your system is like having a big hole blow right through your balloon of energy. Everything can be drained out of you in a matter of moments. It can take hours, day, even weeks to recover. Some people suffer this so frequently, they never "recover." They never experience the kind of clarity that comes with emotional balance.

You often hear people say, "I was having a good time until I lost my temper and exploded." That's like saying you tried to park a car going 70 miles an hour. That's dangerous. It's the head thoughts that get you angry, triggering the emotions and hormones that create temper. Even if temper feels good in the moment, there are a lot of friends lost, rash decisions made, and even deaths caused by unmanaged temper. It's okay to have some feistiness in your system. However, it's important to manage it in a way that you feel at peace with the consequences of your actions.

All of us have had times when we knew our emotions were clouding our judgment. Now you can access the power of your heart to help you manage your emotions in the moment and maintain clarity when emotions start to override your better judgment. Jot down your insights about what you have just read today.

_____

_____

_____

_____

Exercise

It's your own mental, emotional and physical health you promote by reframing your attitudinal approaches to people and issues in life. But these kinds of perceptions will never change if you don't learn how to manage your emotions. To turn emotional deficits into rewarding assets, we first need to recognize emotional stress.

Which of these emotional stresses apply to you?

❑ Quick to get irritated, frustrated or angry
❑ Feeling unloved or unliked
❑ Frequent hurt feelings
❑ Moodiness; lots of ups and downs
❑ Depression
❑ Afraid of losing emotional control
❑ Fears or phobias

❑ Other _____

Your heart can give you understanding and direction to deal with these feelings. FREEZE-FRAME for clarity and guidance on how you can make improvements in emotional management. Jot down your insights.

_____

_____

_____

_____

_____

_____

_____

Often, after a "blow-up" from a head reaction, the energy settles in the heart and you see clearly that emotionally reacting wasn't an efficient way to conduct yourself. Unfortunately, people often get into guilt after emotional blow-outs. They wish they had acted differently, feel embarrassed, etc. Guilt is inefficient—any way you look at it. When you listen to your heart intuition, you gain the insight needed to apologize or work things out, then you pick up the pieces and go on. It's the unmanaged head that keeps replaying the situation, reinforcing the guilt or hurt.

Do you sometimes find yourself replaying an emotionally-charged scenario, reinforcing guilt you might be feeling about a situation where you wished you had dealt with things differently? Focus in your heart to help you find peace and recognize that you do have the ability to regain your balance and security. What's done is done. Use the wisdom of your heart to see the whole picture, not just that time when you were not really being yourself. Jot down any new insights.

_____

_____

_____

_____

Follow Up Exercise—Bonus Insights

Continue to observe your emotions throughout the day and make extra effort to use FREEZE-FRAME if things start to get a little out of balance so you won't have to go back and clean up any spilt milk along the way.

There were many ways of breaking a heart.
Stories were full of hearts broken by love,
but what really broke a heart was taking away its dream
—whatever that dream might be.

Pearl S. Buck

DAY 3

Today's Reading

Continuing in Chapter 5, in *The Hidden Power of the Heart*, "Higher and Lower Heart Frequencies," Sara helps us to gain an understanding about true heart feelings.

Millions of people today are afraid to love because they fear being hurt, rejected, and feeling the pain of a broken heart. Once burned, they don't want to touch hot coals again. Others see the heart as gushy, sentimental and getting them into trouble when they feel deeply about things. A lot of people have experienced so much hurt and disappointment, they have shut down their hearts in self-protection and feel detached, even numb. They have vivid memories, as a child or young adult, of opening their heart, only to have someone they loved trample on it. There are thousands of marriage counselors and therapists trying to help people re-gain a sense of intimacy in relationships. While our society values an honest, sincere heart, it is wary of the vulnerable open heart.

When love turns into attachment, or compassion gets colored with sympathy, your heart energies are pulled into density, often feeding back in your system as hurt and sadness. Love can seem like the cause of that hurt, especially when the initial heart feeling is deep and sincere. In reality, it's what our head does with our feeling of love that determines whether it stays in the higher heart and is fulfilling or leads us into lower heart feelings and stress.

When you have a "broken heart" your mind takes a deep disappointment and keeps replaying that same old sad movie, reinforcing the hurt feelings each time. A broken heart is really the result of a head-on collision between broken attachments, expectations and emotional investment; there is some heart energy mixed in which is why it feels like your heart aches. You really did love, but then your love drifted into the lower heart frequencies of attachment and expectation—expecting someone to love you in the way you loved them. When that doesn't happen, the emotional shock can short-circuit your mind and your emotions. Your security was invested in someone outside yourself and when that security is gone, you feel like a victim, powerless.

Just about everyone has experienced a "broken heart" in one way or another. Reflecting on an experience like that, objectively with our emotions in balance and with heart intelligence, we can understand how our expectations and attachments might have colored our experience. Think about any situations in your life where you felt broken hearted and apply what you have read today for new understanding. Jot down your insights.

_____

_____

_____

_____

Exercise

When you allow lower heart bands (heart feelings colored with sentiment, attachment and expectations) to take over your feelings, they can deplete your system and cause stress. People operate from the heart some of the time, but often believe they consistently do, when it's lower heart bands they are feeling. These frequencies cut off your connection to your higher heart and can easily lead to thoughts of worry, disappointment and fear. That's why the heart is often perceived as being so vulnerable.

Think of a situation where you felt that you were operating from the heart but it did not feel right or the outcome was not to your liking. Look at it more closely to see if you were in the higher heart where courage, compassion, understanding and wisdom are experienced or if you were in a lower heart where your true heart was being colored with attachment, expectation, pity or comparison. Write down what you observed in reviewing this situation.

_____

_____

_____

_____

_____

_____

It's important to learn the difference between emotional pulls and true heart's desire. We can go back and forth analyzing the variables, trying to choose which direction to go. Often our choice is based on an emotional pull—an attachment—and not what our heart truly desires. By Freeze-Framing and going to the heart we can distinguish the emotional impulse from our real heart and gain a balanced perspective. Quite often, what our heart wants is not the same as the emotional pull.

Is there a decision you are trying to make? Are your thoughts about it colored with an emotional pull and attachment or a true heart's desire? You can resolve this dilemma by going to your heart and asking for a readout. Write down your response.

Situation

_____

_____

Heart Response

_____

_____

_____

Follow Up Exercise—Bonus Insights

Observe yourself throughout the day to see if you are managing your life from the perspective of your higher heart intelligence or from emotional pulls. If you're in doubt, ask your heart to guide you. Jot down your observations.

_____

_____

_____

_____

_____

Problems have only the size and the power that you give them.

— *S.H.*

DAY ④

📖 *Today's Reading*

In *Self Empowerment*, Chapter 2, "The Head and the Heart," Doc helps us to realize the power of the heart as our source of strength and intelligence.

People may often sense the promptings of their heart feelings but repress them because they fear becoming vulnerable. Realize that it's living in the head that makes people vulnerable to stress and prone to a profusion of mental and emotional pain. Because the heart frequencies express themselves through feelings, people tend to think of the heart as the emotions. You have probably heard people say, "When I open my heart, people take advantage of me." As you learn more about your heart, you will find the statement to be the opposite of truth. First of all, the heart consciousness is not a mushy, wimpy, sweet and defenseless bag of emotions. Your heart uses emotions to express its inner wisdom which is translated through feelings of "knowing." Heart intelligence embraces head intelligence and is the prime, bottom-line strength of your existence. It represents the real you inside—the essence of the inner child and the responsible adult in a balanced package.

The head often uses emotions to activate insecure feelings in your solar plexus, creating what is called "emotionalism." It's your heart that bails you out after your head runs you aground, especially in the traumatic times of your life. The comfort and security of the heart give you the momentum to start anew after exhaustive, self-image disturbances. The head keeps crying over spilt milk. The heart wisdom helps you appreciate that the "spilt milk" times in your life could have been worse. Bottom line—the heart gives you the strength and understanding to create new self-image attitudes.

Can you recall a time when your natural heart wisdom helped you to deal with an emotionally-charged situation? What was the outcome? Jot down your insights.

_____

_____

_____

Exercise

When you call on your heart intuition for help, you can be surprised with the facilitation you get—if you listen to it. The problem for many people is that they don't listen to what their heart is trying to tell them. They try to change a head attitude by using the head to do it. It doesn't work. You end up in the same old rut, time and time again. With sincere practice, you can learn to draw on your own inner strength and bring self-management into areas of your life which you've wanted to manage for a very long time.

Is there an emotional pattern that keeps repeating and holding you back? Ask your heart for guidance and then remember to follow its advice. Write it down.

Emotional Pattern

_____

_____

Heart Response

_____

_____

_____

Emotions seem hard to manage at times because they come and go instantly as thoughts or attitudes trigger them—consciously or unconsciously. Emotional energy is not positive or negative; it's neutral—like a car idling. You can press the gas pedal and drive to work responsibly or you can press the gas and drive a hundred miles an hour into a concrete wall. The car represents a neutral power that you can use or abuse. Emotional energy is like that. Recall a situation where you let your emotions get the best of you. Now FREEZE-FRAME to determine what would have been a more energy-efficient response and remember to use what you learn if a similar situation comes up for you.

Situation

Heart Response

Follow Up Exercise—Bonus Insights

Observe yourself to see how well you are managing your emotions. Are your reactions becoming more energy efficient? Jot down your observations.

Nothing in life is to be feared. It is only to be understood.

— *Marie Curie*

DAY **5**

Today's Reading

In his book, *Self Empowerment*, Chapter 2, "The Head and the Heart," Doc gives us an understanding of the power of the heart to assist us in dealing with repressed emotions.

> Repression is not management. It's dangerous and can result in psychological and physical disabilities. Repression is a protective mechanism used by the head when it doesn't have the ability to face or resolve a problem. When the heart feelings are shut down, you don't have the power to release and let go. For example: In many traumatic situations, such as the death of a loved one, child abuse or rape, the heart feelings shut off because of shock and betrayal. You may feel like your heart is broken. The heart isn't broken; it's that your heart feelings shut off, and then your emotions run wild or get repressed because of pain, or a sense of loss or remorse.
>
> For long periods of time this can cause a numbness inside which doesn't change until the heart energy re-opens within that individual. The re-opening of the heart makes the releasing of repressed emotions possible. As you maintain heart perspective, you accelerate the process of releasing your imprisonment to past events.

> You can facilitate the heart opening by trying to love and care for more people—any people. Loving and caring for others gives you the incentive to want to clean old repressive patterns out of your data bank. Make sincere efforts from the heart and you'll find the power to manage those old thoughts until they starve from lack of attention. This is the process of self-empowerment. It's heart commitment that gives people the strength to release the old and look forward to the new.

Recall how loving and caring for others—using positive emotions—has helped you to feel better. Write down your observations.

_____

_____

_____

_____

_____

_____

Exercise

People often carry around old emotional hurts and pains. It's definitely not good to repress these emotions but it's also not efficient to keep bringing them up, re-experiencing them time and time again. Transforming them would be more efficient. Depending on the emotional issue, this can take time but it's worth it. Use the power of your heart to dissolve old emotional patterns and experience a new feeling of buoyancy and passion for life.

If you find yourself stuck trying to analyze and figure out or justify some old hurts, you could try sending love to that issue and to yourself to open the door to a deeper understanding. This could sound like a "soft skill" approach to dealing with long-standing emotional issues but the transformational power of your heart—applied with sincerity—may surprise you. Think of a situation that could simply use more heart. Right now, as best you can, try to experience a higher heart feeling (care, appreciation, tolerance, etc.). Just doing this can take the intensity out of emotional issues. Jot down any new insights from taking this short pause to make contact with your heart.

_____

_____

_____

You've probably had situations at some point in life where your mind constantly projected the worst-case scenario. Later, simple stepping stones unfolded into efficient solutions and you bypassed all the stressful results that your mind "just knew you were going to go through." If you can get your mind to chill out long enough for your heart to assess any situation, then you can often save the fear and stress accumulation that come from constant worry and anxiety. That's emotional management that pays off.

Do you find yourself projecting about what might happen? Why not bypass the unnecessary anxiety by asking your heart for an understanding of the situation? For starters you might want to reflect on the many times that you thought something unpleasant was going to happen and it didn't or perhaps what did happen was not nearly as bad as you had thought it would be. Do this written exercise for more clarity.

Situation

_____

_____

_____

_____

_____

What actually happened

_____

_____

_____

_____

_____

_____

_____

Follow Up Exercise—Bonus Insights

Reflect on your week. Have you had insights about your emotions and how to balance them? Perhaps you have uncovered emotional issues and you haven't resolved them yet, but that's okay. Take things one step at a time and keep making the effort to release emotional turmoil through the heart. Your emotions are one of your greatest gifts. Practice managing your emotions and turn their power into a renewed passion for life. Jot down your observations about the week. Start by making a list of the five most important things you have gained from this week's practice of managing emotions.

1. _____

2. _____

3. _____

4. _____

5. _____

MONTH 2
Why Heart Intelligence

WEEK 1
Heart Lock-In®

WEEK 2
Appreciation

WEEK 3
Love Yourself

WEEK 4
Love the People

*What lies behind us and what lies before us
are tiny matters compared to what lies within us.*

— Emerson

DAY ①

Today's Reading

In *Self Empowerment,* Chapter 2, and *The Hidden Power of the Heart,* Chapter 1, Doc and Sara explain the value of connecting with the hidden power of the heart.

> Your "heart feelings" or "heart sensations" are the energy and activity that surround the heart. Heart energy is a subtle activity that one has to attune to, become aware of and amplify—so that you can understanding its significance to you. Your heart sensations give you signals like a traffic light: stop, go, caution. When you feel uncertain, the heart gets mixed in with solar plexus energy, indicating that something needs considering or that there's a fear or insecurity. When your heart signals to you: "Yes, go," it's often accompanied by a more solid, secure feeling inside that's indicating: "This action would be helpful for me, or someone else or some issue I am dealing with."

> Down through the ages, the world's great religions and philosophers have referred to the heart as a source of strength and power. Webster's dictionary defines the heart as "the center of the total personality, especially with regard to intuition or feeling; as the source of one's deepest innermost feelings; as Spirit, courage or enthusiasm." In our modern society, we casually use expressions like, "She sings with a lot of heart," "Go deep in your heart to find the answer," or "Follow your heart." What do these phrases really mean? Most people live for those moments when "our hearts come alive," when we are filled with love and life feels great. However, few of us have ever been taught how to self-activate and sustain love and fulfillment in our lives.

Recall the times in your life when you felt most fulfilled, happy and at peace. More than likely, those were moments in your heart. Imagine being able to access those feelings in the moment. Jot down your insights about those heart-filled experiences.

_____

_____

_____

Exercise

To do a Heart Lock-In® means to focus your energies in the area around your heart—that place inside where you have experienced feelings of love, care or appreciation. Heart Lock-Ins are similar to doing a FREEZE-FRAME except you just focus gently in the area around your heart for a longer period of time and you don't necessarily need to ask a specific question. Also, Heart Lock-Ins are done with the *Heart Zones* music. Music can be effective for enriching the experience. *Heart Zones* was scientifically designed by Doc Lew Childre to connect people with their heart power, and to reduce mental fatigue and emotional burnout. Doc spent several years studying and testing musical tones, harmonic resonances, rhythms and specific chords for their effects on psychological stress patterns. Sophisticated testing of ECG (heart) frequencies showed significant changes in a very high number of people. Studies done on *Heart Zones* have also showed significant improvements in immune system response and in Heart Rate Variability, an important measurement of cardiovascular function and nervous system balance. Try not to compare *Heart Zones* to other music you have heard. It may take a couple of listenings before you adjust to the music and experience the benefits. We will start slowly, just listening to the first one or two songs during these first few days of this section of your study.

Here are the steps of Heart Lock-In:

1. Start the *Heart Zones* music. Close your eyes and relax.
2. Shift your attention away from the mind or head and focus your energies in the heart area.

3. Remember the feeling of love you have for someone now, or have had in the past for someone whom it was easy for you to love. Or focus on a feeling of appreciation for somebody or something positive in your life.

4. Send that sincere feeling of love or appreciation to yourself or others.

5. If head thoughts come in, just bring your focus gently back to the heart area and radiate energy from the heart. If the energy feels too intense or feels blocked, try to feel a softness in the heart and relax.

Now, try your first Heart Lock-In. You'll do a short one this time listening to Song 1 from *Heart Zones*. Just put on your *Heart Zones* tape, follow the steps you have just read and enjoy.

After doing this one song Lock-In, write down any intuitive feelings or thoughts that are accompanied by a sense of inner knowingness or peace. Remember, it does take practice to truly "Lock-In" to deeper heart feelings. It's a refreshing break from the head and will help you activate heart intuition.

Follow Up Exercise—Bonus Insights

During the course of your day, when you feel the need for a break from whatever it is you're doing, try to do a mini Heart Lock-In. This means taking about five minutes to just gently focus in the area of the heart with your eyes closed. You don't have to use *Heart Zones* when doing a mini Lock-In but you can if it is convenient. Mini Lock-Ins are like extended FREEZE-FRAMES but with a gentle focus. They will help recharge your batteries and actually prepare you better for whatever it is you need to do next.

We must always change, renew, rejuvenate ourselves; otherwise we harden.

—Goethe

DAY 2

Today's Reading

In *The Hidden Power of the Heart*, Chapter 8, "Tools for Rapid Self-Adjustment," Sara Paddison explains some of the benefits of a Lock-In, including how it can help release feelings stored in the unconscious.

> As you reap the rewards of loving yourself and others, you will become motivated to build your heart power to love more consistently. The Heart Lock-In is a potent tool you can use any time you want to contact a deeper heart frequency. It can be a refreshing break from the head and, with a little practice, feels good, activates your heart power, and helps you maintain better balance.

> If you've had a combination of lower heart and head creating insecurity and vulnerable feelings in your life, these feelings often are stored in your unconscious. With practice, the Heart Lock-In can release them and take you to a deeper heart security. Security is what finally transforms pain and old hurts. As love increases in quality, the old attitudes of expectation and attachment release bit by bit. View all of your feelings that arise in a Heart Lock-In as love that is growing but is not yet completed in its highest quality.

> The main intention of a Heart Lock-In is to experience your own heart more deeply. If draining thoughts come in, look at them objectively and go to your heart computer for understanding and release. Be consistent, but be casual in practicing your Lock-Ins, then they will flow. If you try too hard from the head, you create mental tension that blocks your higher-dimensional awareness. Take five minutes or more during your day to feel love in your heart for yourself, everyone and everything around you. Try to find a peaceful, still feeling and a warmth around your heart. The more you practice, the easier it will be to feel a deeper heart contact.

J ot down your observations about what you have read.

_____

_____

_____

_____

_____

Exercise

Let's practice another Heart Lock-In. Begin by finding a comfortable place to sit, closing your eyes and relaxing. This time you will listen to Songs 1 and 2 from *Heart Zones*. To Lock-In, shift your attention from your head to your heart, by relaxing your thoughts and focusing your energies in the heart area. Then send a sincere feeling of love or appreciation to yourself and others. Just love people. Appreciate the good things in life. Appreciate your life compared to tougher situations, like people who are homeless or starving. This helps facilitate the deepening of heart resonance. Just let go of mind chatter and release your feelings in the heart. If head thoughts come in, bring your focus gently back to the heart area and radiate feelings of love and appreciation.

If you can't feel love right away, or if you feel some tension in your heart, it's okay. Try to tune into a memory of when you loved someone and it was easy, or a time when you deeply appreciated someone and there was no insecurity or anxiety. Focus on that clean, higher heart feeling in a relaxed way. After your Lock-In, jot down any feelings or insights.

_____

_____

_____

_____

_____

Follow Up Exercise—Bonus Insights

Observe yourself throughout the day and try to increase the length of time that you experience the "heart" you feel when doing your Lock-In. See if you can continue to recall those feelings during your day. Before you end your day, write down your observations about how you felt in the heart today.

_____

_____

_____

_____

_____

_____

_____

_____

_____

> Only in growth, reform, and change,
> paradoxically enough, is true security to be found.
>
> — *Anne Morrow Lindbergh*

DAY ③

Today's Reading

Continuing in *The Hidden Power of the Heart*, Chapter 1, Sara Paddison talks about seeking reassurance, answers and fulfillment from within, by accessing the power of the heart.

It's natural for people to discover some of this power of the heart in times of crisis—such as after the death of a child, rejection by a loved one or when we bottom out in pain, anguish and despair. When there is no other place to turn, people do go to their own hearts and comfort themselves the best they can. Through prayer, meditation, a walk on the beach, we try to get in contact with our deeper self, an inner wisdom to give us some release. We listen for a still, small voice inside, a voice of intuition or spirit. We try to tap into the highest source of intellect that we can find in ourselves to stimulate our understanding ability. This effort to go deep within the heart for an answer has been known to help people change their perspective and outlook on life.

The basis of heart empowerment® as a complete system for fulfillment starts with remembering to quiet your mind, go to your heart and follow your own heart directives to manage the regular day-to-day situations of life. You realize you are responsible for how you manage your system. It's your own inner business. You achieve balance by listening to your heart directives and self-correcting your inefficient thoughts, feelings and attitudes with heart power. It's just common sense to go for that feeling of knowingness inside. Most of us have a lot of old programming to clear out and re-program with wiser, energy-saving attitudes. No one else is going to do it for you. No one else is going to give you fulfillment. Your security lies within you, just waiting for you to find it.

It looks like there's no passing the buck here. It's up to you to find your fulfillment. But then again, maybe you've known that all along—deep inside. And now you have a system to help you go deep inside—to your heart. Jot down your thoughts and feelings about what you have just read.

_____

_____

_____

_____

_____

_____

Exercise

When there's too much stress in your mind and emotions, it's hard to feel love—the hidden power in your heart. The Heart Lock-In is a potent tool you can use anytime or anywhere you want to contact a deeper heart frequency. It's a refreshing break from the head and, with a little practice, helps you regain your balance.

By practicing this tool in moments of peace, you can enrich those moments. At the same time, the more you practice accessing your heart, the easier it will be for you to Lock-In to your heart and regain your peace in moments of stress.

Today let's do a Lock-In to all four songs of *Heart Zones*. The entire length of this powerful, scientifically-designed tape is just 17 minutes. Put on the music in a comfortable place, relax and feel the love inside yourself. If you feel a bit of tension in the area around your heart or if the third song seems fast or a bit jarring, just focus gently and try to find a soft feeling in your heart.

After doing the Heart Lock-In, note the good feelings your heart generates through your system—mentally, emotionally and physically. Jot down your feelings and observations.

_____

_____

_____

Love is not automatic. Most people only love when the mood arises or when someone does something for them. To use love as a power tool, you have to consciously choose to feel love. Your system accumulates the energy of love, just like it accumulates stress. As love accumulates, it keeps your system in balance and harmony. As you consciously use love as a tool, you connect with your heart at deeper levels, then with other people's hearts. You create a tremendous power circuit that becomes an access code to the mysteries of the universe.

Take a few minutes now to Lock-In to your heart, re-experience the peace you may have felt during your Heart Lock-In and send love to someone. Note how that feels in your system. Jot down your observations.

_____

_____

_____

_____

Follow Up Exercise—Bonus Insights

This week, deepen your practice of sustaining the feeling of the Heart Lock-In during the day. Try to take a break during your daily activities and do at least one mini Heart Lock-In with or without music for five minutes to recall the deeper heart feeling and connection.

A little quiet is the only diet.
— *Scottish proverb*

DAY (4)

Today's Reading

In *FREEZE-FRAME*, Chapter 5, "Personal Benefits and Applications," Doc Lew Childre discusses the physical benefits we can gain by locking in to our heart, as well as how it can add sparkle to life.

> As you build your sense of personal power through Lock-Ins and FREEZE-FRAME, you are likely to find physical benefits as well. Each time you Lock-In or FREEZE-FRAME, you are building personal power and recharging your batteries. It's quite amazing how much healing and regenerative power the human system has when body, mind and emotions are in sync rather than fighting each other. The next time you feel run down or having an annoying ache or pain try locking-in to your heart. (This is not instead of taking medication that might be appropriate, but as an add-on.) Let the body shut down for a few moments while you calm the mind and emotions. Frequently, the annoyance we feel when the physical body is hurting or sick only adds to the discomfort and lengthens the healing process.

> We all would love to find the fountain of youth. But to come upon a big waterfall labeled, "Drink here, you've found it!" might not happen. Let's take a subtler look at what youth really means on the inside. Everyone knows how refreshing a child's energy can be. Children have a certain liquid flexibility that "goes with the flow." They play with all their hearts and if they fall down and scrape their knee, once the band-aid is on, they're usually back into the swing of things fast. To find an adult with these same qualities is not so easy. What happened to us? Where did it go? Did our spirits age too? That's what a fountain would be good for—to fill us back up with childlike qualities of enthusiasm, flexibility and the zest for adventure no matter how difficult our life experience has been.

77

The heart offers a simple, scientific approach to health and well-being. Don't let the simplicity fool you. Recall fun-filled moments in your heart. Was there a childlike quality to those times? Imagine being able to access those feelings in the moment. Locking-in to your heart is a powerful tool for health and well-being.

Jot down your insights about the feeling you have during fun-filled moments.

_____

_____

_____

_____

_____

Exercise

To age mentally and emotionally denotes a loss of flexibility and a loss of the ability to adapt. You become a person who doesn't like to do anything you don't usually do—and nobody can change your mind. You are just like that—"set in stone." Doesn't that sound like age, becoming set in your ways? You've lost the childlike feeling that life's an adventure, with new events to experience and enjoy. Aging is a part of life. But to age naturally, with a childlike heart, can keep the sparkle, spontaneity and adventure in your life.

Aging happens when our cells lose flexibility and the ability to adapt. We become crystallized in certain habits and attitudes that are harder and harder to change. But it's being proven in the lab that the positive hormones you create within your own system with positive feelings do more for your regeneration than you might know.

Do you notice yourself becoming stuck in certain habits? (Your socks have to be folded a certain way, you have to have your coffee out of a certain mug, etc.) Is there an area or areas of your life where you've lost the childlike feeling or sparkle? Perhaps so, but here's the good news. Lock-Ins are highly regenerative and can help to re-ignite the youthful qualities of the heart.

Do a Heart Lock-In to all four songs and send love to yourself and all of the cells in your body. This will help to revitalize your system and reconnect you with more of your youthful vitality. Jot down your insights after doing your Heart Lock-In.

Follow Up Exercise—Bonus Insights

Observe yourself throughout the day. Are there definite times when you feel your energy beginning to wane? Try doing a mini Lock-In during those lags and re-boost your system. Jot down your observations about what you experienced from using mini Lock-Ins today.

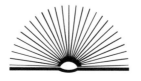

*The body is the soul's house. Shouldn't we therefore
take care of our house so that it doesn't fall into ruin?*

— *Philo Judaeus*

DAY 5

 Today's Reading

In *FREEZE-FRAME*, Chapter 4, "The Scientific Basis of the FREEZE-FRAME Technology," Doc Lew Childre helps us to gain a better understanding of how the heart affects hormones and the immune system.

Let's look at more scientific facts on the relationship between emotions and health. Scientists are proving that repeated episodes of anger and frustration cause nervous system imbalances that are detrimental not only to the heart, but to the brain and the hormonal and immune system. Have you ever had a big argument with someone you loved and, the next day, replayed the situation over and over in your mind, cranking up negative emotions from the day before that made you feel terrible? Even recalling an upsetting episode can produce imbalances and stress. As mentioned earlier, we know that stress creates specific hormonal imbalances, and that these same hormonal imbalances have been shown to damage brain cells. They may even lead to Alzheimer's disease. It doesn't have to be that way once you understand what you are doing to yourself and how you can change it.

Affiliation is a social motive characterized by the desire to establish warm and caring relationships with others. People with strong affiliative motives tend to be loving and caring individuals. It has been shown that loving and caring people have decreased levels of stress hormones and higher IgA levels during times of stress than non-affiliative individuals. They get sick less often and are less vulnerable to disease. Loving and caring people also have increased norepinephrine, a chemical released from the nerves that has a wide variety of functions in balancing the nervous systems. Studies have shown that even if you aren't naturally affiliative, self-induced feelings of warmth and care towards others also increase IgA, resulting in an enhanced immune system.

I magine improving your health by loving and caring for others. It's a win-win situation. The benefits to your system are profound. Jot down your thoughts about what you have read.

_____

_____

_____

_____

Exercise

At least four to five times a week throughout the rest of this study program, try to do your Heart Lock-In to *Heart Zones* to help you go deeper in your heart. In your Lock-In today, send heart energy and appreciation to the patterns you have discovered in yourself that may need adjusting. Then spend some time sending a feeling of love and appreciation to yourself. Listen for your heart's intuition. Write down any new ideas, perceptions or creative solutions to problems that come up. Remember, often an intuitive solution is very simple. Don't let the simplicity fool you. Jot down your insights and observations from today's Lock-In.

_____

_____

_____

_____

_____

_____

_____

Follow Up Exercise—Bonus Insights

Now having completed some of the HeartMath Discovery Program, you know how to practice observing the difference between your head and your heart during your daily activities and conversations. Try to recognize when you are in your head and when you are in your heart. You'll know by how you feel if you pay attention to your inner signals. By now, you know which one feels better. Remember to Lock-In to your heart and try to sustain those good feelings. If you catch yourself off course, simply bring your energies back down to your heart and try to lock them in. Like anything else, it just takes practice.

Write down a few sentences about the progress you have made in your ability to recognize the difference between the head and the heart compared to when you started the program.

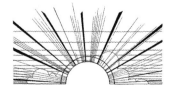

Gratitude helps you to grow and expand; gratitude brings joy
and laughter into your life and into the lives of all those around you.

— *Eileen Cady*

DAY 1

Today's Reading

In *The Hidden Power of the Heart*, Chapter 20, "The Magnetics of Appreciation," Sara Paddison explains the magnetics of appreciation and its power to bring more joy and fulfillment into our lives.

> ...I appreciated just being alive. Instead of always having to recover from some lump or bump, my day-to-day life turned into a fun game of discovery. I discovered the tremendous magnetic power of appreciation and saw the law of magnetics at work: the more I appreciated, that magnetic energy attracted more wonderful people and fulfilling life experiences to appreciate.
>
> The word "appreciation" means to be thankful and express admiration, approval or gratitude. It also means to grow or appreciate in value. As you appreciate life, you become more valuable—both to yourself and others. Appreciation is what I call a "super power tool" for personal growth and universal evolution. It rapidly shifts your frequencies from head to heart, bringing you a quick attitude adjustment and giving your mission in life a lift.

> When I began to explore the power of appreciation, I realized that my deepest friendships were the ones I'd appreciated, the ones I valued enough to look after. I also remembered the relationships that had crumbled. They didn't *grow in value* because I didn't appreciate them. The power of appreciation seemed so obvious, but I also knew how often this simple truth gets lost in judgment and insecurity. Appreciating each other is a true family value, one that will bail out much of the stress on the planet and helps strengthen the universal bond all people have.

It's so easy to get caught up in the "busyness" of our lives that we tend to take things for granted when there truly is so much to appreciate—everything and everyone. Perhaps appreciation needs to be a priority on our "to do list." Jot down your insights about what you have just read.

_____

_____

_____

_____

Exercise

Let's begin to look at the things in life we can appreciate. Make a list of the people, places and things you could appreciate more. Be especially conscious of the little things (getting a parking space, the first bite of that chocolate truffle, etc.). Then do a Heart Lock-In to *Heart Zones* and send a feeling of appreciation to the items on your list. After your Lock-In, jot down any new things that you can now see to appreciate.

Appreciation List

1. _____
2. _____
3. _____
4. _____
5. _____
6. _____
7. _____
8. _____
9. _____
10. _____

Relationships can add fun, sparkle and meaning to life. Think about your relationships, past and present—the ones that are still vital and alive, as well as the ones that have faded. Jot down the people—the relationships—that make your heart come alive. Note how they have added richness to your life.

_____

_____

_____

Reflect on how appreciation has helped some relationships to continue to grow and how lack of appreciation had led some relationships to slip away. Jot down your insights.

_____

_____

_____

_____

_____

Follow Up Exercise—Bonus Insights

This week deepen your practice of active appreciation in the moment. Remember to appreciate someone or something during more moments in your day-to-day life.

If you talk about your troubles
And tell them o'er and o'er
The world will think you like 'em
And proceed to give you more.

— Unknown

DAY 2

Today's Reading

Continuing in Chapter 20, "The Magnetics of Appreciation," Sara Paddison discusses the power of appreciation to shift perception, transform attitudes and bring more fulfillment.

Whenever you activate heart power tools, you open the door to new perceptions. Appreciation is a powerfully magnetic energy that helps you see the wider picture faster. As you appreciate, you see more and understand more. On an energy level, it brings intuitive breakthroughs and helps you realize God is within you. Appreciation magnetizes you to the universal flow. When you sincerely appreciate what you have in life, you magnetize more of your true heart's desires. Mathematically speaking, if people spent half as much time appreciating what they have as they do complaining about what they don't have, life would have to get better.

What you put out comes back. The more you sincerely appreciate life from the heart, the more the magnetic energy of appreciation attracts fulfilling life experiences to you, both personally and professionally.

Learning how to appreciate more consistently offers many benefits and applications. Appreciation is an easy heart frequency to activate and it can help shift your perspectives quickly. Learning how to appreciate both pleasant and even seemingly unpleasant experiences is a key to increased fulfillment.

Appreciation is truly the gift that keeps on giving. Not only does it grow in value, but so do we. We can always appreciate the good things; that's simple. It's learning to appreciate the "seemingly unpleasant" that can be more of a challenge and a valuable practice. Jot down your insights about what you have read today.

_____

_____

_____

_____

Exercise

It seems that life always presents us with small challenges. As you learn to value them in your day-to-day life, you begin to see how they are designed for your growth. Were there any lumps or bumps in your day? Let's challenge those challenges by going to your heart for a wider perspective and find something to appreciate about these incidents. Pick at least one and make an effort to find something to appreciate about the situation.

Situation

_____

_____

Appreciation Insight

_____

_____

_____

Appreciation is like looking through a wide-angle lens that lets you see the entire forest, not just the one tree limb you walked up on. In our culture, most people remember negative events more quickly than they do positive ones. Focusing on the negative comes easy to the head, while focusing on the positive comes easy to the heart. Appreciation is an opening frequency.

You receive new intuition when you can sincerely say, "I'll find the good in this situation no matter what. I'll plug in this program from my heart computer—appreciation."

Is there an event in your life which you perceive as negative? Perhaps you're only looking at that one tree limb. Why not take a step back so you can see the bigger picture? Using your heart computer, find another perspective about this situation. Allow your heart to provide you with insights. Write down the things that you can appreciate about this situation.

Situation

_____

_____

Appreciation Insight

_____

_____

_____

Follow Up Exercise—Bonus Insights

Put your appreciation into action by taking time to show your appreciation. Tell one or more people something you appreciate about them. Remember, what you put out comes back. What did you experience from doing this exercise? Write down your observations.

_____

_____

_____

The head does not know how to play the part of the heart for long.

— *La Rochefoucauld*

DAY ③

Today's Reading

Continuing in Chapter 20, Sara Paddison helps us to gain an understanding of the power of appreciation and its regenerative effect. It's time for us to appreciate appreciation.

When positive feelings are activated, hormones are released that regenerate your mental, emotional and physical systems. IHM research has shown that feelings like care and appreciation improve immune system response and cardiovascular efficiency. There are always deeper levels of appreciation to be realized and wider perspectives to be seen. The sincerity of our appreciation is the key. Appreciation in action is an act of love. By making an effort to appreciate more often with sincerity you are able to see and experience more of the good things in life. Using appreciation as a tool brings enhanced health and overall well-being. On all levels, appreciation is a regenerative frequency. It feels wonderful and has a magnetic quality.

Positive feeling states like appreciation produce coherent patterns in the frequency spectra of the ECG. IHM research has confirmed correlations between these coherent patterns and improved immune and hormonal response. In addition, each time you stop to appreciate, you build more self-empowerment and more quality.

Appreciating something positive in a negative event sends a signal to the heart that magnetizes balanced understanding. Why not remember the positives? They're the fuel for your self-empowerment. It doesn't really matter what you appreciate—as long as it's sincere. The activation of this particular heart frequency is what counts. Appreciate that you have food to eat, a job, your health, a place to sleep instead of the sidewalks and all the positives you take for granted. Create an attitude of gratitude and you'll magnetize more rewarding experiences.

The power of this simple tool is awesome and appreciating feels good. It magnetizes more good things to you and simultaneously regenerates your system. You can reap a bountiful crop when you sow seeds of appreciation. Jot down the insights you have gained as a result of beginning to appreciate more sincerely.

_____

_____

_____

_____

_____

Exercise

As you appreciate in the moment, the magnetics make the returns come back even faster. This gives you more truthful perceptions of events or situations that are unpleasant. Of course tough situations are harder to appreciate. But if you go to the heart, you realize that things could be worse and are worse for a lot of people. It's all a matter of perspective. Find something about a tough situation that you can appreciate. Start by appreciating that no matter what the problem is, there is a wider perspective yet to be uncovered.

With this in mind, think back to a difficult situation— either from work or your personal life—where you felt frustration, fear, perhaps even defeat, but where later, in retrospect, you could look back and see how the situation actually helped you become more resilient.

What was the situation and how did it help you grow? Jot down a few words about your discoveries, appreciating them as you write.

_____

_____

_____

Here's your next step. Sometimes when we are in the middle of things, we feel like we are in the dark. We can't see clearly. But later on, when we look back, we suddenly gain new insight. Things become clear. Hindsight is 20/20. Appreciation is a tool that can bring new clarity to a tough situation right when it's happening.

Now think of a difficult situation you are currently facing. Try to find three things to appreciate about it. Here's a helpful hint if you're stuck—things could always be worse. Remember to feel appreciation as you write your insights.

_____

_____

_____

Follow Up Exercise—Bonus Insights

In your Heart Lock-In today, send heart energy and appreciation to yourself. This will help you feel more confident, secure and self-empowered. Sending appreciation to yourself as well as others is regenerative and good for your entire system—mental, emotional and physical. Appreciate your observations and jot them down.

_____

_____

_____

The meaning of things lies not in the things themselves,
but in our attitude towards them.

— *Antoine de Saint-Exupery*

DAY ④

Today's Reading

In *The Hidden Power of the Heart*, Chapter 10, "Releasing Judgments," Sara Paddison explains how judgments of ourselves and others get in the way of appreciation, and, most importantly, how we are really hurting ourselves.

> ...The power of appreciation seemed so obvious, but I also knew how often this simple truth gets lost in judgment and insecurity. Appreciating each other is a true family value, one that will bail out much of the stress on the planet and help strengthen the universal bond all people have.
>
> How you perceive life—people, places and things—is of the utmost importance. There is such a fine line between assessing a situation and judging it. Assessments, when not made from the heart, often become judgments. Judging oneself and others is such a mechanical habit, a commonly accepted frequency in our society. But it generates a tremendous amount of stress. In using the word judgment, I'm not talking about the ability to discriminate. I'm talking about the judgmentalness that comes from mind-sets or insecurities that color your perceptions and affect your ability to discriminate truth. You are hurting yourself if you don't give yourself a wider perception of a situation by taking the data objectively to your heart, and then using your heart intelligence to make a clear assessment.

—◦◦◦—

> Judgments are often subtle, formed from old hurts, pressures, stress, haste and comparisons between yourself and others. Comparisons are tricky. It's extremely easy for a comparative assessment to turn into a judgment....

Teach yourself to make heart assessments. Recognize a quality or character trait in someone, but if you disagree with it, don't judge them, just love them to find understanding. Try to see what it's like to be in their shoes. Your heart frequencies could help their behavior improve, and you won't be adding more stress by judging them. Give people the latitude to be themselves. You would want someone to give that to you.

I t's easy to judge, but not if you are appreciating. Judgments can be blatant, or sneaky and subtle. Think about what it feels like to be judged. It's a common habit that needs to be unlearned. But don't judge yourself for it! Jot down your feelings and insights about these statements.

_____

_____

_____

Exercise

Judgments block you from connecting with the essence of another person. They create imbalance and disharmony in your system. As justified as they can seem, judgments have never been known to help anyone. If you're judging someone, you're draining your energy. You pay the price, not the other person. People and life are always changing, so judgments often limit your perceptions and stop your next level of knowingness.

You can choose either to judge or be open. One drains energy, the other accumulates energy. Judgments create separation and alienation. Openness leads to connectedness.

Why not stop that subtle energy leak in your system by turning your judgments into appreciation? Think of someone you tend to judge—someone in your family or workplace or a public figure. Now find some things to appreciate about them—sincerely. Let's turn an energy deficit into an asset. Write down what you find to appreciate.

_____

_____

_____

_____

_____

What are self-judgments? They are those head processors: "I'm too fat, skinny, clumsy, dumb, I did wrong, I blew it, I'm not efficient, effective or good enough." Self-judgment can drain you as fast as judging others. Self-judgment destroys the feeling of connection with your heart, your source of power. Not only does self-judgment deplete you, often it isn't even the correct perspective.

Learn to give yourself the gift of appreciation. Write a list of all your good qualities, character traits, etc. Try to see yourself through the eyes of appreciation. Perhaps it's time to stop taking yourself for granted!

1. _____

2. _____

3. _____

4. _____

5. _____

6. _____

7. _____

8. _____

9. _____

10. _____

11. _____

12. _____

Follow Up Exercise—Bonus Insights

Observe yourself throughout the day. If you catch yourself judging (yourself or others), find something to appreciate and broaden your perspective. Notice how you feel when you switch from your head to your heart. Jot down your feelings and observations at the end of your day.

It is in the enjoyment and not in mere possession that makes for happiness.

Michel De Montaigne

DAY ⑤

📖 Today's Reading

Continuing in Chapter 20, "The Magnetics of Appreciation," Sara Paddison has given us an understanding of this simple, yet powerful tool for enriching our lives. It's worth appreciating!

Appreciation can provide a "wake up" call. It helps you wake up to what's slowing down your growth and opens a doorway to new possibilities. You're probably familiar with the saying, "You can't put new wine into old wineskins." Another way of saying it is, "If you want to put new furniture in a room, you clean the room and take out the old furniture." Old "furniture" means habitual thought patterns that don't serve you anymore. Appreciation is a heart frequency that helps transform inefficient frequency patterns within the human system. It helps clear out the old while it magnetizes the new. As you feel and put out the heart frequency of appreciation, life will mirror back to you the missing pieces of your puzzle.

If you make a sincere effort to follow your heart directives every day, you'd magnetize transformation and all the fun "add-ons" in life....Add-ons are those extras in life that make it fun. They are the unexpected benefits that life brings you—in ways better than you would have imagined. They are what your deepest heart would enjoy.

...Appreciating gave me a feeling that somehow everything would be okay....It was as if a kaleidoscope had turned—what had been bleak, gray colors were now sparkly, bright hues. Humbled, I appreciated the fact that I am always taken care of. Sometimes it takes a humbling experience to help us appreciate. I appreciated the gift of appreciation itself, and the rest of the day seemed to fall right in place in an almost magical way.

It's much easier to learn and grow by choice, rather than being forced to learn. Taking the time to appreciate is a more efficient and pleasant option. It's almost as if when you appreciate life, life, in turn, will appreciate you. Jot down your observations about Sara's insights.

_____

_____

_____

Exercise

Your inner security, your heart power, doesn't need to be dependent on anyone else, on what they say or do or don't do. Feeling misunderstood, taken advantage of, not getting the proper credit—those times in life when someone or something has done you wrong and you feel justified in getting out of your heart—can be summed up as the "poor me's." Science is proving that self-victimization really does affect health.

It's time to shift that perspective and do some inner house-cleaning. Make a list of any old hurts, resentments or issues where you still feel unresolved or have feelings of "poor-me." Try to find at least one thing you can appreciate about each item on your list and write that down next to the item.

Situation	*Appreciation*

There are times when appreciating can be a real challenge, especially in those "tough" situations. As we move through our lives, we meet people and situations that can drain our energy, sap our vitality. If you practice appreciating the little things in life, then when bigger problems or situations arise, you find you'll have an easier time dealing with them. Appreciation is simply a magnificent feeling in the heart that becomes the compass to find more good.

Remember, it's dealing with the little hassles on a daily basis that keep draining your energy and are often inefficient responses. If you decide to no longer view them as "hassles," but rather as opportunities to practice appreciation, you're going to add to your energy bank account. So make a list of those daily hassles (like dealing with traffic jams, your spouse leaving the cap off the toothpaste—yes again—or having to help your restless child with his homework, etc.) and find something to appreciate about them. If you can remember to practice this exercise in the moment, you're going to feel better at the end of the day. That's something to appreciate.

Situation	*Appreciation*

Follow Up Exercise—Bonus Insights

Remember, anything can be appreciated. Why not make a fun game of appreciation and during the course of your day look around you for something to appreciate—even if it seems silly. Look at a lamp and appreciate Thomas Edison. Look at a chair and be happy you don't have to sit on the floor. Just keep looking and keep on appreciating!

To love oneself is the beginning of a life-long romance.

— *Oscar Wilde*

DAY 1

Today's Reading

In *The Hidden Power of the Heart,* Chapter 7, "Heart Power Tools," Sara Paddison helps us gain an understanding of the importance of feeling love for ourselves.

> To be able to love others more deeply, you need to know how to love yourself at a deeper level. Often loving yourself seems harder to do than loving others. We can see past other people's shortcomings and love them. We can see their inner beauty and potential. But since we are with ourselves all day long, we're our own worst critics. It is one thing to put out love, but it is also important to appreciate the love you feel from others and from yourself. In appreciating love, you are able to receive, feel and utilize more of the love someone is sending to you. It increases the value.

> Most of us pay a lot of attention to how we're doing in life, where we want to improve, and so on. We tend to judge ourselves if we don't measure up to our own wishes or expectations. By confronting any uncomfortable thoughts and feelings you have about yourself with love, you interlock, connect and balance your system. In learning how to send love to your negatives, you neutralize self-judgments and gain more power to self-correct. Each time you self-correct with love, your energies come more into alignment and you begin to see your own inner beauty and radiance. You are not really loving to your fullest unless you are receiving and appreciating the love of others too. Practice feeling loved. Don't be afraid to have self-respect enough to understand that you are lovable too.

Sometimes we're so busy loving and caring for others that we forget to love and care for ourselves, or perhaps we might feel uncomfortable about loving ourselves. Regardless of the reason, we all need to embark on loving that important relationship—the one with ourselves.

Jot down your reflections on what you have read.

_____

_____

_____

_____

Exercise

It's time to let go of any uncomfortable thoughts or feelings you have about yourself. How do you do it? With love! That's right. Make a note of those things about yourself that you are having difficulty accepting. Then do your Heart Lock-In and send them love. Remember, with love comes understanding. So radiate love to yourself and bring your energies into alignment so that you'll have a chance to see more of the real you—"your own inner beauty and radiance." Write down your insights.

Uncomfortable thoughts or feelings

_____

_____

_____

_____

Insights gained from your Lock-In

_____

_____

_____

_____

Observe how the areas on your list where you don't love yourself are energy leaks that dilute your power to love others. How does a lack of loving yourself in these areas affect your family, your friendships, your career, your inner peace? Listen to your intuition and write down your answers. If any of these uncomfortable feelings come up during the week, try to just keep loving them.

Heart Intuition Response

_____

_____

_____

_____

_____

_____

_____

_____

Follow Up Exercise—Bonus Insights

We often hear people talking about acts of kindness towards others. How about acts of kindness towards oneself? Let's begin this life-long romance by doing loving things for yourself—watch your favorite movie, have your favorite meal, go for a walk on the beach, indulge in a bubble bath—things that nourish and nurture! Hey, you're worth it! This is the week to romance yourself. Do something loving for yourself today!

> A good garden may have some weeds.
>
> — *Thomas Fuller*

DAY ②

 *Today's Reading*

In *The Hidden Power of the Heart*, Chapter 18, "Deep Heart Listening," Sara Paddison explains how she deals with insecurities. She first plays a game called "No I.D." and then deep heart listens to hear the real truth.

> If you practice deep heart listening to yourself during the day, when emotional whirlwinds stir, you have a better chance of not being pulled into the tornado of thoughts. You can intellectually know that everything is frequencies, but when emotional identification is strong, knowledge often goes out the window.
>
> Honest communication can put you in a vulnerable spot, feeling like you're giving your power to someone else. I got over this insecurity by playing a game called "No I.D.," which means you practice having no identification with insecure thoughts and feelings when they pop up. You surrender them to your heart and get a truer perspective.
>
> After putting a control knob on self-identification during communications, I found deep heart listening to personal critiques to be a fun challenge. The "No I.D." game helps balance your emotions so they can't run away with you.

> Deep heart listening keeps unfolding new math. It gets more refined with practice. Don't let your thoughts be colored by past associations or head band distortions. If my head and heart still won't agree on a solution, then my heart lets my head express itself further. Afterwards, I try to keep my head calm and my mind open to hear the heart's response. Whenever my head sincerely listens, heart intelligence brings understanding and unravels solutions to the problem.

R emember, if you identify with just your head, it will lead you down the road to insecurities. If you follow your heart, you'll find the path to security and understanding. Write down your thoughts and feelings about what you have read.

Exercise

Think of a situation where you didn't listen to your heart and ignored that inner voice trying so hard to get your attention. How did things turn out and how did you feel? Write down your recollections. This would be a good example of not truly loving yourself.

Situation

Outcome

Listening to your heart and then acting on its wisdom is an important act of self-love. Why? Because it produces a higher percentage of thoughts and actions that are efficient and beneficial to your well-being.

Now think of a situation where you did listen to your heart and recall how things turned out and how you felt. Write down your recollections.

Situation

_____

_____

_____

Outcome

_____

_____

_____

_____

Follow Up Exercise—Bonus Insights

How about playing a game this week of listening to your "real teacher"—the one inside you? When we ignore that real teacher, we create stress. Mind-sets, stubbornness and recycling old problems keep bringing us back to square one and we find ourselves saying, "If only I'd listened to my heart in the first place." Don't beat yourself up when you forget. That would not be loving to yourself. Just start listening deeply again, caring for yourself from that moment. We all have moments when we get disappointed in ourselves. No one is perfect. Remember, just love those weeds. They're a part of the garden, too!

Jot down your perspectives about these statements.

_____

_____

_____

Be a friend to thyself, and others will be so too.
— *Thomas Fuller, M.D.*

DAY ③

 *Today's Reading*

In *The Hidden Power of the Heart*, Chapter 8, "Tools for Rapid Self-Adjustment," Sara Paddison shares her experience and success in learning how to deal with energy-draining thought loops, and how in the process she learned to have compassion for herself.

> Thought patterns are those "random dialogues" or "inner soundtracks" of your perceptions of life. As you observe them, you'll see they tend to run in loops. We've discussed how some of the most common thought loops are repetitive patterns of worry, anxiety, fear, resentment and unfulfilled desires. They keep you on that inner (and not very fun) merry-go-round. Sometimes multiple thought loops run continuously without resolution. Try the FREEZE-FRAME game when you want to quit replaying stressful tapes like, "I should have said this," or "I should have done that." Thought loops like these used to keep me upset all day, and constantly bleed my energy.

> When you get caught up in a thought loop, FREEZE-FRAME and say to yourself, "Oops, no big deal," and don't self-judge or analyze. As simplistic as this may sound...It helps you look at yourself like a child learning to walk. You wouldn't beat a child for falling down or stumbling as he was learning his first steps. You'd say, "Oops, no big deal." That creates a heart frequency of care, compassion and forgiveness for the child so he can learn faster. You can do the same thing for yourself to help bypass thought loops. You'll grow faster because it keeps the learning process lighter and fun....Don't judge yourself if you stumble or get tired, just move on to the heart and you'll get stronger. "Oops, no big deal" teaches you to self-adjust without self-judging. It's like a stepping stone back to your heart.

How wonderful to have an option. We can actually have compassion for ourselves. "Oops, no big deal." Just pick yourself up, dust off your knees and keep going—to your heart. Write down your thoughts and feelings about this potential for actualizing more self-love—with love!

Exercise

We've talked about the importance of loving yourself and the various forms of expression it can take. Here's another way—direct and simple. Do a Heart Lock-In with *Heart Zones*. Feel love for yourself as you focus your energies in the soft heart and practice keeping your energies in the heart. That will help you activate feeling frequencies to find the flow of love. Then you can build on it.

You can use imagery if you like—such as imagining your heart as a waterfall flowing through your whole being, or as a power generator pumping out energy. Prime the pump of love for a few moments until it flows on its own. Then love yourself with that love. It could feel odd at first to be sending love to ourselves instead of out to some other person or issue. There is truly nothing wrong with using your love to regenerate your system. Practice loving yourself and watch your sense of self expand! Jot down your feelings and insights from your Lock-In.

Part of loving yourself means having compassion for yourself. It's not about being perfect. It's about learning and growing and appreciating the steps you are taking in your growth. As you feel more love for yourself, you unfold deeper perceptions of yourself and others. You activate the energy equation: Feeling + Perception = Understanding.

If there are still some uncomfortable feelings rumbling around inside, remember to have compassion for yourself, "Oops, no big deal," and send love to those feelings. Through love will come understanding. Jot down any feelings or insights about having compassion for yourself.

_____

_____

_____

_____

Follow Up Exercise—Bonus Insights

Observe yourself throughout the week. Do negative thoughts about yourself still creep in? The most efficient thing you can do in the moment is to remember to love yourself. Treat yourself the way you would want others to treat you. Wouldn't that be with compassion?

Today make an extra effort to love yourself and write down your observations about this exercise before you go to bed tonight.

_____

_____

_____

_____

No one can make you feel inferior without your consent.

— *Eleanor Roosevelt*

DAY 4

Today's Reading

In *Self Empowerment*, Chapter 4, "Intui-Technology®," Doc Lew Childre gives us an understanding of self-esteem, its importance and value, and how to attain it.

> The word "self-esteem" is an attempt to describe an electromagnetic energy that flows through the human system, creating self-confidence and "on-the-move" type feelings. Self-esteem is actually a description of certain isolated frequencies of spirit manifesting through one's system. If spirit were a pie, then self-esteem would be one of the slices— not the whole pie. Realize that high-achievers in business or school can win awards for self-esteem, yet their personal or social lives can be stressful and chaotic. Just because self-esteem can manifest in one isolated area of achievement doesn't mean that you have a high ratio of spirit manifesting in other areas of your life.

> Managing from the heart helps bring complete balance into your system, thereby allowing your inner spirit to increasingly manifest in your day-to-day world. This adds fun and fulfillment to your life, even if you've never heard the word self-esteem. Self-awakening through heart contact leads to the beneficial essence of what people call self-esteem, but in a complete package, not just in a few isolated areas. Self-esteem is a by-product of being yourself. It's not a magical potion or a quick fix for life's problems by any means. However, as you experience more self-esteem (or more spirit flowing through your system) through heart management, it gets easier to dissipate the resistance of stress and find new areas of sparkle and achievement in your life.

The key here is balance and the balancing point is the heart. Not only does the heart harmonize and balance all our systems, it is the doorway for spirit to come in. Let's keep that door open! Jot down your insights about what Doc has said about self-esteem.

_____

_____

_____

_____

Exercise

Self-esteem (an aspect of spirit) is simply an intelligent magnetism that generates balance and synchronicity between the heart/emotions/mind and brain. That's why people who are considered to have high levels of self-esteem often operate with more effectiveness, flexibility and adaptability. One spirit-generated attitude can start to rearrange and uplift the frequency patterns of a depressing day—just like turning a radio dial back to a good station. Self-negating attitudes or poor self-image create inner frequencies of distortion and static—like a radio stuck between stations.

Sounds simple and it is. If you find yourself stuck between stations, listening to that inner noise or static, let's adjust that dial. Turn it to that station (the heart) that radiates a frequency 40 to 60 times more powerful than that other one (the head) to which we frequently listen. A Lock-In can help you find that station. Do a Heart-Lock-In and try to tune into a higher heart station—one that feels good and adds to your self-esteem. Write down your insights about the power of shifting your own inner radio stations.

_____

_____

_____

_____

Heart intuition can efficiently guide you through a step-by-step transformational process of re-educating your insecurities, fears and mind-sets. Remember, mind-sets are crystallized attitudes that hinder the expansion of intelligence; they keep you bound to insecurities and tunnel vision. With practice, you can transform mind-sets and insecurities into flexibility and peace with being yourself. It won't be the long journey that you might anticipate if you start now.

Identify any insecurities, fears or mind-sets that still pop up from time to time. Ask your heart for an understanding. That would be loving yourself. Write down your insights.

Follow Up Exercise—Bonus Insights

Try to be aware of your thoughts and feelings during the day. Those self-negating thoughts will sneak up on you if you're asleep in the moment. It could be time to wake up and love yourself. Write down what you gained from observing and eliminating self-defeating thoughts today.

> How shall we expect charity towards others,
> when we are uncharitable to ourselves?
>
> — *Sir Thomas Browne*

DAY **5**

📖 *Today's Reading*

In *Self Empowerment*, Chapter 5, "An Overlooked Relationship," Doc Lew Childre explains the ramifications of self-judgments and the need to replace them with compassion for ourselves.

> The tendency to judge (or self-judge) is often caused by a lack of security to isolated areas within yourself. It's the bondage to fears, envies and insecurities that keeps humanity from enjoying the freedom of spirit and real quality in experience. As you learn to live from the truth in your heart, your feelings of security increase and your judgments decrease. Self-security replaces judgments with compassion. Compassion and understanding facilitate, while judgments debilitate and create stress....
>
> Habitual patterns of judging crystallize you into "knowing what you know." If you're too rigid in "knowing what you know," you put ceilings on your capacity to learn and experience. This can inhibit mental and emotional growth and fulfillment and eventually lead to disease.

> Self-judgments can dilute your system as fast as judging other people. Practicing sincere compassion for your own growth process is a remedy for that. Realize that self-judgments and self-beating only make things worse....You often hear people say, "I've got to quit judging myself because I know it's making matters worse." That's their heart coming through—the inner voice of wisdom.
>
> If you're self-judging and being hard on yourself, just wake up one morning and affirm in your heart that you're going to quit it. Then when you

111

find yourself chewing on self-judgment during the day, practice RE-MEMBERING that you were going to quit that. As you use the power of your heart, you can, at times, gently release those thoughts and quit giving them energy to exist.

S elf-judgment and self-beating get you nowhere and sure don't feel good in the process. Self-judgment is certainly not self-love. It's just an overly familiar habit that needs to be broken. Know that you're not the only one who does this. Have compassion for yourself and ask your heart to help you. Jot down your insights about this information on self-judgment.

_____

_____

_____

Exercise

Take that recurring self-judgment and love it. After all, it is a part of you that needs love, just like any other part. Oftentimes, with love comes understanding. Lock-In with *Heart Zones* as you send love to yourself and your negative thought pattern about yourself. Remember, self-judgment is a self-imposed block to your personal progress. It stifles that energy that could be supplying you with more happiness and fulfillment. After your Lock-In, write down any new self-loving perspectives.

Self-judgment

_____

_____

Heart Response

_____

_____

_____

After your Lock-In to *Heart Zones,* reflect on this: Remember how it feels when people love you and keep that love flowing through your heart to love yourself and others more deeply. Love your body, too; it is the structure that holds the light of experience, the feeling world.

Write down any insights about the statement you have just read.

_____

_____

_____

Follow Up Exercise—Bonus Insights

So how's your romance coming? It's going to be a long courtship, perhaps longer than any other relationship—for the rest of your life. It takes sincerity and commitment, just like any other relationship. The only difference is that this one will affect the quality of all the others. Do remember to love yourself and practice feeling love for yourself each day. See all of the good aspects of yourself instead of over-focusing on the things you see as weaknesses or imperfections. A balanced, heart-based perspective of yourself will give you new power and freedom.

Jot down the three most important things you gained from your practice this week on learning how to better love yourself.

1. _____

2. _____

3. _____

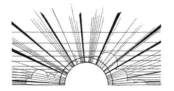

A man's growth is seen in the successive choirs of his friends.

— *Emerson*

DAY ①

Today's Reading

In *The Hidden Power of the Heart*, Chapter 17, "Return to Family Values," Sara Paddison gives us an understanding of the simple power tool "loving the people" and a glimpse of its power from her own experiences.

> Loving your neighbor doesn't just mean the person who lives next door or on the same block. Planet Earth is but one big yard—the evolution of one family tree from the original DNA. We're all neighbors and we're all part of the family of Mother Earth. You would want to love your neighbor if only to gain an understanding of loving your total self.

> Practicing the heart power tool of "loving the people" facilitated a tremendous expansion in my awareness. It's my tool of choice. If I ever want more understanding about anything— whether a predicament in my life, direct perception of another person, or about some aspect of the universe—I start by loving the people.

> ...Connecting with your own deeper heart, and then with other people's hearts, creates a tremendous power circuit. It creates the access code to the mysteries of the universe. The answers don't necessarily come in the way you might expect. They come as your next step in unfoldment, the next frequency of your blueprint that you need in order to understand the next, and so on.

It seems that the more we love, the more we benefit, not to mention the benefits others will receive as well from our love. By loving, we can create Heaven on Earth.

Write down your insights about these powerful statements.

_____

_____

_____

_____

Exercise

Unless you love people, you can never understand them. When you love enough to put yourself in someone else's shoes, you discover compassion. True love and compassion release other people to be themselves because they finally feel understood. Care and compassion are heart frequencies that are activated by a sincere attitude of wanting to help. They are power tools that, if used, strengthen your connection with your own heart and your ability to love.

Think of an area in your life that could benefit from you having more compassion. Do a FREEZE-FRAME and ask your heart to give you understanding. Refer to the steps on page 21 if you need to.

Heart Response

_____

_____

_____

_____

Somehow it's often easier to be compassionate to others and we tend to overlook ourselves. However, we're an important part of that compassion equation. Love doesn't discriminate and neither does compassion. So don't discriminate against yourself!

Is there a part of you that could use a little more compassion? Remember, your ability to love others will depend on your ability to love yourself. Take some time during your Lock-Ins to send compassion to yourself. After doing today's Heart Lock-In, write down your insights.

Heart Intuition Response

_____

_____

_____

_____

Follow Up Exercise—Bonus Insights

Just keep loving the people—anyone who crosses your path. Why not make a game of it? If you're stopped at a red light, send love—to the person in the car next to you, the person in the crosswalk, or someone who pops into your heart. Your acts of love don't need to be "gushy" or overly sweet. Just caring, respectful and compassionate attitudes towards others.

Before you end your day, write down your insights from doing this exercise.

_____

_____

_____

_____

Life is not lost by dying; life is lost minute by minute,
day by dragging day, in all the thousand small uncaring ways.

— *Stephen Vincent Benet*

DAY 2

Today's Reading

In *The Hidden Power of the Heart*, Chapter 17, "Return to Family Values," Sara Paddison continues to give us an understanding from her experiences of the expanded concept of family and helps us to realize how sincere "family feelings" are the hope for security and peace in this stressful world.

> As I practiced loving the people in all situations, or at least made the effort to try, I came in touch with the essence of the "Family Frequency." This frequency is the deeper, personal love and care for every person, plant or animal on the planet. The Family Frequency embraces the earth as all one family, a global or planetary family. This frequency comes from the higher dimensions as a truly new understanding. It's the realization that everyone really is connected to each other in the heart. The family frequency band unfolds as people align themselves in the heart, communicating, working, and living as all for one and one for all. It's a powerful band of energy that helps you realize, understand, feel and experience the eternal security of oneness.

> Humanity is regaining an appreciation for "family" and will continue to do so. In a support group of family, people look out for each other and accept people for who they are. A family grows and moves through life together, inseparable in the heart. A family acts as a buffer to external distortions. A family made up of self-secure people generates a magnetic power that can get things done. As people live in this family frequency, they animate other people's heart bands, making it easier for them to wake up and experience the love and security needed to understand all that is.

Now we can understand why family is so important. Of even greater importance is the realization that we are all a part of the family of man. In order for that family to truly manifest we all must learn how to love all the people all the time. Jot down your insights about what you have just read.

_____

_____

_____

Exercise

Real family values don't demand a return to old family structures. There are thousands of traditional nuclear families who are family in name only. Real family is a deep feeling inside, the recognition of an inner need for support and security. Family would include the extended family, people attracted to each other based on heart resonance and mutual support.

Think of some of the people with whom you have a natural resonance. They can be actual family members or others. The point is that you love and care for them—that's real family. Make a list of these people and recall how you feel towards them. Then take a few minutes to send love to each one. If any new insights about these people come up, write them down next to the person's name.

People	*Insights*
1.	
2.	
3.	
4.	
5.	

Now make a list of some of the people you still have difficulty loving. Lock-In to *Heart Zones* and send radiant energy from your heart to each person on the list. If any insights come up about how you can love them more, write them down next to that person's name.

People   *Insights*

1. _____

2. _____

3. _____

4. _____

5. _____

Follow Up Exercise—Bonus Insights

Your heart resonance increases when your communication is more sincere with all people in business, social and personal matters. It's about learning how to treat people the way you want to be treated. Be aware of the sincerity of your interactions with others. Remember, heart resonance always feels good—no matter with whom! You can make that heart connection in an elevator, at the car wash, at the bank, etc. It doesn't have to only be with your immediate family. It can be any member of your family on the planet. Make an effort to love other people more today and write down your insights about doing this at the end of your day.

_____

_____

_____

_____

_____

A friend is a gift you give yourself.
— *Robert Louis Stevenson*

DAY 3

Today's Reading

In *The Hidden Power of the Heart*, Chapter 17, "Return to Family Values," Sara Paddison sees the hope of the world residing within each individual and the depth of their heart connection with themselves. At the same time, she emphasizes extending that love to everyone!

Most people feel that children today are not learning the basic core values of life. These are values that people believe are essential, involving a sense of personal and social responsibility. But if we want our children to be more efficient and mature with their energies, then we need to reach a new level of efficiency within ourselves. We can only give what we have.

If children are taught how to be responsible for themselves, then they would have the ability to serve and become responsible for others, their environment, their society, their world. The heart is our only hope for rebuilding common values in our stressed-out world. As people experience heart resonance through understanding and care, real "family values" will be re-integrated in our society. As you experience the Earth as one global family, you pave the way for balance and fulfillment.

Greet everyone as family. Family is warm and nurturing; it feels good. Family loves without caring what your imperfections are. It doesn't necessarily have to agree with all your choices, but loves, supports and nourishes you to help you make the best choice. Caring for all people, on continually deeper and more sincere levels, is the fastest way for family, businesses, schools, government, the world, and you, to grow. This degree of family care can only come from going from a deeper heart connection with yourself—and with each individual you meet.

C an you just imagine how wonderful the world would be if everyone treated all people like family? You're an important part of creating that reality. Why not start now? Make it a fun game for yourself and today, try to greet everyone as family in some way. Write down your insights about how the world might look if people considered at least starting out with love instead of judgments in relating to each other.

_____

_____

_____

_____

Exercise

Do a Lock-In to *Heart Zones*. Ask your heart which "people" to send love to during your Lock-In. Take the love you feel from your Lock-In and continue to love whoever and whatever comes your way during your daily activities. Jot down any insights.

_____

_____

_____

_____

Create a "Love the People" action plan of your next step in loving those people you have the most difficulty loving. Your next step might be sending them appreciation or forgiveness, having compassion for their situation, listening to them more deeply, talking with them, etc. Ask your heart for guidance.

Write down three ideas for your "Love the People" plan.

1. _____

2. _____

3. _____

Follow Up Exercise—Bonus Insights

Take one whole day during the week just to love everybody you come in contact with. Use it as an experiment to see what it brings to you. Expand your radius of love. Love the people you see walking down the sidewalk, the gas station attendant, the people in the news—everyone. Everyone will benefit, especially you!

At the end of the day, record your feelings. Were there any differences in your energy level or vitality at the end of the day? What was the quality of this day like compared to other days?

> Be kind, for everyone you meet is fighting a hard battle.
>
> — *Plato*

DAY 4

 *Today's Reading*

In *Self Empowerment*, Chapter 5, "An Overlooked Relationship," Doc Lew Childre explains how disharmony in relationships can be a major energy drain. He suggests plugging up those leaks by replacing judgments with compassion.

If you could record your stress deficit for one year—stress that was accumulated from disharmony in relationships—you would realize why you sometimes feel less vitality and spark than you should or why you don't enjoy life the way you used to. Not everyone experiences this, but many do. Just as positive energy creates assets in return—so does disharmony create deficits in return. Energy goes out and comes back, (that's physics).

Have you ever noticed how it feels when someone judges you and the stress that it can create if you let it? Yet it's so mechanical and natural for people to judge each other without even thinking twice. Well, it's really not natural to judge people. Nature doesn't judge. It allows. Judging is the opposite of allowing people to be. Your true nature is to live and let live, while attending to your own turf. That's the most efficient thing you can do for yourself and for the people you would judge.

It's comfortable to pass judgments off as assessments until they are directed at you. Then you keenly realize that people's assessments of you are often judgments in disguise. In life, we need to make assessments and discernments, and use discrimination. These processes of evaluation facilitate when done from the heart. When done from the head, without care and latitude from the heart, these evaluations create separatism, condescension, self-righteousness and hurt. Until people learn to assess, discern and discriminate with the heart, these words will remain hiding places for outright judgments.

We all know what it feels like to be judged. You can tell when it's being done to you. So what makes you think that the person you might be judging can't feel it coming from you? Judgment is not loving people. If you catch yourself about to judge, switch to compassion. You'll feel better and so will the other person. Jot down your insights about the need to love instead of judge.

_____

_____

_____

_____

Exercise

There's an emotional starvation among people to be accepted, understood and not judged. This need won't be filled until people individually accept the responsibility to put out to others what they would want in return. As you learn to filter life through your heart, then mechanical head judgments will cease and be replaced by more compassion and care.

Make a list of the people you tend to judge: family members, someone at work, a public figure or anyone. Ask your heart to help you have self-security and compassion as you send love to these people. Write down your insights next to the person's name.

People	*Insights*
1.	
2.	
3.	
4.	
5.	

It's important to be free from judgmental mind-sets so you don't limit YOUR possibilities for richer relationships. You can free yourself from mind-sets and pre-judgments by the practice of relating to all people from the sincere heart. Then your heart intuition will allow you to experience the real essence in people—and not miss it because of judgments or pre-conditioned opinions.

Bearing the above in mind, think about the people on your list again. Perhaps it's not really just about them, but about you as well. What is it you need to learn about yourself in this relationship? Ask your heart for guidance. Jot down any insights.

_____

_____

_____

_____

_____

_____

Follow Up Exercise—Bonus Insights

Observe yourself this week and be aware when judgmental attitudes creep in towards yourself, other people or issues. Then make efforts to replace these attitudes with latitude. In others words, give yourself and others more latitude. Wouldn't you want someone to do that for you?

The family the soul wants is a felt network of relationship, an evocation
of a certain kind of inter-connection that grounds, roots, and nestles.

— *Thomas Moore*

DAY 5

Today's Reading

In *Self Empowerment*, Chapter 6, "The Family Concept," Doc Lew Childre
further clarifies the concept of family and nurturing, for ourselves and
especially for men.

> Family is determined by the degree of heart resonance you feel with
> someone. This explains how you sometimes have a deep connection
> with certain friends or co-workers, similar to the one you have with
> family at home. In many cases, people feel more resonance with friends
> (because of other interests) than they do with their own families. As
> people become heart-conscious, they will experience family resonance
> with more and more people. This doesn't take away from the special
> feeling you have with your family or your closest friends. Extended
> family resonance has the power to stimulate a tonic and healing effect
> among individuals and society. Heart-generated interactions release
> positive hormones into your body that act as protective soldiers to
> your immune system.
>
> As you love the people, energy is released through your system. Loving
> is highly regenerative and nurtures your entire being. It's not as impor-
> tant who you love or what you love as it is important that you are just
> loving. Love, however, is not automatic. It takes practice and heart
> focus to love people in a universal way.

> Men have within them tremendous nurturing frequencies. With prac-
> tice, these energies can be brought from the subconscious and create a

more enriched relationship to all life. Don't be someone who thinks that nurturing is putting food on the table and a roof over the family's head. That's providing, not nurturing. Many divorces have taken place because of this one misunderstanding. It's nice to provide but it's a good place to hide—from the understanding of nurturing. Food on the table can feed your face but nurturing kindles the spirit of a person's existence. Communication at the essence level is where real strength is exchanged in relationships.

So what's the real difference between providing and nurturing? For one thing, they feel different. One takes care of the body; the other takes care of the soul.

Jot down your insights about Doc's statements.

Exercise

If you are interested in learning to enhance your nurturing aspects, then practice caring at a deeper and more sensitive level for whomever you are with. Nurturing starts with a sensitive caring and an appreciation of someone more deeply than just at the personality level of communication.

The family frequency bands are the feelings and intuition contained within your heart. They give you access to love, care, security, nurturing, bonding, family interaction, relationship frequencies and more. We all came from families. Perhaps they did not meet our expectations in one way or another, or perhaps they did. Nevertheless, they are our family. Today in your Heart Lock-In to *Heart Zones*, send at least 10 minutes of heart energy to the people you consider to be "family." Write down your insights after this Lock-In.

_____

_____

_____

_____

Follow Up Exercise—Bonus Insights

It's the deeper, more sincere, family-type-caring-for-people that's the missing ingredient in the recipe for harmonious living. It's a powerful solvent for eliminating the stress in the world and its people. So remember to love the people! You'd be helping yourself and everyone else. Make it a fun game to see how many people you can love each day. You're the one who knows the score.

Take a few moments to Lock-In to your heart and consider where you are now compared to when you began a month ago. Have you been able to create more peace in your life? Are your days more energy-efficient? Are you remembering to take time out during your day to make contact with your heart? Send heart energy to yourself and appreciate the efforts you have made to learn and practice HeartMath. Jot down your insights and observations.

_____

_____

_____

_____

_____

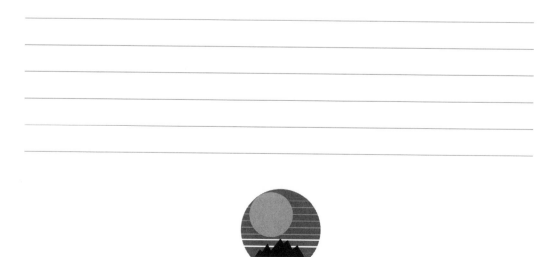

MONTH 3
Intuition

WEEK 1
Intuitive Listening—
Deep Heart Listening

WEEK 2
Heart Talk—
Speak Your Truth

WEEK 3
Intui-Technology®

WEEK 4
Power of Neutral

> Just by listening deeply we alleviate pain and suffering.
>
> — *Buddhist saying*

DAY 1

Today's Reading

In *The Hidden Power of the Heart*, Chapter 18, "Deep Heart Listening," Sara Paddison explains the value and power of deep heart listening.

Most of us have vivid memories of conversations where we felt we weren't really being heard. Maybe our words were heard, but not our feelings or real meaning. Remember these times when someone speaks to you and listen to them as you'd like to be listened to. This means caring to make sure your own thoughts aren't going a mile-a-minute, which will block you from hearing their essence. Listening is a true art and there's always room for improvement.

Deep heart listening means to sincerely listen and receive what another is saying. Deep heart histening helps you experience more textures and achieve static-free reception. It creates deeper truth. Your feedback to others becomes a deeper insight into your own knowledge. Deep heart listening is loving and respecting others, but you are also helping yourself. As you deep heart listen, you help others feel understood and cared for at the heart level, which helps their own heart to open and connect with their higher intelligence.

Forming assessments or opinions while people are telling their story is a form of mental interruption. You don't have to agree with what someone is saying but if you wait until they're done speaking before you address your own thoughts, you'll actually have more to offer them. When people feel heard at the essence level, they connect with their heart. Often they come up with their own insights because you were loving them and listening deeply. It's a joy to see their face light up when they find their own solution.

J ot down your insights about what you have read.

_____

_____

_____

Exercise

There are three essential elements to be aware of while deep heart listening:
1. Word level—what is actually said.
2. Feeling level—the feelings or frequencies behind the words.
3. Essence level—the real meaning.

Through listening to a person's heart, not just the words, you can tune to the frequency, meaning and words all at the same time. Your intuition will allow you to hear someone in a way that incorporates both understanding and kindness.

Here are the Steps to Deep Heart Listening:

1. Listen deeply from the heart to the other person. In other words, be conscious of focusing gently in the area around your heart when listening. Play "don't open your mouth" until the other person is completely finished talking. Keep your head thoughts quiet by letting them go and bring your attention back to focused listening from the heart.

2. Mirror or reflect back the essence of what was said in your own words. Repeat the essence, the feeling and the real meaning you heard as well as the key words.

3. Fine-tune your hearing ability by asking the person if you were accurate. Have the speaker fill in the parts that were missed. Then reflect back the additional parts as well.

4. Now respond with your own heart truth. Before this time you had been listening and reflecting. Perhaps now you have an add-on, an insight you would like to share about what was communicated.

5. Ask the speaker if he/she feels heard.

Now it's time to practice deep heart listening. If you can, find someone who is willing to play this game with you so that you can begin to develop this skill and share the steps with them. If you don't have someone available to do the exercise with, just make a sincere effort to practice the steps of deep heart listening during a conversation with someone today. Just try to remember to deep heart listen whenever someone is speaking. Over time, it will become a more natural way to listen. Before the end of the day, jot down your observations about the conversation you were in where you consciously practiced deep heart listening. Notice any differences in the quality of the communication.

Follow Up Exercise—Bonus Insights

During your daily activities try to remember to deep heart listen. When you really care about something, you do listen deeply and you don't forget much. Remembering to deep heart listen while in the thick of activity is real care in action. Sincerity is the generator that increases your ability to deep heart listen more effectively. Observe other conversations and in a non-judgmental way, think about how deep heart listening might improve these communications. At the end of the day, jot down your observation of practicing and observing deep heart listening.

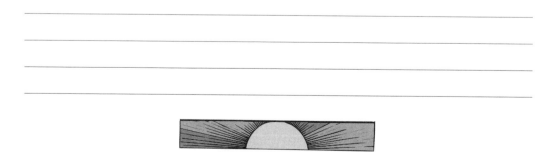

132

Communication leads to community,
that is, to understanding, intimacy and mutual valuing.

Rollo May

DAY ②

Today's Reading

In *The Hidden Power of the Heart*, Chapter 8, "Tools for Rapid Adjustment," Sara Paddison describes the riches we and others can reap by deep heart listening.

> FREEZE-FRAME taught me how to listen more deeply to other people's hearts as well as my own. I practiced what we call "Deep Heart Listening" by focusing the energy in my heart while I listened to someone talk. I learned to hear their being, their essence speak.
>
> Try not to listen with the head. Nine times out of ten I'd find myself doing that. As I practiced loving and deep heart listening, a miracle happened. I experienced a wider perspective of my consciousness which led to a more sensitive, essence-based understanding of what the other person was really trying to say. There was a real heart connection with the other person's heart. I found that making that connection plugged me into a current, and it took less effort to keep it going. I had a deep realization that people are not our enemies; they are our friends. They all have hearts, even if they often perceive things differently. My mind had known the truth of this before, but to have the intuitional light bulb turned on and directly feel it was truly enlightening.

> It's so important to have someone understand you. If we don't have anyone who can, we feel alone. People often turn to prayer, hoping that God understands. Feeling understood at the heart level is a frequency of the Creator. We all yearn for that because it's part of our complete DNA blueprint. When we feel understood, we understand more. It's like a switch that activates your DNA template for fulfillment.

Recall the times when you've been listened to at a deep level and how that felt. It really does create a wonderful connection with you and the other person. Experiences like these add to the riches of life, making it fulfilling and meaningful. Now you can give that gift to someone. Jot down your insights about a time or times that you were sincerely listened to.

Exercise

How do you deep heart listen to others? With focused attention in the heart while making an effort to be caring and sincere. Then you can hear what they are saying between the lines, which makes them feel really understood. That releases their own heart wisdom. Then they feel heard and cared for. And you feel good because you've connected deeply with another person and perhaps facilitated an insight for them.

Practice deep heart listening in at least three conversations today. During your daily activities, consciously practice staying relaxed in the heart and deep heart listen during conversations at work, in business meetings, or when speaking casually at home, over the dinner table, with children, on the phone—anytime someone is speaking to you. To make sure you have heard what the other is really saying and help them feel understood, remember to use the mirroring or "reflecting" tool when it is appropriate. You can do this casually in conversations by sincerely saying, "So what I hear you saying is..." People will appreciate that you cared enough to ask. Just put aside your thoughts, opinions and assessments, and keep listening. If an insight pops in, just keep focusing on the other person's essence, words and meaning and the insight will reappear at just the right time.

Before you end your day jot down any insights from your practice of deep heart listening.

_____

_____

_____

_____

Follow Up Exercise—Bonus Insights

Observe yourself and others as you practice deep heart listening. Is your practice helping others feel more cared for at the heart level? Is your feedback giving you deeper insight into your own knowledge? Are others coming up with more of their own insights and answers as a result of you listening more deeply to them? It's fun to take a step back and watch it all happen—almost magically, as you deep heart listen.

Jot down your observations about how deep heart listening seems to make you and others feel.

_____

_____

_____

_____

_____

We cannot teach people anything;
we can only help them discover it within themselves.

Galileo Galilei

DAY ③

Today's Reading

In *Self Empowerment*, Chapter 2, "The Head and the Heart," Doc Lew Childre offers us a compassionate viewpoint at our first endeavors to deep heart listen to ourselves and further explains why it's worth our while to keep on practicing.

People know what heart promptings feel like in different situations (such as the feeling that gives you the urge to show someone appreciation, or the feeling that tells you not to take that third drink, or to release old resentments). As you get more familiar with those promptings and listen, your heart intelligence unfolds, giving you moment-to-moment self-management in all situations in life. Remember, when the head is not in a joint venture with the heart, you can make decisions that you may regret, resulting in more stress than efficiency.

Don't get frustrated with your first few efforts to decipher which are your heart feelings. After of few days of self-listening, you'll start to recognize the intuitive feelings—and more easily distinguish them from the scattered, unmanaged mind chatter or the emotional solar plexus reactions. As it becomes automatic, it facilitates the integration of your spirit (the most fulfilling and fun manifestation of your real self) into your day-to-day life.

———— ⋘●⋙ ————

The heart is not just for bailing you out of problems. It's especially good for preventing problems. It's a source of strength and commitment, adding quality and buoyancy to your relationships or activities. You can notice the difference in the quality of a lecture or a talk when it is given from the heart with sincerity. People tell each other to play and sing from the heart. This brings another level of obvious quality and texture to their performance.

It looks like the heart is the missing ingredient in any recipe for success and fulfillment. You can add it at any time, especially when you remember to deep heart listen to yourself. Jot down your thoughts about how you feel about the importance of the heart in achieving success and fulfillment.

_____

_____

_____

Exercise

How do you deep heart listen to yourself, you may be wondering? Deep heart listening to yourself means to be more attentive to your inner dialog. To do this will take some practice. Start by asking your heart to help you become more acutely aware of the thoughts and impressions that flow through your consciousness. Try to tune out the static or thoughts that don't seem efficient, productive or in many cases, even necessary at all. Right now, observe your inner dialog for a few minutes. What do you hear? Now, make contact with your heart, focus in the area around your heart and activate a higher heart feeling. Try to find a peaceful frequency or feeling within your system. Observe how your inner dialog begins to change. What are you talking to yourself about now? Is there a difference? A difference that feels more productive and beneficial? Jot down your observations about this exercise.

_____

_____

_____

_____

_____

Try deep heart listening to yourself today. From time to time, remember to stop and pay attention to what you are thinking. Is there rambling inner dialog going on—static on the inner radio—or do you have thoughts running through your system that are adding quality to your life, feel good to your system and are coming from your connection with your heart?

Follow Up Exercise—Bonus Insights

Find time before your day ends to write down the insights you have had from making the effort to deep heart listen to yourself today. Was there a shift in the quality of inner dialog when you made an effort to slow down the mind and listen to your heart?

You should not have your own idea when you listen to someone.... To have nothing in your mind is naturalness. Then you will understand what he says.

— Shunryu Suzuki

DAY 4

Today's Reading

In reviewing Chapter 2, "The Head and the Heart," in *Self Empowerment*, we find that Doc Lew Childre gives us a perspective on the gap between the generations and suggests we might be able to fill it by communicating from the heart.

> The lack of heart communication constantly increases the gap between younger and older generations. It's obvious that children seem to be born today with an extreme innate awareness and mental quickness. Confusion in communication between the generations is on the increase—and without a lot of hope or solutions being offered. However, when adults and children alike learn to communicate and make decisions from their heart sensitivity, then the so-called "communication gap" will dispel itself. Technology and science alone cannot create the remedy for this social quandary; it will have to be dealt with through individual self-awareness and responsibility.

> Following heart directives may not be the "instant" panacea for bridging the generation or communication gaps among people, yet it will be one of the first advance initiatives proposed. As you personally ponder the situation, you can intuitively realize that it's the heart connection that has been missing all along—with oneself and others.

> When communication is approached from the heart, you experience sincerity and resonance. Without the heart engaged, communication can be dry and dull—and you can't wait to get away for a break. Have you ever noticed workplaces where people seem to coexist in a me-

chanical, robotic way, without much sincerity or care in their communications? It's like being in a sleepwalking environment. The absence of heart energy sterilizes an environment.

It stands to reason then, that listening from the heart would add quality to communication, and as we have already learned, take it to a deeper level. What could be more meaningful than connecting at the heart—the missing ingredient? Jot down your insights about today's reading.

_____

_____

_____

Exercise

Think of a meaningful or enjoyable relationship you have now or one from the past with someone older than you. Do you feel the difference in your ages or is age irrelevant because you are connecting at the heart level? Similarly, recall the same scenario with someone younger. Do you notice a difference that interferes with your communications or with your relationship?

The heart doesn't discriminate or set up barriers because of age. It just loves. It's our head that sets up limitations. Sincere communication from the heart can leap over barriers. Jot down your thoughts and feelings about what you recalled about your relationship with older and younger people.

_____

_____

_____

Pay attention to the people you speak with this week. Notice how easy it would be to dismiss them because they're too young or too old. Think of the rich experiences you might be missing because of a mind-set regarding age. Everyone has a gift to give. But you have to be present to receive it.

Think of conversations you might have missed because you felt that some-one didn't speak your "language." Remember, everyone can speak the language of the heart. Actually, they are waiting to be heard. Through deep heart listening, you can hear at the essence level which goes beyond just the language.

Make it a point to speak to some of the people who you have some difficulty communicating with. Use deep heart listening when you do. Jot down your observations after you have communicated with them using your new heart tools.

_____

_____

_____

_____

Follow Up Exercise—Bonus Insights

Keep on practicing deep heart listening. Today, especially practice not inter-rupting before someone has finished speaking. Put your thoughts and judgments on hold so that you can sincerely listen from your heart. A day of deep heart listening can be fun and fulfilling. Jot down what you experienced today as you practiced not interrupting.

_____

_____

_____

My lifetime listens to yours.

— *Muriel Rukeyser*

DAY ⑤

Today's Reading

In *Self Empowerment*, Chapter 6, "The Family Concept," Doc Lew Childre explains how personal experience led to his insights on the importance of deep heart listening and its relationship to nurturing.

> The development of a deeper "hearing ability" helps to awaken your nurturing capabilities. Deeper listening will do much to eliminate what men call "nagging." Nagging is often a cry in despair to be understood. After a year or so of not being heard or understood, nagging evolves into (so-called) bitching. Finally, how could it not. This will dissipate tremendously as men develop their nurturing side....
>
> As men and women become more balanced within themselves, they will naturally develop the understanding and sensitivity that they demand or expect. Then, they'll be able to give children the understanding and nurturing needed for future self-security.

> One of the most helpful things I discovered was that I needed to develop a deeper hearing ability. When dealing with women, I tended to know all the answers before they even stopped talking. This doesn't work. It creates out-of-phase communication. The less aggressive person usually ends up misunderstood or stifled in these situations. By listening more sincerely, my sensitivity increased. That brought my nurturing side into balance with my assertive male nature. Sincere listening and care can nurture male/female communication and understanding into a new level of awareness.

S incerity and care are the keys to enhance all communication. That means being present in the moment and in the heart. Deep heart listening is a conscious choice—one that nurtures. Jot down your insights about what you just read regarding male/female communication.

_____

_____

_____

Exercise

How can you tell if you're deep heart listening?
* *Do you interrupt or finish other people's sentences for them?*
* *Do you try to figure out what they are going to say next?*
* *Are you busy solving their problems for them while they're talking?*
* *Do you quickly give them advice?*
* *Do you try to talk them out of their feelings?*

If you answered "yes" to any of the above questions, chances are you are not deep heart listening. But you can start now. You'll surprise yourself at the results if you make the effort to sincerely listen from the heart.

Are there certain friends you turn to when you have a problem or need to be listened to? Think about this:
* *Are they compassionate, understanding and nurturing?*
* *Are they totally present, giving you their undivided attention?*
* *Do they try to solve your problems for you or do they help you to get clarity so that you can solve your own problems?*
* *Do they let you talk until you're done?*

Chances are the people you turn to for support and understanding are good listeners. You can develop these qualities as well and take them even deeper into "essence understanding" through mastering deep heart listening.

Reflect on your practice of deep heart listening this past week with family, friends, co-workers. Are you remembering to use the reflecting tool? Are your conversations improving? Are your conversations nurturing for you, as well as the other person? Ask your heart for help. And remember to deep heart listen for answers. It will nurture you!

What areas in communication still need to be improved on? Jot them down.

_____

_____

_____

_____

Follow Up Exercise—Bonus Insights

Continue to observe yourself during conversations. Are you remembering to deep heart listen? Ask your heart to remind you. Words can be a source of misunderstanding. But with deep heart listening, you can go beyond the words, into the feelings and real essence of what is being conveyed. This tool enables you to have heart-to-heart communication. What could be more nurturing? Jot down the three most important things you have gained from practicing deep heart listening this week.

1. _____

_____

2. _____

_____

3. _____

_____

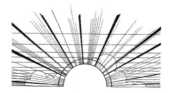

Words and magic were in the beginning one and the same thing,
and even today words retain much of their magical power.

— Sigmund Freud

DAY ①

Today's Reading

In *The Hidden Power of the Heart*, Chapter 9, "Speak Your Truth—Honest Communication," Sara Paddison explains the other half of the communication equation—speaking your truth. She helps us find a way to deal with the fear which inhibits honest expression of feelings.

Deep listening from the heart is one half of true communication. Speaking from the heart is the other half. They are like two sides of a coin. When you remember how you like to be spoken to, that helps you speak from your heart and helps the other person listen better.

To completely release certain issues and move on, you may need to speak your truth. Honestly communicate your feelings and thoughts about a situation—speak sincerely from your heart—and be open to feedback. Speak your truth is frequently one of the last tools people will use out of fear of the other person's response. If your heart is prompting you to talk and try to work things out, you are rejecting your own heart when you don't.

If you find you're not speaking the truth, access your heart and ask it to help you understand the reason why. Are you just scared and don't know why? Heart intelligence can help you overcome insecurities by giving you clarity and understanding. Ask your heart for the steps you need to take to start speaking your truth. Your heart can tell you when speaking your truth would be energy-efficient or not and advise you on the best timing. It can turn any deficit into an asset. The heart is not about right and wrong. The heart is like a friend who wants to help you reach understanding whether it's with yourself or others.

Were there times when you were fearful about speaking your truth? Now if those feelings resurface, you can go to your heart to understand your hesitancy and perhaps find it easier to speak your truth in the future. Jot down the usual insecurities that come up often for you when you find yourself not being able to speak your truth.

_____

_____

_____

Exercise

Do you still have unresolved issues with people because you were fearful of speaking your truth? A good place to begin is by sincerely sending love, appreciation or forgiveness to them. Then ask your heart for clarity and understanding about your hesitancy. During your Heart Lock-In, ask yourself with whom you need to speak your truth and have more sincere communication. (That's right. Please remember to do Heart Lock-Ins regularly). Write down your heart read-outs from your Lock-In today.

Heart Intuition Response

_____

_____

_____

_____

Oftentimes we may decide not to speak our truth. However, it's important to know whether this decision is due to a head reaction of insecurity or true heart intuition. There's one way to find out. Your heart will help you determine which is which. Sometimes your heart might want you to wait for a more opportune time to speak.

Is there a matter now about which you haven't expressed your feelings? Check in with your heart to see if your insecurities are getting in your way or is your heart trying to tell you to wait for a better time?

Write down what your heart says.

_____

_____

_____

_____

_____

Follow Up Exercise—Bonus Insights

Observe yourself throughout the day. Do you find that you're hesitant to speak your truth? Ask yourself if your reason for not speaking is coming from your head or your heart.

Write down your observations.

_____

_____

_____

_____

_____

> The best of life is conversation, and the greatest success is confidence,
> or perfect understanding between sincere people.
>
> —*Emerson*

DAY ②

Today's Reading

Continuing in *The Hidden Power of the Heart*, Chapter 9, Sara Paddison talks about the value of deep heart listening and speaking your truth. She truly believes they have enriched her life.

> The combination of speaking my truth and deep heart listening is one of the best gifts I've found in life. It's taught me I can be myself, my whole self. What an elated feeling to finally understand something about myself that's been like a tree limb blocking a panoramic view! When you sincerely want to know what another person has to say, you receive more power to deep heart listen which opens wide the windows of perception. Real communication is from the heart. Deep heart listening and speaking your truth generates an exhilarating "heart talk" frequency. "Heart talk" is care in action and builds friendship. As you learn to see everyone as your friend, and not as an enemy, you release judgments. Just keep your heart open to them as you speak your truth.

> Being vulnerable doesn't have to be threatening. Just have the courage to be sincere, open and honest. This opens the door to deeper communication all around. It creates self-empowerment and the kind of connections with others we all want in life. Speaking from the heart frees us from the secrets that burden us. These secrets are what make us sick or fearful. Speaking truth helps you get clarity on your real heart directives.

Recall a time when you were afraid to speak your truth. How did you feel? Chances are you didn't feel great. Did you end up draining your energy because the thoughts would resurface or those feelings would re-emerge, making you feel off or uncomfortable? Which was the better choice: living with the discomfort and bottling everything up inside or risking and speaking your truth? A lot has been said in what you have read today. Jot down your insights.

_____

_____

_____

_____

Exercise

We can always find reasons for not speaking our truth. In the moment they might feel justified. But are they justified? Your heart can tell you. Do any of these reasons ever apply to you?

"I already know what they are going to say."
"They never listen. Why should they be different now?"
"It won't change anything anyway."
"I'm hoping the problem will go away."
"They probably won't like what I have to say or like me for saying it."
"They might judge me, think less of me, or reject me for saying what I feel."
"They won't understand."
"I don't want to offend or be rude."
"I'm not clear, so I won't talk until I'm clear."
"I should be past this."
"I do it too, so why point out areas where they need to fine-tune?"
"It will just turn into an argument."
"I might say it all wrong."
"I'm waiting for the right time to speak."

Sound familiar? We've all been there at one time or another. It's very easy for the head to come up with all kinds of reasons. But are they really in your best interest? Is it energy efficient or inefficient when you don't speak your truth?

Recall a recent situation that became more stressful because you were hesitant to speak your truth. Would the same scene have played out differently had you spoken sooner or at all? Perhaps speaking up might have been stress-reducing rather than stress-inducing. Ask your heart for an understanding of this situation.

Heart Intuition Response

_____

_____

_____

Follow Up Exercise—Bonus Insights

Being vulnerable can be scary without heart security. But if you risk and speak your truth you might be surprised by the results. Remember to speak the way you would like to be spoken to. It will help the listener hear what it is you're saying.

Try speaking your truth to someone you know you need to communicate with. Jot down your observations about how this attempt at communication went.

_____

_____

_____

_____

If you wait until the wind and the weather are just right,
you will never plant anything and never harvest anything.

— *Ecclesiastes 11:4*

DAY ③

Today's Reading

In reading the previous day's information from *The Hidden Power of the Heart*, Chapter 9, we learned the value of speaking our truth. Sara Paddison has also given us a deeper understanding of the rewards of being vulnerable. Additionally, she offers valuable insights on gaining self-security.

> Have courage to be vulnerable and be your own self. It opens the rest of the gifts of life. Sincerity is being vulnerable to your own heart. There may be times when you sincerely speak your truth to someone who isn't able to respond from his or her heart. You will find that the strength of your heart is there to give you the satisfaction of having spoken from your heart without attachment to the other person's ability to respond in kind. Your vulnerability is to your own heart, not the other person.

> In being vulnerable, opening yourself up and saying what you think, you take a chance of receiving fine-tuning from others. If you are in a sensitive space, your feelings inside could feel like you are open to attack, but an honest response from the other person is just the fine-tuning of frequency bands. It's learning and growing and opening to new heart frequencies to find more of an understanding of your own being. It's like saying, "This is ME, what do you think?" It is head frequencies, mind projections or your self-image that may feel under attack. By stretching to express yourself, you gain an increased bonus of more of your true self. But if you are closed up inside and don't try, then people won't be able to see the total beauty inside you. Sincere communication is respect for others and for yourself. It indicates maturity.

151

B eing vulnerable can feel uncomfortable, but it's worth the risk because it's an opportunity for growth. Remember, your self-security—your heart power—is not dependent on anyone else or on what others say, do or don't do. It's dependent on you! Jot down your insights about today's reading.

_____

_____

Exercise

Whether you are in a relationship with someone—a romance, a mate, a parent-child relationship or alone—you still have a relationship with every person you meet and a relationship with your own heart. Your self-security does not have to depend on anyone else. By deep heart listening, you maintain your own self-security by using the power of your own heart to listen and speak your truth.

Is there still some unresolved issue because you have not yet had the courage to speak your truth? First deep heart listen for guidance in dealing with this situation. Your heart truly does want to help you. Then speak your truth from your heart. Risk being vulnerable. It might be better than living with the emotional pain or discomfort it could be causing. Do the following FREEZE-FRAME exercise to determine what steps to take regarding a communication issue where you may need to be vulnerable.

Unresolved Issue

_____

_____

Head Reaction

_____

_____

_____

Heart Intuition Response

Follow Up Exercise—Bonus Insights

Today, practice speaking your truth from the heart, not a reactive head, during your day-to-day activities. At the end of the day, ask yourself how well you did. Identify where you might not be communicating honestly and vulnerably. If you were not open and honest in some of your communications, write down your reasons for not speaking your truth. Are they head or heart reasons? It could be that the timing was not right or it could be that your insecurity got in the way. Have courage to be vulnerable when doing this exercise and then follow your heart to security.

Remember to play the game of not over-reacting to the response from others when you speak your truth. Don't allow your head to identify with what others might say. Go to your heart for your real security. Risk, be vulnerable and don't be attached to the outcome. Just be open as you speak your truth. Adopt an attitude of "Okay, I'm going to risk. Let's see where this is going to go." You just never know!

We know the truth, not only by the reason, but also by the heart.

— *Pascal*

DAY ④

Today's Reading

In *The Hidden Power of the Heart*, Chapter 13, "The Power of Surrender," Sara Paddison helps us gain a deeper understanding of the power of love and a broader perspective on the concept of surrender.

> Surrender helps you to love whatever comes your way in life and stay empowered. From my experience, life is full of the gifts of learning and growing. Some gifts feel quite terrific, so surrender is just a matter of opening without fear to an experience you might have thought to be impossible. If an experience feels unpleasant or painful, true surrender would give you the eyes of the heart to see the gift of growth and embrace it. You can soften and smooth out the jarring feeling of the unexpected with loving surrender.

> When we know love matters more than anything, and we know that nothing else really matters, we move into the state of surrender. Surrender does not diminish our power, it enhances it. Surrender is not giving power away, it is actually joining power. It is the synergy of all your powers, not a weakening but a powerful strengthening inside you. Surrender releases the charisma of the spirit, an invisible energy with visible effects. You become of the moment. You come into possession of your greatest asset for changing the world: your capacity to change your perspective about the world.

We tend to think of surrender in terms of giving ourselves up. But when you give yourself up to love, you are surrendering or uniting with a powerful force. In that moment you become greater than before.

Surrender to your heart for your true power. Remember, the young sapling that doesn't bend in the wind has difficulty surviving the storm.

Jot down your insights about what you have read.

_____

_____

_____

_____

Exercise

Recall a time when you felt something was off—a situation, person or issue—and you felt compelled to speak your truth about it. (Perhaps your heart had been prompting you.) How did you feel afterward? Did you feel empowered, relieved, at peace, etc.? Start speaking your truth with the "little things" and then if a big thing comes along, it will be much easier for you to speak up. And the more you speak your truth, the easier and more natural it will become. Jot down your recollections about a time when you spoke your truth from the heart.

_____

_____

_____

_____

Speaking your truth means communicating authentically with everyone—your significant other, your children, co-worker, delivery man, etc. How else will they know how you feel? Speaking your truth is not about just popping off from the head, "telling it like it is" and so on. It is a sincere, balanced communication done from heart intelligence that frees you and opens the door for greater understanding. Sometimes speaking your truth means to express sincere thanks, acknowledgment, appreciation or even forgiveness. Speaking your truth means to share what you are feeling in your heart. For some, this can feel awkward or embarrassing. But once again, you'll probably feel a whole lot better after you've spoken. Additionally, by not speaking, you are not giving people the benefit of your wisdom. Just speak from your heart and don't be attached to the outcome. Try it today!

Is there a current situation where you need to speak your truth? Ask your heart for clarity and understanding. During your Lock-In, send heart to the person you want to communicate with. Write down your insights about this Lock-In. What did you feel about the situation and the other person/people?

_____

_____

_____

_____

Follow Up Exercise—Bonus Insights

Being an example of speaking your truth in the moment and deep heart listening is the most important factor in helping others open up and express themselves. So seize those opportunities to help others as well as yourself by using these two powerful tools. Write down your feelings about the power that can come from using a combination of speaking your truth and deep heart listening.

_____

_____

_____

_____

If you do not express your own original ideas,
if you do not listen to your own being, you will have betrayed yourself.

— *Rollo May*

DAY 5

Today's Reading

Continuing in *The Hidden Power of the Heart*, Chapter 13, "The Power of Surrender," Sara Paddison emphasizes the value of speaking your truth and deep heart listening, as well as the importance of keeping yourself open.

> Holding back, when the heart is prompting you to have courage and be open, is often what creates the very reaction or loss people fear. As you learn to see everyone as your friend, and not as an enemy, you release insecurity and find more love. You don't have to let speak your truth be the last tool you use. If you talk things out when issues first come up, you often find more appreciative perspectives that allow creative solutions to unfold. But realize it's never too late to try to work things out. Just keep your heart open as you speak your truth and tune into people's essence. Once there's sincere heart, then all things can come out and be heard that are for the whole.

> Surrender is giving up our attachment to how we think things ought to work out—the outcome of a situation. It means letting go of the crystallized thought patterns, mind-sets and box-ins that leave no room for a wider perspective. Growth never stops, no matter who you are or how aware you may be. When the mind sets up a temporary truth, and you are sure you know what you know, you don't leave any room for a higher truth to come to you. Leave the box open, give your heart a chance to breathe. Then it can show you new possibilities for fulfillment. New truths will feel good to you once you have gotten the mind-sets out of the way.

S o often we get stuck in mind-sets—thinking we know how something will unfold, so why bother risking and speaking our truth? Why box yourself in to what you believe is the predictable? Perhaps the fact that you have made a change within yourself, whether large or small, may create a new dynamic in your interactions with others. It's worth finding out. Jot down your insights about the possibility for improvement in relationships that can come from the changes you have been making.

_____

_____

_____

_____

_____

Exercise

It's not uncommon to have someone in our lives with whom we are hesitant to speak our truth. Our fears set up a road block to communication—fear of being judged or intimidated, fear of becoming tongue-tied or appearing inept. To help you get through these obstacles, agree that for five days you will set aside at least five minutes during your Lock-In to send heart to any person with whom you'd like to speak your truth. You can begin by locking-in now and writing down any insights that come up.

_____

_____

_____

At the end of the five days, promise yourself you will speak your truth to them. Make a list of other people with whom you still need to speak your truth. Then do a mini FREEZE-FRAME and ask your heart how you can have more honest communication with them. Write down your heart read-outs and have the courage to act on them.

People

_____

_____

Heart Intuition Response

_____

_____

_____

Follow Up Exercise—Bonus Insights

Begin with the little things, before they turn into big things. Speak your truth in the moment as things come up. And remember to speak the way you would want to be spoken to—from the heart. If it's uncomfortable for you, start with the dog and tell him "No" when he jumps up on the sofa. Then try speaking your truth to your child after you've tripped over his toy that he did not put away. Then move on to your spouse who continues a pattern that is not beneficial. Finally, say something to that coworker who never returns your stapler. You get the idea here. Essentially, if you speak your truth on the little things often enough, with care and balance, when bigger things come up, it will feel quite natural to express yourself. Try it and see if you agree. Jot down your observations about this week's work on learning how to better speak your truth. What have you gained from this week's practice?

_____

_____

_____

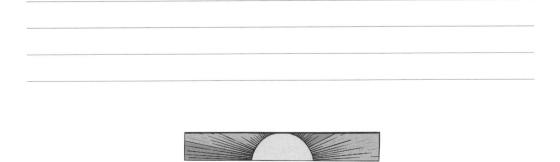

It is the heart always that sees, before the head can see.

— *Thomas Carlyle*

DAY ①

Today's Reading

In *Self Empowerment*, Chapter 4, "Intui-Technology®: A New Dimension of Efficiency," Doc Lew Childre clarifies the misconception that intuition originates in the head, when in actuality it emanates from the heart.

The heart gives voice to the intuition if you learn to listen and apply its free wisdom. In religion and philosophy, they call it "the still, small voice," or people say, "listen to what your heart tells you." Both are referring to intuition, yet people still try to find it from a head approach. They think intuition is a flash inside the head that releases wisdom. Intuition from the heart sends illumination to the head center, then the head flashes with knowingness and facilitates in manifesting the idea or realization. That's why it seems like the head gives birth to intuition, yet the frequency band of intuition enters your system through the heart, from your source of light and understanding. The heart quickly transmits the intuition to the head, which acts as a substation of the heart. Your heart is the mainframe "intelligence center" in your system.

Intuitional development can facilitate all areas of human activity, even your day-to-day, routine decision-making. Many people think that intuition is only useful for discoveries, such as the invention of the light bulb or a "flash" that gives you the winning lottery number, etc. Yes, it has to do with that, but that's only one slice of a larger pie of possibilities. Intuition can be just as efficient in directing relationship problems, business affairs, social affairs, managing your time, the way you dress, the way you eat, and on and on. It provides you with the directions for effective unfoldment in any given area of focus. Intuitive development can make all areas of your life more productive—and therefore much more enjoyable and complete.

I magine being able to run all aspects of your life with total efficiency. The key is learning to develop your intuition. Intuition is the answer for the answers. It's there inside of you. Write down your intuitive insights about Doc's understanding of intuition.

_____

_____

_____

_____

Exercise

Everyone has the capacity to recognize and develop their inner knowingness. Listen more deeply to your inner truth and you can prove this to yourself. Start by asking your heart what steps you need to take to develop your intuition. That would be a fun first step. You might be surprised by the answers. Begin by breathing love through your heart and then send sincere love or appreciation to engage your heart. Then ask your question. Write down your insights, and more importantly, remember to apply them.

_____

_____

_____

_____

Your intuition can offer you efficient guidance in simple or complex situations. It will develop to the degree of your efforts. As you practice following the heart, your intuition becomes more user-friendly and accessible. Is there a situation you would like more clarity about, perhaps a change in your diet, plans for your vacation, a decision at work, etc.? Use your intuition to help you find the answer. Pick a situation, then consult with your heart—the entry point in your system for intuitive intelligence—then record what it says.

Situation

_____

_____

Heart Intuition Response

_____

_____

_____

Follow Up Exercise—Bonus Insights

Try to be aware of when you need to respond to something during the day—a situation, a person, a problem—and take the time to let your intuition guide your response. It could be as simple as "What should I have for dinner tonight?" or "Which shortcut should I take home tonight?" Make it a game to play when you have the opportunity and see what happens. Before the end of your day, write down your observations about trying to make intuitive decisions about the big and small things throughout this day.

_____

_____

_____

_____

Man's main task in life is to give birth to himself.
— *Erick Fromm*

DAY 2

Today's Reading

Continuing in *Self Empowerment*, Chapter 4, "Intui-Technology," Doc Lew Childre gives us a scientific understanding of intuition and the actual process that takes place within the heart, mind and brain.

> Your heart intuition has the capacity to engage your mind in producing subtle electrical frequencies which bring balance to the left and right hemispheres of the brain. These encoded electrical patterns regulate the brain chemistry to increase the efficiency, integrity and effectiveness of the brain and its functions. The balance of the two brain hemispheres creates one unified electrical signal. This signal then integrates with the heart and mind frequencies creating a triangulation of electrical resonance. As these three frequencies build in resonance, they form an energy field of intelligence that for all practical purposes translates into a third brain (which is electrical in nature, not physical).

—⚬—

> This third brain is designed to transmit and receive quantum intelligence and to differentiate it down through your physical brain network for practical use in day-to-day life. As the electrical triplicity between the heart, mind and brain builds into a standing wave of resonance, it creates a unified field of energy within the individual human mind that widens your perception. This electrical integration progressively activates the unused percentage of brain potentials that science acknowledges is dormant. Who would dare to believe that this can be achieved by learning how to follow your heart intuition and become your true self? Probably not science—yet.

It's apparent that there is incredible untapped potential within each one of us—for effective and efficient living—by remembering to access the heart. What tremendous power is there waiting for us to use. We each have the ability within us to create fulfilling lives. We just need to do it—go to the heart! Jot down your insights about Doc's theory.

_____

_____

_____

Exercise

Intui-Technology starts with becoming more consciously sensitive to your inner structure—your mental, emotional and intuitive natures—and isolating them objectively. You can do this by Freeze-Framing, which creates a window of opportunity for intuitive insight.

FREEZE-FRAME changes the quality of your energy and activates your heart power, making it easier to quiet the inner noise and static. Heart attunement often brings clear, unclouded perspectives that result in practical solutions. This comes from heart intelligence—it's a feeling of knowingness.

Freeze-Framing is not meditation or a mystical practice. It's just a deliberate, inner stillness so that the dust from the mind and the emotions can settle. Then it's easier to see a different reality without distortion. Freeze-Framing works especially well for anxiety. When the mind is slowed down, the heart intuition can more easily manifest into your conscious awareness. That starts to eliminate fears, anxieties, anger and the "poor me's" from your catalog of attitudes.

So give yourself a chance to let the dust settle from the mind and emotions. It's no fun getting lost in that dust storm. But you can get out by Freeze-Framing. FREEZE-FRAME and allow your intuition to answer a question that's been rumbling around. Ask a question that you would like more clarity on, FREEZE-FRAME it and write down your response.

Question

Heart Intuition Response

FREEZE-FRAME is not only useful for solving problems, it's also good for creative inspiration. During a creative project like writing, designing, carpentry or any hobby, Freeze-Framing can expand and develop your creativity. It yields more intuitive perception at any time. If there's a project you've been working on, why not FREEZE-FRAME for additional ideas and write them down?

Project

Ideas

Follow Up Exercise—Bonus Insights

Don't allow yourself to get caught in any dust storm. When you feel those winds begin to stir, head for shelter—the shelter of your heart. Today, remember to FREEZE-FRAME even if there's just a little breeze rustling—and let your intuition give you direction.

Be patient toward all that is unsolved in your heart.
And try to love the questions themselves.
— *Rainer Maria Rilke*

DAY **3**

Today's Reading

In further reviewing Chapter 4, of *Self Empowerment*, Doc Lew Childre offers a new perspective on time management—management from the heart.

> The popular time management programs are evolving processes. They ultimately lead to self-management in their highest unfoldment. True self-management is actually a dimensional shift in intelligence compared to time management as it's understood today. As you achieve self-management, managing time becomes an automatic process. This doesn't mean that you discard all your tools for time organization. It means that you are no longer boxed-in by them.
>
> People who practice time management programs often feel like they've trapped by time rather than truly managing it. This happens when the head gets so involved in the procedures that it stifles the intuitive link to the heart. If you over-focus on managing time, you can short-circuit your possibilities for the next level—intuitive time management.

> Quantum intelligence unfolds through the heart via intuition. As you learn how to activate this process, your relationship to time dramatically shifts into another level of freedom and creative innovation. Time management disciplines are valuable, like training wheels on a bike. They can guide you into the awareness of a more direct intuitive management that works at high speed. Intuitive management automatically accesses what action or direction would be the most effective in a moment of time measurement—an hour, day, week, month, etc.

Y ou'll be able to use that daytimer or organizer better if you've got your heart with you too. It's just a matter of remembering to check in with your heart for your next action. Jot down your insights about what you read today.

Exercise

Intuition is "knowing without knowing how you know." Intuition doesn't necessarily rely on information or data, but it can bring in new perceptions about any information. It can be a correct hunch about another person, a clear feeling on how to sort through all the information on your desk or a clear perception that gives you an "Ah ha" answer on a personal problem.

Your intuition is always there. Just remember to access it in the moment. Remembering in the moment saves time. That's a form of time management. If you're like most people, there's never enough time. If you're scrunched for time, ask your heart for a more efficient way to manage the moment, the day or the week. Think about what you have to do today or perhaps tomorrow. Now, ask your heart, "How can I organize this day most efficiently? How can I accomplish these things in less time with less stress? What do I really want to accomplish today? Write down your observations.

As you develop your heart intelligence, your intuition will come in at the appropriate times so you don't have to keep circulating the same list of reminders in your head. At times, your intuition will tell you to write down a thought on your "to do" list and get it out of your head. Some of those whisper thoughts might be helpful, but some are nagging, insecure thoughts. As you release them, you will experience a new level of intuitive organization. As you develop your intuition through FREEZE-FRAME, you start to notice your multi-level inner processes. You become sensitive to the whisper thoughts and feelings that are energy draining.

Does any of the above sound familiar? Why not go for efficiency by relying on your intuition to take care of your "to do" list and eliminate the constant background noise that can wear you down. You might find your list becomes shorter and not as overwhelming. Ask your heart for guidance as you plan your day. In the first part of this exercise, you wrote down what you really wanted to accomplish today. Now, let's do some planning. Ask your heart what your priorities are for today.

Priorities

1. _____

2. _____

3. _____

Follow Up Exercise—Bonus Insights

By practicing the HeartMath tools such as the Heart Lock-In and FREEZE-FRAME, you'll soon discover that in many cases you have been able to still the mind. And, it's when the mind is still that your intuition can speak to you. Otherwise it has trouble getting through because of all the static coming from the head. The more you keep that frequency dial tuned to your heart during the course of your day (through love, care, appreciation), the more insights or intuitive flashes you will have. So check in with yourself during the day to see if that dial is tuned to a heart frequency. Then pay attention to those intuitive flashes. Assess how well you were able to stick to the plan that you created from doing your daily exercises. Write down any intuitive insights you have today.

_____

_____

_____

The secret of success is constancy to purpose.
— *Benjamin Disraeli*

DAY ④

📖 *Today's Reading*

In *Self Empowerment*, Chapter 4, Doc Lew Childre continues to give us a deeper understanding of time management, explaining that heart management is a state of being that enables us to access an intuitive flow for more efficiency and effectiveness.

> Following the heart is like using a master time management computer. It empowers your mind and brain to give you access to another dimension of time management. Managing time is not necessarily the same as being productive within a time span. It's similar, but there's a qualitative difference. Time management is about planning. Heart management is about being. In the state of being, planning becomes more of an intuitive flow, allowing you to make more effective choices regarding your use of time. Balancing the brain hemispheres with the heart activates both its creative and linear functions, creating a joint venture of efficiency and effectiveness.

———— ✦ ————

> Without heart intelligence, the mind tends to get so involved in the pieces of the puzzle that it can lose sight of the bigger picture. While the mind is well-equipped to orchestrate linear time management programs, the overview of intuitive intelligence is required to orchestrate the mind. Heart intuition is designed to manage the mind.

> If you practice time management programs, then you know the importance of writing down your true values and the purpose you want to accomplish. Write down your priorities, but attempt to do it from the heart level and not just from the head. The heart will reveal what you're truly looking to achieve, while the head will tend to reach for the sky

before building a bottom line foundation. It's okay to shoot for the sky, but go a step at a time and build solidly so that a gust of wind doesn't wipe out your whole intention.

Your heart knows what is truly important, while the head has the tendency to make *everything* important. Prioritizing from the heart gets to the heart of the matter. Write down your insights about the advantages of prioritizing from the heart.

_____

_____

_____

Exercise

Heart intuition is designed to put first things first, especially knowing what *is* first—what your true goals are. Heart intuition illuminates the mind with high-speed intelligence that is aligned with your deeper values and intended purpose. When you manage the mind from the heart, you have more focused energy for carrying out your real priorities.

How often do we find ourselves putting our job first before family, or skipping a meal because we have to meet a deadline, or going faster than the posted speed limit because we're late? Which is the real priority? What do we stand to lose if we have our priorities mixed up? You'll find that when you make love and care your first priority, everything has a way of falling into place better than you had expected. That's real time management.

Are priorities sometimes a dilemma for you? Why not ask your heart for the bigger picture and prioritize according to what really matters. Make a list of your real priorities—your true core values.

1. _____

2. _____

3. _____

4. _____

5. _____

Doc Lew Childre has clarity on his priorities. "My first priority is to arrange time to allow for sincere interactions with people. Building deeper relationships with people is valuable in anyone's bigger picture plan. It creates bonding and nurturing, which empower true quality experiences at work or at home."

Here's an opportunity to refocus on your priorities. Ask your heart for insights on your priorities at home and at work. Make sure you write them down for effective time management.

Home   *Work*

1. _____

2. _____

3. _____

4. _____

5. _____

6. _____

Follow Up Exercise—Bonus Insights

Listen more deeply to the quiet wisdom of your heart feelings for the most effective guidance throughout the day. This will take you past the present understanding of time management and into the capacity to effectively and efficiently arrange time as you see fit. How did you do today at staying on track with your real priorities? Before you end your day, write down a few sentences about how you did with this exercise.

_____

_____

_____

_____

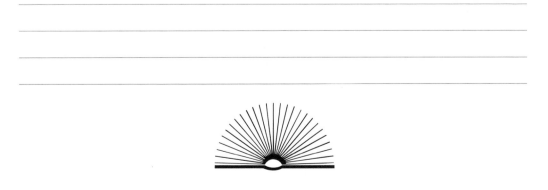

What it lies in our power to do, it lies in our power not to do.

— *Aristotle*

DAY ⑤

Today's Reading

In *Self Empowerment*, Chapter 4, Doc Lew Childre once again emphasizes the power of the heart and planetary ramifications if we all make the heart our priority.

> True self-management will be a featured aspect of the next level of human intelligence, which is already expanding fast. It will be the "in thing" to pursue in the coming years. The next practical step in humanity's advancement will be to actually live our beliefs and "walk our talk," rather than turning others off with aggressive information that hasn't first been soundly proven in one's own backyard. People are looking for proof in action. They've heard all the self-righteous prescriptions for peace and are listening less.

> ...It's time for individual mental and emotional management to be taken more seriously by all. This type of management would be evidence of higher intuition manifesting through human consciousness.

> A self-responsible method of energy management will facilitate business, medicine, science, politics, social affairs, religion, economics—you name it. Intuitional innovation is much needed in all of these isolated areas. Still, new breakthroughs in these areas will only provide patchwork solutions for the whole, until we apply management to relationship and communication problems as well. As people realize the efficiency in care and cooperation, this will magnetize techno-biological advancement according to the need of the "now." First things first.

D oc has said a lot in these few paragraphs. Think about what you have read and jot down your insights.

_____

_____

Exercise

Many people are only vaguely aware of their intuition. They mechanically seek outside answers for problems that develop within, rather than accessing the capabilities of their own heart computer. The heart is similar to a mainframe computer and has unexplored potentials of power and high-speed efficiency. View your heart as your center of control (mainframe) and your head (mind) as a sub-terminal used to help manifest the intuitive directives from the heart.

Recall how you used to handle problems in the past, searching everywhere for answers. HeartMath tools simplify and shorten the search and also remove a lot of the stress. Select a situation from the past that caused you difficulty and write down how you handled it. Then ask your heart how you would handle it now. Notice the difference in your responses. If there is a similarity, perhaps you were already relying on your intuition!

Situation

_____

Before HeartMath

_____

After HeartMath

_____

_____

173

Have you ever been driving along a road and then there it is—a fork? Which way should you go? Well, you could analyze, digitize and calculate—all from your head—and not get anywhere. You might still be sitting at that fork trying to make up your mind. Or you could go to your heart and see what your intuition has to say. It might offer you a shortcut.

The next time you come to a fork in the road, and you probably run across them frequently during the course of your day, ask your heart for guidance. Intui-Technology is the compass to common-sense guidance through life. Are you stuck at a fork right now? Ask your heart to direct you and write down what it says.

Heart Intuition Response

_____

_____

_____

Follow Up Exercise—Bonus Insights

"Let your heart be your guide." There's a whole lot of truth in that statement! Allow it to guide you. It would be similar to being lost somewhere and having a compass in your pocket to guide you but refusing to look at it. Think of the stress and wasted time because you didn't take a moment to use your compass. Life can be just like that if you don't follow your heart. Think about what you have accomplished this week from learning about and practicing Intui-Technology. Write down your observations about this week's study.

_____

_____

_____

_____

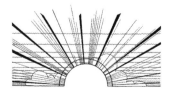

*None of us is responsible for all the things that happen to us,
but we are responsible for the way we behave when they do happen.*

— *Unknown*

DAY 1

Today's Reading

In *FREEZE-FRAME*, Chapter 3, "The Steps of FREEZE-FRAME," Doc Lew Childre gives us an understanding of the importance of neutral.

> There is a great power in learning to be neutral about issues until you have added awareness of the options. When you're in neutral, you can adapt more quickly even if things don't go the way you'd wish. With a neutral attitude you don't waste energy prejudging a person or situation before you have a deeper comprehension of what is happening. Unfortunately, many people spend years worrying about the future, wasting tremendous energy. You lose the power to create a better future if you miss the opportunity of living in the "now."

> There will be times when you are trying to intuitively listen and you don't get any answers. Or you may be reacting to something that happened or to something said. Mental or emotional reactions cut off intuitive listening. When you don't get an answer or if you find yourself reacting, go to "neutral" in the heart.

> Neutral is a conduit for objectivity in the moment. However, if you're unable to hold that objective position and find yourself right back in the heat of things, don't give up and think there's no hope...Try to FREEZE-FRAME and find that neutral point again....If the emotions and racing mind don't just go away on command, try not to be impatient. Have some compassion for yourself...

Most people are looking for quick fixes—immediate reinforcement. Sometimes patience is the key. You would slam on the brakes in your

175

car, if it was an emergency. There are also times when we need to slam the brakes on the mind, (emergency or not) so you just slow things down. Then your mind gets the picture and says, "Oh yeah, I guess we're stopping here," and then the heart takes over. Jot down your insights about what you read today.

Exercise

To practice the power of neutral:
FREEZE-FRAME and stay focused in the heart. Practice breathing through your heart to help keep your focus there. If you can't find any peace or any positive feeling, then just hold on to any neutral feeling you have in the heart. Don't look for a positive feeling or answer. When you can't feel the heart, the mind tends to try to take over to figure out what's wrong or what to do next. Practicing the *power of neutral* is Freeze-Framing to stop the mind's search, staying in neutral and asking your heart to help you see with new understanding. While you're in neutral, stay in a soft heart and let your heart energy have a chance to recoup. You may have to keep trying to stay in neutral for a few minutes, a few hours, or even a day or two before you get the intuitive breakthrough and release. Just know that neutral is fertile ground for new possibilities to emerge from.

If there is a current situation that is troubling you and you can't seem to get an answer from the heart, neutral would be the most efficient and effective way to deal with it. Whenever the mind brings it up, know that's when you need to go to neutral. Remember, the mind thinks it has all the answers, but without management from the heart, it will just keep dragging you around. So do your best to stay in neutral. Take some time now to get there. Just relax as best you can and gently focus in the area around your heart. If any insights pop in, write them down.

The mind can be subtle and sneaky when we're in the thick of something and our emotions are about to take off. There are definite times when neutral would be the way to go:

- *When you find yourself complaining, judging or blaming*
- *When you sense strong attachments or expectations*
- *When you can't feel your heart or can't get an answer and think the HeartMath tools don't work*
- *When you are mentally or emotionally reacting to people, situations or life*

The more you observe yourself and the more aware you are of your mental and emotional processes, the sooner you'll be able to catch yourself and at least get to neutral. Once you're there, you won't be causing yourself as much stress. And however long you have to stay in neutral and stop the mind projections, fears or concerns—you will be saving time and energy. The power of neutral will bring you perspective shifts and new intelligence about any issue.

Follow Up Exercise—Bonus Insights

It's real easy to get so caught up in our day that we aren't even aware of our thoughts and feelings. Don't get stuck on that treadmill. Try to be awake in the moment. Go to neutral as soon as you catch yourself out of sync. By practicing neutral on little stresses and irritations, you build your inner heart muscle, making it easier if you have bigger problems and crises. Try to maintain a balanced state of neutral throughout the day and write down any observations you gain from making this effort.

To attain knowledge, add things everyday.
To attain wisdom, remove things every day.

— *Lao-tse*

DAY ②

Today's Reading

In *The Hidden Power of the Heart*, Chapter 3, Sara Paddison explains the value and importance of neutral.

> The heart understands that it can take some time to find peace in a crisis situation. Using your heart intelligence will speed up the process. The efficient way to dissolve pain is to go back to the heart for a deeper understanding rather than let the head processors run wild and distort any insight your heart wants to give you. You achieve this by keeping the mind in neutral, so that the heart has a chance to give you a read-out. Putting the mind in neutral means simply trying not to think anything about the particular subject anymore. Just make an effort to put it on the shelf, still your mind and "be" the best you can until you can feel your heart again. This isn't burying the problem. It's having the hope and understanding that allows your heart to give you the love and intelligence that can help.

> The longer you let negative thought patterns run, the more intensified they become and the harder they are to stop. You don't have to let stress build and accumulate to the point of anguish, tears of despair and numbness. That's where unmanaged head processors can and do take most people in a crisis. Once numbness sets in, release seems far away, and the process of recovery feels like it will take forever. It can take people months, years, sometimes their whole lifetime to forgive and make peace with an event. (Some people never do.) But, by managing your head processors with your heart, a release will come so you can survive and move on with your life.

Neutral becomes a safe haven in a storm. Seek it for shelter and stay there as long as you need to. Allow your heart to tell you when it's time to come out.

Jot down your insights about Sara's perspectives on neutral.

_____

_____

_____

Exercise

It can be difficult to shift to a positive feeling if a situation is emotionally highly charged. But the effort made to shift helps you neutralize your reaction, allowing the space for a new perspective to arise. When you're neutral, you can adapt more quickly even if things don't go the way you wish. Neutral is powerful. In neutral, you don't add energy to your reaction and you don't drain energy worrying. Stay in neutral until the reactive mind and emotions calm down, and your nervous system comes back into balance.

If there is a situation that is draining your energy and you're not getting anywhere with it, why not go to neutral? It's like giving yourself a time-out—like sports teams do in the middle of a game—so you can recoup your energy, come up with the next play or even decide if you're ready to go back into the game. If your energy is drained, you can't play efficiently nor can you think clearly. Take the time to go to neutral now. Apply neutral to this situation, big or small, and write down any insights that come up.

_____

_____

_____

_____

Neutral is designed to help you see clearly without the mind racing into the future or fretting about the past. We often stress ourselves needlessly about things we can't change. For example, if you FREEZE-FRAME in a traffic jam, it won't make the traffic disappear, but Freeze-Framing and at least getting to neutral can save wear and tear on your system and keep you from aging needlessly before the traffic moves. Why not try it the next time you're in a traffic jam or any of the little jams life presents you? Remember, neutral is neutral. It's like driving a car—in neutral you're not going forward or backward. Just keep idling in neutral.

Follow Up Exercise—Bonus Insights

You know how the water gets muddied after a storm and then you have to wait for all the mud to settle before the water is clear and serene? Well, we're no different. After a storm, our waters get pretty muddy, too. We can't think clearly and we're not at peace. That's when it's time to go to neutral and wait for everything to settle. So during the course of your day, if you feel the water getting muddy, go to neutral so that things can begin to settle rather than getting more stirred up. Observe yourself during the day. If you can't see yourself, then you know the waters are pretty muddy. Write down your observations about practicing the power of neutral today.

_____

_____

_____

_____

_____

Be still and know.

— *Psalm 46:10*

DAY ③

 Today's Reading

In *The Hidden Power of the Heart*, Chapter 8, "Tools for Rapid Self-Adjustment," we gain a deeper understanding of the value of FREEZE-FRAME and the power of neutral.

> The effects of FREEZE-FRAME can be seen physiologically by scientists converting time measurement into frequency measurements through Fast Fourier Transform (FFT) analysis. Using electrocardiogram (ECG) and heart rate variability (HRV) measurements, scientists are able to see three unique stages of autonomic nervous system order from FREEZE-FRAME practice. When we are frustrated or angry, the HRV pattern is irregular and disordered—our heart function is not normal. Practicing FREEZE-FRAME takes us to the first stage: neutral. In neutral, the reactive mind and emotions calm down, and the autonomic nervous system comes back into balance, re-establishing normal heart function. Neutral is powerful. When you're in neutral, you can adapt more quickly and you don't waste mental, emotional or physical energy, or damage your health. Neutral clears the static from your mind and is the doorway to new intelligence.

———— ❧ ————

> Freeze-Framing works better when you *remember* to activate a positive heart frequency. As you put your movie on pause, make a sincere effort to feel something in your hearts, such as love, care or compassion. This sets the stage for your heart intuition to come in. It's no different than fine-tuning your radio dial to get a clear station and tuning out the static. You may not always be able to feel a deeper heart feeling right away, but stay focused in the heart. The sincerity of your effort can reconnect you to your heart current and start the juices flowing. To plug in, think of someone you love or remember what feels good, maybe

181

a fulfilling experience. Feelings help you remember. You become sensitive to the difference between head reactions and heart feelings—they really do feel different. Remembering this difference helps you go back to the heart more often—it feels better.

The power is yours—heart power. You just have to remember to access it in the moment. If for some reason you're feeling off, you really can't blame anyone because it's your choice in every moment: head or heart. Sincerity, intention and Freeze-Framing can get you back to your heart and to neutral. It's the best place to be. Jot down your insights about what you have read.

Exercise

FREEZE-FRAME and neutral are not meant to:
- suppress your emotions
- make you become a doormat
- make you accept abuse or delay positive action

FREEZE-FRAME and neutral are meant to:
- give you time to calm the mind and emotions
- allow you to get clarity
- allow you to come up with efficient perspectives and actions

These are valuable qualities or attitudes that help you be more efficient and effective in the moment. But tools like FREEZE-FRAME and the power of neutral won't work if you don't remember to use them. Here are some simple examples where neutral could be applied:
- Someone just cut you off in traffic.
- The checkout line at the counter is exceedingly long.
- You want to have a heart-to-heart talk with someone and they tell you they don't want to talk about it.
- The copier doesn't work and you have a deadline.

- You're about to leave for an important meeting and your car battery is dead.
- Your teenage daughter has missed her curfew.
- You lose something important.

These are commonplace scenarios that most people don't see as a big deal but yet mechanically reacting to situations like these bleeds away your vitality. What isn't commonplace is having a tool that can give you more peace in the moment, and keep you from wearing yourself out and aging unnecessarily. Next time something like this happens to you, be prepared—FREEZE-FRAME and go to neutral! If scenarios develop during your day that are causing you stress, try going to neutral. At the end of your day, make an effort to write down what you experienced from practicing neutral.

Follow Up Exercise—Bonus Insights

Continue to observe yourself throughout the day. Are you remembering to FREEZE-FRAME and go to neutral? Neutral will get you where you want to go faster than your head ever will. Your head will just keep you going round and round, sort of like a cat chasing his tail. Neutral is a good place to hang out until you're ready to make your next move. It's a lot wiser and safer than the alternatives. Remember, it's the inner knowingness that comes from stilling the mind that will give you the answers and clarity you seek.

What do you have coming up tomorrow where you feel practicing going to neutral might be important? FREEZE-FRAME any worry or anxiety and go to bed tonight with a knowingness that you can at least be neutral about any challenges that may come your way.

A moment's insight is sometimes worth a life's experience.

— *Oliver Wendell Holmes, Sr.*

DAY ④

Today's Reading

In *FREEZE-FRAME*, Chapter 5, "Personal Benefits and Applications," Doc Lew Childre helps us to understand the effects of unmanaged emotions and the value of neutral in these situations.

> People know their emotions can be like a dark cloud, making it difficult to see solutions. FREEZE-FRAME will help you calm your emotions so they won't keep rampaging the mind. When the emotions are managed, your mind has a chance to achieve clear common sense. In talking about the necessity of managing the emotions, I'm not trying to imply that your emotions are the bad guy in the human system, or that FREEZE-FRAME is intended to suppress them. I am saying that you'll save energy when you learn to first neutralize their intent before you engage them. When the heat of the emotions is turned down, the mind can see more options and more solutions.

> As research has proven, when your unmanaged emotions fuel negative thought patterns, you pay a price in accelerated aging, weakened immune system and impaired cardiovascular function. Letting excessive negative emotions blow through your system is like having a big hole blow right through your balloon of energy. Everything can be drained out of you in a matter of moments. It can take hours, days, even weeks to recover. Some people suffer this so frequently, they never "recover." They never experience the kind of clarity that comes with emotional balance.

> When the emotions are managed, not suppressed, they can be used to add more fun, texture and quality to life. They are like free fuel for your system; but if left unmanaged, they're highly flammable.

D id you ever notice how at the end of some days you're totally drained and exhausted, like you just ran a marathon? Perhaps it was a marathon of emotions because an issue came up and you allowed your emotions to run you. On days like these, neutral can save a lot of miles on your system.

Write down your observations about how emotions can drain you and how learning to consciously activate the state of neutral can be beneficial to you.

_____

_____

_____

Exercise

When you feel the emotions beginning to smolder, that's the time to go to neutral before they really begin to flare. If you ever find yourself confronting the following emotional stresses, then you know it's time to go to neutral:

• Quick to get irritated, frustrated or angry
• Feeling unloved or unliked
• Frequent hurt feelings
• Moodiness—lots of ups and downs
• Depression
• Afraid of losing emotional control
• Fears or phobias

Learn to rely on your heart during these times. Come to know the power of neutral. Sincerity, intent and practice will take you where you really want to go.

People live in fear—fear of rejection, fear of being hurt, fear of the future, fear of public speaking—the list of phobias is long. Many fears can be lessened by Freeze-Framing and going to neutral in the moment. The technique gives you a chance to engage the power of your heart to calm fear reactions and gain more objectivity. With practice, the technique will activate positive feelings and perspectives that can actually release the fear.

List some of the fears that might still sneak in from time to time. Remember to go to neutral when they arise in your system. For now however, just ask your heart for an understanding and insight to deal with them.

Fears

_____

_____

_____

_____

_____

Heart Intuition Response

_____

_____

_____

_____

_____

Follow Up Exercise—Bonus Insights

Continue to observe yourself throughout the day. Learn to build the state of neutral. It's like switching stations within your system. Eliminate the static and get better reception by tuning in to your heart. Neutral is a recoup station which creates a zone where you can start regaining lost energy. For a little Bonus Insights make a little more effort to apply neutral to manage your emotions throughout this day.

When you come to the end of your rope, tie a knot on the end and hang on.
— *Unknown*

DAY 5

Today's Reading

In *FREEZE-FRAME*, Chapter 6, "Social Benefits and Applications," Doc Lew Childre gives us a perspective of the global ramifications of the power of the heart and FREEZE-FRAME.

> It is possible to consciously develop a superconscious brain that operates on a software package which comes totally from the heart. When all human beings function at this capacity, conceptual understanding will become secondary. Through high-speed intuitive understanding, people will bypass the conceptual process and have direct knowing instead. FREEZE-FRAME guides you through this unfoldment as you practice at deeper levels. With Freeze-Framing, you gain the power to choose between a) real inner silence, b) intuitive analysis from your heart computer, or c) digital head analysis. Developing this flexibility heightens your common sense on any issue. It creates a harmonious flow where people and digits both get taken care of. This is why HeartMath is a system for peace in action.

> FREEZE-FRAME is not only a power tool—it's a shift in consciousness. As you FREEZE-FRAME at deeper levels and shift your perceptions, you help shift the perceptions of humanity. Since all are interconnected, each time you forego an inefficient frequency pattern, it lessens the density of that pattern in the mass consciousness. Our brains holographically and mathematically construct our perceptions by interpreting frequencies that come through our senses, feelings and thoughts. The frequency patterns that humanity experiences collectively form the mass consciousness.

It appears that by taking care of yourself, which would mean going to the heart in the moment, you are actually contributing to the welfare of humanity. We each have a responsibility to ourselves and to the planet and it begins in the heart. Jot down your insights about this powerful concept.

_____

_____

_____

_____

Exercise

Some people might tend to think of neutral like they do vanilla ice cream. There doesn't seem to be much happening. But to those vanilla lovers, there's a lot happening. Vanilla is not bland or tasteless. And neither is neutral. Neutral has a power all its own. It's not dull, bland or boring. It's an opportunity to recoup, reprogram and re-enter. You won't truly understand its value until you have sincerely used it.

We'd have a lot more peace in the world, both inner and outer, if people would go to neutral. Think of the unnecessary arguments, fights and needless lives lost because of the lack of emotional and mental self-management. A lot of regrets could have been avoided by Freeze-Framing first and acting later.

Are there some areas in your life where you could spend more time in neutral? Pick a situation in your life that needs neutralizing. Then FREEZE-FRAME and go to neutral. Write down your insights.

Situation

_____

_____

_____

_____

Heart Intuition Response

_____

_____

_____

_____

_____

Sometimes we're so busy doing that we don't allow ourselves to just "be." Here's a fun variation on FREEZE-FRAME. Practice Freeze-Framing for observation in a neutral heart—still frame—then receive information as if you are a video camera videotaping an event. You can relax in a soft heart, not trying to put out heart or appreciate or do anything but observe, receive and just "be." You might want to try this little practice when you Lock-In to *Heart Zones* and see what it feels like. Just "be" in neutral. Write down any insights.

_____

_____

_____

_____

Follow Up Exercise—Bonus Insights

What are the five most important things you gained from doing the HeartMath Discovery Program this month? Write them down.

1. _____
2. _____
3. _____
4. _____
5. _____

You're already half way through the program so for more Bonus Insights, write down the five most important insights you have gained from doing these first three months.

1. _____

_____

2. _____

_____

3. _____

_____

4. _____

_____

5. _____

_____

Mycroft's Books

https://www.mycroftsbooks.com/

FREE SHIPPING
ON ALL ORDERS

Happiness is an expression of the soul in considered actions.

— *Aristotle*

DAY ①

Today's Reading

In *The Hidden Power of the Heart*, Chapter 21, "Care or Overcare?" Sara Paddison explains the physiological benefits of true care and offers a deeper understanding of its value.

Harvard psychologist David McClelland did studies which proved that the feeling of care enhances a person's immune system through increased production of the hormone Salivary IgA, which protects against colds and flu. A clinical study on caregiving among nurses revealed that care is what gives nursing its real meaning; it provides nurses with an over-arching sense of connectedness to all life....It is one of the most regenerative, productive and powerful frequencies for health and well-being. Care is an oil that lubricates the entire mental, emotional and physical system. If you run your system without care, it's like running your car without oil—resulting in friction and breakdown.

❦

Without care, life grinds metal on metal. True care regenerates both the sender and receiver. It's a nurturing and healing energy....

Care creates security and support for all involved. It is the cohesive substance that saves a relationship once the initial romance or novelty has worn off. Care is the ingredient that keeps true friendships alive despite separation, distance or time. Care gives latitude to another person and gets you past the dislikes and annoyances. Quite simply, caring sustains love.

Recall a time when you cared about someone and how that felt. Also recall a time when you were sincerely cared for and how that felt. Care is a powerful frequency that pays big dividends for both the giver and receiver. Sincere care can make everyone happier. What could be better than care—a gift for everyone! Jot down your insights if you like.

_____

_____

_____

_____

Exercise

Make a list of the people, places and things you sincerely care about. The items on your list make you feel good, and caring about them nourishes and regenerates your system. Then take five minutes sending heart to them and give yourself an extra boost.

People	*Places*	*Things*

Are there areas in your life where you could care more? Remember, caring is a win-win situation, so why not add more to your system to keep it running smoothly? Jot down a list of those areas that could benefit from your care. Then ask your heart how you could add more care to them.

Areas to Care More

_____

_____

_____

_____

_____

Heart Intuition Response—Adding More Care

_____

_____

_____

_____

_____

Follow Up Exercise—Bonus Insights

Observe yourself during the course of the day. Are you remembering to care? You can care by sincerely asking someone how they're doing, or by suggesting an idea to assist a coworker, or by offering to do some little task around the house, etc. You can also show your care to someone by expressing your appreciation of them. How does it feel to your system when you're caring?

Jot down your insights about the effects of care you experienced today.

_____

_____

_____

_____

_____

The pure relationship, how beautiful it is! How easily it is damaged, or weighted down with irrelevancies just life itself, the accumulations of life and time.

— *Anne Morrow Lindbergh*

DAY ②

Today's Reading

Chapter 21, "Care or Overcare?" in *The Hidden Power of the Heart,* is a real eye-opener about the subtle differences between care and overcare. Apparently, care can be just the tip of the iceberg. It can easily slip below the surface and plunge into overcare, or you can becomes so frustrated just trying to stay afloat that you reach a point where you don't care at all. Overcare is care that becomes a burdensome sense of responsibility, worry and anxiety. Sara Paddison shares her personal experience of overcare.

> On the other hand, there are many people so cut off from their hearts they don't care at all and have become numb. There has been a time or two in my life when it seemed so right to care, so important, that I would get stressed out over the outcome and decide it was better not to care at all. That just made things worse. I cut off my own heart and the results were more stressful than caring too much. Both overcare and not enough care create stress and can lead to burn-out.

> Parents often think they have to overcare and worry about their children to feel they are really caring for them. This is a terrible misconception. Worry never brings balanced solutions to problems. In fact, most of us recoil from people who are overcaring and worrying about us. Overcare actually blocks the flow of sincere care between the sender and recipient.

> Care is the essence of service, yet overcare is probably the biggest energy drain and stress producer for teachers, nurses, counselors, environmental and peace workers— people who want to do good for

others and the world. Overcare is what leads to burn-out among care-givers in our society. This could explain why psychiatrists have the highest suicide rate in the country.

Care is no longer care when it slips into overcare. If your care is stress-producing, you know that you've crossed that fine line into overcare. It's subtle, but now that you know there is a difference, you can save a lot of unnecessary wear and tear on your system. This explains why in certain instances your care didn't feel quite right or perhaps didn't feel good. Put this bit of ammunition in your arsenal of information. It's a valuable insight for peace—yours!

Jot down your insights about the difference between care and overcare as you understand them so far.

_____

_____

_____

Exercise

Simply said, overcare drains energy and limits perception while true balanced care adds energy and new perspectives. So let's take another look at that list you made yesterday of the people, places and things you care about. Look a little deeper and see if any of these things you care about also cause you to overcare. Do you see the culprit lurking on the borders of care luring you away from your original care?

Now from yesterday's list, jot down the items which cause you overcare.

_____

_____

_____

_____

_____

Interesting how the things we care about can also cause us to overcare. That's how subtle overcare can be. As soon as you notice any uncomfortable feelings sneaking up on you, like worry, anxiety, etc., it's time to grab a tool. FREEZE-FRAME and ask your heart what would be needed for sincere care. Find true, balanced care from your heart. And remember, at least you cared.

Select an item from your list that gets you into overcare, FREEZE-FRAME and ask your heart for a more efficient way to deal with the person, situation, etc., so that your care can again be regenerative.

Situation

_____

_____

_____

FREEZE-FRAME Response

_____

_____

_____

_____

Follow Up Exercise—Bonus Insights

If you should find yourself worrying or anxious during the day, you know you're into overcare. Appreciate that you cared, but remember to FREEZE-FRAME and find true, balanced care from your heart.

> Doubt and mistrust are the mere panic of timid imagination,
> which the steadfast heart will conquer, and the large mind transcend.
>
> — *Helen Keller*

DAY ③

Today's Reading

Reviewing in *The Hidden Power of the Heart*, Chapter 21, "Care or Overcare?" we can understand the importance of learning the difference between care and overcare.

It's essential to learn the difference between true care and overcare. Choices based on true care feel good to your heart, while choices made from overcare create feelings of stress. Overcare feelings can be subtle or obvious—ranging from a vague sense of unease to uncomfortable feelings in the area of the heart, to feelings of strain, drain, worry and feeling burned out.

Overcare starts with true care, then spirals down into the lower heart frequencies. Quite often, when we care for someone, some project, some issue, all kinds of concerns pop up. If your energies slip into lower heart frequencies of attachment, expectations, sentiment, sympathy, insecurity, etc., then in comes the head processing and feelings that drain you.

Care defined in the lower heart is: sorrow, afflictions, anguish, grief, heartache, heartbreak, regret, woe, anxiety, uneasiness, disturbed or vague insecure feelings, worry, trouble, too much concern. As overcare stacks in your system, over time it can lead to breakdown and illness.

Care defined in the higher heart is: balanced concern, consciousness, regard, supervision, custody, guardianship, nourishment, safekeeping, trust. Sincere care is love in action and regenerates both the caregiver and receiver.

It's really not that difficult to tell the difference between care and overcare. Your meter is found in your feelings—how good you feel in your heart. Jot down your insights about what you have read today.

_____

_____

Exercise

This week's practice is to pin-point lingering overcares, then change perspectives back to the original point of true, balanced care. This will help release and transform overcares into clear perception, which is true care. Have compassion for yourself as you learn the subtle difference. When you catch yourself in overcare, appreciate that at least you did care! The more you practice FREEZE-FRAME and sincere, balanced care, the easier it will be to recognize and release overcare. Start to notice the direction your head thoughts take right after you FREEZE-FRAME. Recognize if they are lower or higher heart-directed. If they start to go into overcare, softly bring the thoughts and feelings back to the heart, back to sincere care.

Many times heart intuition will give a clear read-out, but due to overcare, people don't listen. Start to notice how your subtle attachments to people, places, money, job, performance, approval or anything can stack, drain your energy, create stress and leak away the power you need to feel good and see clearly. Learn to tell the difference between care or overcare. Remember, your meter is your feeling world—how good you feel in the heart.

Make a list of overcare feelings you frequently experience, e.g., worry about what someone may think about you, money concerns, health concerns, anxiety about work performance, social issues, your spouse, children, etc.

_____

_____

_____

_____

199

Now pick one of these overcares, FREEZE-FRAME and ask your heart for a balanced perspective to help you get to sincere care. Jot down what your heart says.

Situation

_____

_____

_____

Heart Intuition Response

_____

_____

_____

Follow Up Exercise—Bonus Insights

Continue to observe throughout the day. Don't allow your care to create a crisis for you. If any uncomfortable feelings come up, check to see if you've slipped into overcare. Ask yourself whether your care is stress-producing and then you'll know if you crossed over that line. Ask your heart to help you get back to true care. Jot down your observations from today's practice.

_____

_____

_____

_____

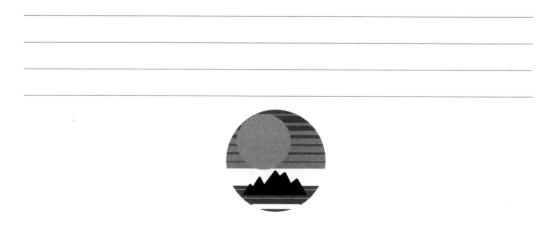

We are more often frightened than hurt:
our troubles spring more often from fancy than reality.

— *Seneca the Elder*

DAY ④

Today's Reading

In *Self Empowerment*, Chapter 3, "Care and Overcare," Doc Lew Childre gives us a perspective on the amount of energy that is wasted daily in overcare.

> Overcare is a human condition, a social dis-ease, and most have experienced it. You find overcare in different degrees—concerning people, places, things, issues, attitudes, vanities, etc., etc. As you understand its disguises, you will realize the hundreds of ways that people overcare daily throughout the planet. If you calculated the energy lost and the distortion created by the millions of people who overcare in just one day, the energy deficit would amaze you. What a waste when it all started with care—care that became unmanaged.

> Care has strength. It can help. Overcare bleeds your strength and can eventually exhaust the people you are (over) caring for. Why keep putting yourself through the wringer, when you tell yourself constantly that you're not going to do it again? That's your heart telling you to stop overcaring! After you get more sensitive to following your heart guidance, you will efficiently balance your over-attachments, allowing people the same freedom to experience growth as you demand for yourself....

> Once you realize how much stress you can accumulate in one day from overcaring (and then multiply it by 365), you'll want to make efforts to bring your care into balance. Self-imposed stress can make you feel aged, weary and tired. Managing overcare closes up energy leaks in your system, one by one, which is a common-sense strategy for stress management.

W hat could be more nonproductive and inefficient than overcare? If you practice self-management by sincerely listening to your inner voice, you will be able to get back to care and feel a whole lot better! Perhaps you've known the difference all along. Life is about learning and growing, so be glad you're learning!

Jot down your insights.

_____

_____

_____

_____

_____

_____

Exercise

So what can you do to keep your care from crossing over the line into overcare? Here's a list of things to be alert to. Start watching yourself daily for these signs of overcare concerning people, issues, attitudes or events.

Overcare Checklist

- Observe the overcare which causes you stress when life doesn't seem to accommodate you.
- Assess where you might over-identify or be overly attached to issues or other people's approval.
- Begin to notice how long you mentally chew on things in your spare time that are already "spilt milk" and need to be wiped out of your focus of attention.
- Check to see if you have a lot of grudges or resentments.
- Observe yourself to see whether you cry in people's beer with them when you're trying to help. Have the heart to help people, but learn when to let go and let grow.

If you find yourself doing some of the things on this list, then you know you're into some form of overcare and it's time to go to your heart for a more efficient way to deal with the situation. At any moment you can go to your heart and ask, "Is my caring truly efficient? Is it helpful for both myself and the other?" Be honest with yourself. Your heart intuition will guide your discrimination as you practice using it. Today do a Heart Lock-In and just relax in the heart to renew your system and provide you with clarity. Overcares can be tough to beat but don't worry (an overcare)—your heart power can help you.

Follow Up Exercise—Bonus Insights

Observe yourself throughout the day. Are you able to identify and catch your overcares more quickly? At least now you know what overcare is, so give yourself credit for that. Your next step is learning to manage overcare. Remember, it's sly, so don't let it sneak up on you.

Jot down what you saw today while trying to be observant of overcare.

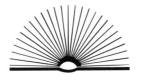

There is no purifier like knowledge in this world:
time makes man find himself in his heart.

— *Bhagavadgita*

DAY 5

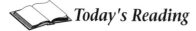

Today's Reading

In *The Hidden Power of the Heart*, Chapter 21, "Care or Overcare?" Sara Paddison explains the negative effects of overcare.

> If care is oil for your system then overcare is an oil leak. Whether you're troubled over small things or over big things like the world situation, the principle of how to deal with them is the same. Go back to your heart and re-start. If you're sitting at home just worrying about someone or worrying about the global stress report on the evening news, you aren't doing anyone any good. Most importantly, you are harming yourself. Overcare will drain you, physically, emotionally, mentally and spiritually.

> There are many people who can't work, sleep or eat because of worrying over someone else's problems. If your care about someone is producing stress, realize it has become overcare. Use your heart computer to know when your concern has become a deficit instead of an asset. As you recognize and understand when your energies slip into overcare, you will see how it's no longer efficient for you or anyone else. FREEZE-FRAME and go back to your heart for re-direction. Appreciate that at least you did care and have compassion for yourself. Overcare is just a third dimensional human inversion of care. Don't get confused. We all have some overcare to deal with because we're all living in a stressful third dimensional world. It's easy to feel like a tight-rope walker in the middle of a three-ring circus.

Overcare is commonplace on the planet. It's become a way of life for so many, thinking they are really caring. Only your heart can tell you if it's true care. If you're doubtful which is which, ask your heart and find out. Of course, the next steps are equally as important. Ask your heart for a more efficient way to deal with the situation and then follow your heart directives. Remember to allow others to "lean gracefully and freely." Jot down your insights if you'd like.

Exercise

From a heart perspective, simply and sincerely sending love to someone is conscious care in action. But, quite often, when you send love to someone, all kinds of thoughts pop up. If you've focused your energy in the heart, your intuition can facilitate these thought patterns, allowing you to understand a wider perspective. Your next thoughts could lead you to an intuitive breakthrough. But if the energies slip into your lower heart frequencies of sentiment and sadness, in comes the head chatter—the worry and stress. The motivation often starts with care.

The key to managing overcares is first to be aware of them. Be diligent in monitoring your thoughts and feelings. As soon as you catch yourself, FREEZE-FRAME. If thoughts still keep coming up that are lower heart frequencies, remember to go to neutral. It's a doorway to higher intelligence.

Is there a situation that still bothers you—concern about your spouse, your child, your job, etc.? FREEZE-FRAME and ask your heart for a more efficient way to deal with the problem. Remember, worry isn't going to help you, the other person or the situation. If anything, it can only make matters worse. Let your heart help make things better.

Situation

_____

_____

FREEZE-FRAME Response

_____

_____

_____

_____

Follow Up Exercise—Bonus Insights

Now that you've learned the difference between care and overcare, the game is to eliminate overcare and still be caring. For so many, it's just a habit, a natural thing to do. Like any bad habit, it has negative side effects. In this case, you really do need to kick the habit for your health. Just say "No" to overcare.

Jot down three important things you learned this week during your overcare practices.

1. _____

_____

2. _____

_____

3. _____

_____

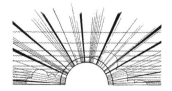

We live, as we dream—alone.

— *Joseph Conrad*

DAY 1

Today's Reading

In *The Hidden Power of the Heart*, Chapter 21, "Care or Overcare?" Sara Paddison explains the importance of caring for oneself to build inner security and self-reliance.

> Care flowing through your system gradually reconnects you with your spirit and vitality. Care enough about yourself to go to your heart to get peace, clarity and direction before you act. True self-care has to come first. Take a moment and ask yourself two things, "How do I feel when others truly care for me?" and "How do I feel when I care about other people?"

> ....Life seems to give us these lessons so we don't totally depend on others for our strength. We have to find it in our own heart instead. Then care from another person is a great gift, but we aren't destroyed if it's not there. Developing your own caring at deeper levels brings an inner security that allows your heart to stay open, regardless of what others do.

Your inner security is dependent on one person—you! Just like a house needs a firm structure to stand, so do you. Build yours from the inside so you can stand freely on your own. Jot down your insights if you'd like.

Exercise

Caring for yourself often means not relying on people, places and things for your happiness but without cutting yourself off from others. Expectations, agendas and attachments can undermine your peace.

Are there new ways in which you could enrich your life—ways you could care for yourself more? Or are you expecting others to do it for you? Look at both your personal and professional life to see what you can do to add more self-care. Ask your heart for guidance and then jot down your answers.

Self-Care Personally   **Self-Care Professionally**

Self-care would be celebrating yourself. What are some things you can do for yourself that are fun and regenerative? It could be shopping, reading a good book, riding a motorcycle or anything that helps you feel good in a balanced way. Make a self-care list of fun things you want to do for yourself.

Appeciating ourselves is an act of self-care. Following through on the things you wrote on your list could seem difficult to do or selfish. See them instead as ways that you can show appreciation to yourself.

Follow Up Exercise—Bonus Insights

Do one fun, self-caring thing for yourself today. Make sure it's regenerative to you and then enjoy without overcaring.

A man cannot be comfortable without his own approval.

— *Mark Twain*

 DAY 2

 Today's Reading

In *The Hidden Power of the Heart*, Chapter 11, "Inner Security—Your Key to Self-Esteem," Sara Paddison offers an understanding of how to build real self-esteem.

> ..."Self-esteem is the amplified essence of heart power. It's the energy your system generates as you gain confidence in yourself." Self-confidence is based on your true level of inner security. You build inner security by trusting in your heart, clearing out old head programs and learning to follow your heart directives. Inner security is like coming home.... "Home is where the heart is." Inner security and self-esteem are by-products of managing your energies from your heart, which releases powerful energy into your system.
>
> Inner security is like fire power for self-esteem. Becoming secure in the heart builds powerful energy accumulators which magnetize all the aspects of complete self-esteem, like personal magnetism, charisma and other leadership qualities. It creates a life of balance and fulfillment—and a feeling of being at home wherever you are.

In the third dimensional perceptions of self-esteem, people try to get self-esteem in different areas. They look for confirmation from "outside" to tell them whether they have self-esteem. People acquire self-esteem in isolated areas—such as physical fitness, sales success, becoming a movie star, etc. Look at a scholar who wins a "Who's Who" award or a talented salesman who wins the trophy for highest sales volume. They each shine with self-esteem in that one area. But at home, the salesman may have an alcohol problem, a poor relationship with his wife or be abusive with his children. The scholar may have many secret insecurities. Well-rounded or complete self-esteem is the result of building well-rounded inner security and heart empowerment....Self-esteem energy accumulates in your system and helps release old problems and old thought patterns. You feel free, limitless and capable of doing anything. Then spirit rushes through your system.

How wonderful to be a complete package unto yourself, so well-rounded that you can roll with whatever life presents you. That's self-esteem and self-empowerment tied up in a pretty bow. And it's attainable—just by following your heart. Self-esteem will grow naturally as you learn the importance of caring for yourself. In other words, you can't experience your true fulfillment without learning how to incorporate balanced care into your life. Quite a formula for success! Write down your observations.

_____

_____

Exercise

Self-care would mean acknowledging, accepting and loving those parts of yourself you might not appreciate—those parts you would rather choose to ignore, deny or wish away. If you want to magnetize more good to you, you need to release self-limiting perceptions. That would be true self-care. It nurtures your spirit and gives you an extra boost of vitality. A seedling has difficulty growing if it's not nurtured, watered and loved. There are parts of you which need that same care. Make a list of them—without grimacing— and then spend five minutes sending them love. Just love them and maybe they'll allow you to blossom! This will help to boost your self-image/self-esteem which is a natural by-product of learning how to care for yourself.

Nurture List

_____

_____

_____

_____

_____

_____

Oftentimes we're harder on ourselves than on our friends. If a friend makes a mistake, we tell them we know they did the best they could and maybe there's something to learn from the particular situation, and certainly, it's not the end of the world. However, if we make a mistake, we wish it were the end of the world and tend to beat ourselves up and have little or no compassion. Self-care would be having a buddy-talk with yourself—with your heart.

So if there's something you've been giving yourself a hard time about, let your heart be your buddy and get a wider perspective about the situation. Your heart truly is your best friend. It will be helpful right now to remember the tool "Oops, no big deal" which you learned a few months ago.

Situation

_____

_____

_____

Heart Intuition Response

_____

_____

_____

_____

Follow Up Exercise—Bonus Insights

Remember those items on your "nurturing list"? Today make an effort to be kind to yourself. If self-limiting thoughts and feelings do come up, send them a little heart. That's self-care. Write down how well you did at nurturing yourself today. How did it feel to be looking out for yourself with care? What did you gain from it?

The beautiful souls are they that are universal, open, and ready for all things.

— *Montaigne*

DAY 3

Today's Reading

In *Self Empowerment*, Chapter 3, "Care and Overcare," Doc Lew Childre gives us an understanding of how a lack of heart energy in the system affects health and vitality.

When people live for years in the head, it upsets their psychic equilibrium which is the result of not enough heart energy flowing through their system. When heart energy is scarce in your system, you tend to develop crystallized patterns in your physical, emotional and mental natures. Mental rigidity keeps you stuck in ruts, seriously hampering your ability to adapt to new situations. When adaptability is low, your immune system suffers. Many illnesses can and do develop from these patterns. But that's not all. YOU miss the quality of life day-to-day and moment-to-moment that you could have had by loving and caring more.

Remember: Care is your engine oil, the lubricant that slows down the aging process because it keeps your mental and emotional nature flexible and filled with spirit. Once you start losing contact with your spirit, life gets dusty and pale. "Is it worth it?" you wonder at times.

Your spirit houses your fun and zip in life. Yet, because of excess stress in the game of life, many people hardly experience their "vitality and spirit" and feel lucky to get through a week without croaking. This is what I mean by living on nerve energy, which is unnatural since it creates "dues" to be paid. Learning to follow your heart will naturally integrate the flow of your spirit into your entire system. You just have to care enough for you to do this for yourself.

Research has often evidenced the power of love and care in the process of self-healing. So, preventive maintenance would be to practice generating more love and care consistently. You can do this by living more from your heart intelligence which is naturally designed for self-maintenance and creative living.

Imagine being able to break out of ruts, boost your immune system and add more zip to your life. Sounds too good to be true. Why not test it for yourself? The only way you'll know for sure is by trying it. Take care of yourself, live life from your heart by loving and caring more and see how you feel at the end of a day, a week or a month.

Write down a little pledge or contract with yourself to make an extra effort to be loving and caring today especially to yourself. Sign it and then be true to your commitment to yourself.

I will

_____

_____

_____

Signature

Exercise

Often we get stuck in ruts, routines or habits that seem comfortable and, therefore, contribute to a false sense of security. Varying that routine or altering a behavior pattern can be difficult. But the more we repeat those old patterns, the more we restrict and constrict our energy, thereby narrowing the channels for our spirit to come through. Life becomes dull and lackluster. Why not add sparkle and spontaneity by risking and modify some of the perpetual ways you do things? This would be caring for your true self.

Are there areas of your life that could use a little sparkle or polish? As an act of self-care, make a list of them and then ask your heart how you could add a little more zip or spontaneity to your day.

215

Areas to Polish

_____

_____

_____

_____

_____

_____

_____

Heart Intuition Response

_____

_____

_____

_____

Ask your heart if there are any areas where you might have become rigid and inflexible. By being more flexible and spontaneous, you can have more fun. This in turn will enable you to be flexible if anything serious should come up. Then it will be easier for you to adapt. Besides, what was true for you yesterday may no longer hold true today, since you are learning and growing. And remember, life isn't exactly the same everyday. It does require adaptability.

Is there a situation (a minor or major one) where you could be more flexible? Ask your heart for an insight on how to adapt to this condition. (It could be as simple as trying a new food, a different route home, an innovative procedure at work or surprising the family with an outing you've repeatedly said "No" to in the past, etc.)

Areas for More Flexibility

_____

_____

_____

_____

_____

_____

_____

_____

Heart Intuition Response

_____

_____

_____

_____

Follow Up Exercise—Bonus Insights

Remember to be flexible as things arise during the course of the day. Catch yourself automatically saying "No" to something new and say "Yes!" And yes to spontaneity! Doing this adds energy to your system. It's like taking an inner vacation.

The best
Thing we can do is to make wherever we're lost in
Look as much like home as we can.

— *Christopher Fry*

DAY ④

 *Today's Reading*

Continuing in *Self Empowerment*, Chapter 3, Doc Lew Childre talks about the importance of making peace with whatever occurs and emphasizes the need to manage overcares.

> Within your heart, you connect with the most trustworthy counselor you can depend on when the bottom falls out in different areas of life. People chase systems of peace, but they are only effective to the degree that they help you contact your real heart truth. Your heart is your personal built-in discriminator. Don't just use it for picking up the pieces when tragedy strikes. Use it daily to become more efficient in all things....

> ...Adapting to the large earthquakes in California had to be extremely stressful for the people immediately involved. It was a stress they couldn't control so they had to either adapt the best they could or experience mental distress. Psychologists observed people who shared similar losses, but noticed extreme differences in their psychological adjustment times. They also observed some who had minor losses experiencing extreme overcare and distress, while others who lost much were caring and appreciative that they had their lives and experienced minimal stress. It's the heart security that helps you to adapt in a crisis and re-establish mental and emotional equilibrium.

> When people use only their minds to adapt after a crisis or a trauma, it can take longer because they find themselves constantly replaying the painful memories and mentally itemizing all the things they lost. This is normal for a while because of the human reaction to shock. How-

ever, if you allow this overcare to continue unchecked, you destroy your peace in this moment as well as diminish your chances for peace in the future. It's your heart security and power that can get you out of the same old mental rut...

The mind is the path of least resistance and can continually lead you in the wrong direction. Your heart can re-route you and get you back on the road to inner peace. Reflect on what you have read today and jot down a few words that summarize what you have learned from these statements.

_____

_____

Exercise

You may be wondering, "What has this got to do with self-care? It sounds like work." Here's how it relates. Creating peace in the moment is important for your well-being. Overcares can rob you of your peace. The key here is to first recognize when you're not at peace and sometimes that recognition is not immediate. The next step is to do something about it—FREEZE-FRAME and ask your heart for a more efficient response. Self-care means creating more moments of peace for yourself—in spite of what is going on around you and what just happened to you. If you're not at peace, you pay the price! Is there a particular area in your life where you're not at peace? During your Heart Lock-In today, ask for guidance on how to have more peace in your life. Write down any new insights or impressions you gain from this Lock-In.

Heart Intuition Response

_____

_____

Do you notice little things that disturb your peace daily—the coworker who always tells "dumb jokes," your carpool buddy who's never ready on time, the waiter who always messes up your order, etc.? Caring for yourself means making peace with situations like these. Sooner is better than later because it saves wear and tear on your system. However, later is better than not at all. So if there are any irritants hanging around the recesses of your mind, ask your heart to help you get to peace with them.

Irritants

_____

_____

_____

_____

Heart Intuition Response

_____

_____

_____

_____

Follow Up Exercise—Bonus Insights

Today become a peace crusader—for your inner peace. It's just caring for yourself. After all, if you saw someone else who wasn't at peace, wouldn't you try to help them? Then be a buddy to yourself and go for inner peace!

All that we are is the result of what we have thought.

— Dhammadpada

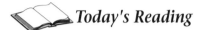

DAY 5

Today's Reading

In *FREEZE-FRAME*, Chapter 5, "Personal Benefits and Applications," Doc Lew Childre explains the important difference between thinking positively and shifting attitudes. He emphasizes heart feelings as the key to shift attitudes and assist in the decision-making process.

> People often attempt to think positively without first making an attitude shift and then wonder why nothing changes. It's because attitudes contain feelings and it takes more than a few positive thoughts to re-route the feelings contained in an attitude—especially a negatively-slanted attitude (like resentment, poor self-image, etc.). On its own, the mind struggles and usually fails in building attitude shifts without the strength and forbearance of the heart's commitment. Approaching attitude changes from the heart-feeling level makes it easier to secure a lasting shift.

> People will achieve more of their personal goals in the future as they truly learn to "put heart into what they do." Freeze-Framing is a window of opportunity to engage your heart feelings in your decision-making. It offers you a deeper understanding of issues the mind often overlooks. With practice you can shift gears and produce energy-saving attitude adjustments throughout the day. You gain what I call "leveraged intelligence" with practical applications. It's leveraged intelligence that restrains you from inviting and repeating the same stress patterns that drain your system and dilute your peace. Leveraged intelligence emerges when the mind and the heart share the same "think tank" before taking action.

A dopting a "heart attitude" is the real attitude shift you want. It will help you approach life in a more efficient manner. Wouldn't you want to give yourself the best possible chance for success and fulfillment? Caring for yourself would be living from the heart. Jot down your insights, if you'd like.

_____

_____

Exercise

Positive thinking and affirmations are steps to self-care. Heart power behind affirmations is even more effective. However, a major step toward true self-care would be making attitude adjustments to pave the way for positive thinking and affirmations. Otherwise, it would be the same as a painter adding a new coat of paint to the house without scraping away the old, decayed, chipped paint. You'd have a superficial finish that just won't stick. As an act of self care, begin now by identifying an aspect of yourself that you'd like to change. Be kind, nurturing and understanding to yourself. Do a Heart Lock-In and then ask your heart how to make a change you would like to make. One that will give you more peace and fulfillment.

Desired Change

_____

_____

Heart Intuition Response

_____

_____

Is there an area of your life that isn't as smooth as you'd like? Maybe not a big deal, but just a little bumpy? If the road is repeatedly bumpy in the same places, perhaps it's time to shift attitudes. Sometimes it's amazing what happens when we make one little change within ourselves and then watch what happens around us. Of course, it's best not to have any expectations. Ask your heart for a read-out to help you shift an attitude and take the bumps out of the road.

Attitude

_____

_____

Heart Intuition Response

_____

_____

_____

Follow Up Exercise—Bonus Insights

Make extra effort to love yourself more today. Do something that feels good or is good for you. Don't worry about the little things. Today is a day of self-care. Write down the three most important things you learned from this week's practice.

1. _____

_____

2. _____

_____

3. _____

_____

*There came a time when the risk to remain tight in a bud
was more painful than the risk it took to blossom.*

— *Anais Nin*

DAY ①

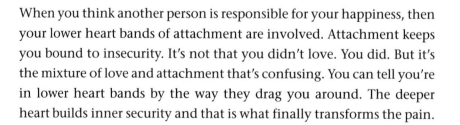

Today's Reading

In *The Hidden Power of the Heart*, Chapter 12, "Uncovering Compassion," Sara Paddison explains the importance of finding fulfillment independent of anyone or anything else, including our overcares. She also gives us a deeper understanding of love and that "special feeling."

> You'll discover that real love is millions of miles past falling in love with anyone or anything. When you make that one effort to feel compassion instead of blame or self-blame, the heart opens again and continues opening. It's only a mind-set (but a strong one) that says you need to have a certain something to feel that special feeling in your heart. Life will bring that feeling back to you, but you have to be open—it may come gift-wrapped in a different package than before. Your spirit wants more than anything for you to feel that total fulfillment, without dependency on someone or something for your security.

~◦~

> When you think another person is responsible for your happiness, then your lower heart bands of attachment are involved. Attachment keeps you bound to insecurity. It's not that you didn't love. You did. But it's the mixture of love and attachment that's confusing. You can tell you're in lower heart bands by the way they drag you around. The deeper heart builds inner security and that is what finally transforms the pain.

Attachment can develop from insecurity and overcares and rob a relationship of its sparkle, or even cause it to dissolve. Developing security from the heart is the real key to happiness and fulfillment. Whether or not you are in a relationship, your happiness still depends on you creating it for yourself. Jot down your insights about Sara's statements.

_____

_____

_____

Exercise

Knowing that you can create your own happiness and that you are whole are important steps to a healthy relationship. Perhaps your present relationship could benefit if you or the other person had more self-security. Take a good look at it and see if there's any overcare that might be getting in the way, leaking your energy and taking the joy out of the relationship. Allow yourself to blossom on your own. Ask your heart for guidance and write down what it says.

Relationship Overcare

_____

_____

_____

Heart Intuition Response

_____

_____

_____

No one likes to be the recipient of overcare. Those who overcare are frequently called "naggers." Nagging can range from "Why didn't you call?" to "You forgot to take out the trash—again." Nagging sounds like a record that's stuck in the groove—going nowhere. So if you're the nagger, stop sounding like a broken record. It's not helping you or the other person. Go back to the point of original care and then speak your truth from the heart. And if you're the "naggee," you might politely make the other person aware that they're in overcare and have a heartfelt talk with them about what's really going on and how their care might have run amuck into overcare. You can both appreciate that the origin of the situation was care!

If these scenarios apply to you, jot down your insights as the nagger and/or the naggee. Remember, your heart will give you a wider perspective on the situation.

_____

_____

_____

_____

_____

_____

_____

Follow Up Exercise—Bonus Insights

Today is a "nag-free day." If an overcare comes up that you wish to express—don't—until you go to your heart first and have gone back to that point of true care. After your heart gives you an understanding, you may not even have to say anything, or if you still do, what you have to say will stand a better chance of being heard because you are speaking your heart truth.

One learns people through the heart, not the eyes or the intellect.

— *Mark Twain*

DAY 2

Today's Reading

Reviewing in *The Hidden Power of the Heart*, Chapter 5, "Higher and Lower Heart Frequencies," we discover an explanation from Sara Paddison about attachment and how detrimental it can be to a marriage.

> ...The feelings of true love and care are very different from feelings like attachment and overcare. As you practice bringing your emotional pulls back to your higher heart, you will gain a peaceful feeling of true love, care or compassion.
>
> Many marriages are based on intimacy, but when this turns into physical or emotional attachment couples often become insecure and the relationship can get sticky. The stickiness often causes one partner to want to pull away. By learning the difference between this isolated frequency of intimacy and all the other frequencies of the real heart that are clear, compassionate and caring, you can bring new love, depth and fulfillment to a marriage.

> As you understand your higher and lower heart frequencies, you start building an efficient relationship between them. Your experience of life deepens as you bring your energies back to the higher heart as soon as you notice unsatisfying feelings. Your intuition will wisely guide you into the balanced and intelligent heart frequencies of true love.

Higher heart frequencies always feel good. Lower heart frequencies don't feel so good. When any uncomfortable or unsatisfying feelings come up, try to view them as an opportunity to make positive changes in yourself, which in turn will enhance your relationship. Jot down your insights if you'd like.

_____

_____

_____

Exercise

Unconditional love is free from judgment, fear, impatience, resentment, self-pity, worry and sadness. Since it comes from the heart, it doesn't have any of these overcares generated by the head that can interfere with a relationship and drain it of its fun, vitality and intimacy. Unconditional love is a great concept, but it has to be worked on and refined.

Are there any overcares that creep into your relationship? Take a sincere look at your feelings and make a list of any overcares that might be undermining your relationship. See if you can identify conditions that you have put on your love for someone. Then ask your heart for a deeper understanding of the situation.

Overcares that Contribute to Conditional Love

_____

_____

_____

_____

Heart Intuition Response

_____

_____

_____

_____

In a relationship, we can get into overcare about ourselves, as well as about our significant other. Then we have double trouble. In either case, it's an inefficient use of our energy and doesn't help the situation. Do you ever find yourself overcaring about your mate? If you do, remember to go back to true care. It might not fix the situation, but it might help you get to peace in the moment. You can't control the outcome of some situations. You can only control how you feel about them. From a place of peace, however, you can gain a better understanding and determine your next step—which might be one of action or one of simply sending love and care.

List any particular overcares you might have about your significant other and ask your heart for any insights so that you can get back to peace and care. Remember, when you can care without going into overcare, the effects of your real care will be more potent.

Overcares

Heart Intuition Response

Follow Up Exercise—Bonus Insights
Throughout this day make extra efforts to manage any overcares that come up in regards to your relationships. Observe how doing this makes you feel.

Nothing so needs reforming as other people's habits.

— *Mark Twain*

DAY ③

Today's Reading

In *Self Empowerment*, Chapter 5, "An Overlooked Relationship," Doc Lew Childre talks about improving relationships by improving yourself!

> Many people separate or get divorced when they really are (or were) compatible. Because of a lack of individual management, their compatibility didn't get a chance to gel. So, if you really want to help a troubled relationship, assess yourself at a deeper heart level. As you rebalance your own self through heart management, you begin to see others from a different perspective and understand them through different feelings. If people do that, they'll have a good chance of saving a relationship or at least maturely separating.

> Lack of self-maturity is the leading cause of relationship problems. Becoming your true self progressively develops that maturity. Start by performing spring cleaning on your own inner junk, while at the same time becoming more sensitive to the other person's needs....It's a mechanical habit of the mind that causes people to think it's others who always need to change. You can drain yourself trying to arrange people to suit your mental and emotional needs. Rearranging your own attitudes puts you on the fast track to self-security and peace.

> Build a heart-secure relationship with yourself, so you can enjoy relationships with others without crossing the line into over-dependency.

Over-dependency is an easy trap to fall into. And there's only one way out—through the heart. Your heart will give you the security you need. The relationship you have with yourself is really the most important one. It's the only one you can change and affect the others. Doc has said a mouthful in these last few paragraphs. Jot down your insights.

_____

_____

_____

Exercise

Are there areas in any of your relationships where you've become overly dependent? This can be with your child, friend, spouse, etc. You can tell by the way the relationship feels. Honestly ask your heart if there's some area where you need to be less dependent and then ask it for guidance.

Area of Over-Dependence

_____

_____

_____

Heart Intuition Response

_____

_____

_____

_____

Overcare in any relationship usually stems from a lack of security within ourselves, leading to over-dependence and overcare. Make a list of your overcares that might cause you to be over-dependent. These could include jealousy, fear of breakup, too eager to please, wanting to "fix it" for the other person, etc.

Overcares

1. _____
2. _____
3. _____
4. _____
5. _____
6. _____
7. _____
8. _____

Follow Up Exercise—Bonus Insights

Today, observe attachments and over-dependency on others for your security. It's okay if you see some things about yourself that you were not aware of. Don't be hard on yourself. You are learning and growing very quickly.

Jot down your observations before you end your day.

_____
_____
_____
_____

Life is not a "brief candle." It is a splendid torch that I want to
make burn as brightly as possible before handing on to future generations.

— *George Bernard Shaw*

DAY (4)

Today's Reading

In *Self Empowerment*, Chapter 3, "Care and Overcare," Doc Lew Childre talks
about overcare in parents and the stress it creates not only for the parents,
but for their offspring as well.

> ...Overcare ranks close to the top of the list of human energy drains.
> It's in the same family as worrying, and worrying hasn't won you many
> trophies. Here's a common example of overcare to give you a "hands-
> on" understanding.
>
> Many parents have a hard time emotionally releasing their children
> when they leave home, go to college, get married, etc. They spend
> much time worrying about their children's welfare and suffering from
> a sense of loss. This often leads to a smothering involvement with their
> offspring as they are trying to get on with their own lives.

> Much ongoing stress is created in these overly-attached relationships.
> The parents stay stressed because of their overcare; the children stay
> stressed because of their parents' over-involvement in their affairs. Not
> only is it hard for some parents to release young adults to live their own
> lives, they often want to govern the lives of their grandchildren as well.
> It all originates from care—but when it crosses the line into overcare,
> the family relationships get drained. Everybody thinks that everyone
> else is wrong. This can lead to family fussing, fighting, feuds and sepa-
> ration.
>
> ...It's wonderful to love and care, but the overcare blocks the pathways
> of love, becoming a hindrance and a continuing source of stress to all
> concerned.

233

Well, we've all been children, so chances are we might have experienced being overcared for at some point in our life. The question is, however, is it genetically programmed or can we stop it from being passed on to the next generation? If you have children, they'll let you know how successful you've been. Jot down your insights about what you have read today.

Exercise

Do you really think that someday your children will look back and say, "Boy, my mom and dad really loved me because everyday they reminded me to take a jacket so I wouldn't get cold and to wipe my nose if it ran." Perhaps, or they could look back and say, "Boy, my parents really undermined by self-confidence because they thought I couldn't tell if I was cold or I wouldn't know to wipe my nose if it was running." They might think, "Boy, my parents were really into overcare."

No matter what the answer is, the real question is, why overcare? Why not take another approach? During a Heart Lock-In today, ask your heart how to deal with situations similar to these that may be in your life, so that your true care can come through.

Raising children is quite a task and good parent/child relationships can be tough to maintain. One sure way to develop a block to communication with children is by nagging them. They'll learn to tune you out real fast. Instead of persistently reminding them about something, why not get their input on how they feel? "Do you think you need a jacket today?" When do you think is the best time to do your homework?" "Do you want to take out the trash before or after dinner?" Empower your child by giving him/her a choice and a chance. Let them learn to make their own decisions, when appropriate, and learn to trust their feelings. If their decision wasn't quite the most efficient one, it will have been a good learning experience. This way you are supporting your child in his/her growth, not stifling it. (This, of course, would not necessarily apply to more serious matters.)

Are there areas in dealing with children (you may not have children but may have situations where you interact with young people) where you could take another approach? Ask your heart for guidance. Write one down and then go to your heart to see what you would determine as a better way to deal with an adult/child communication issue.

Situation

_____

_____

_____

Heart Intuition Response

_____

_____

_____

Follow Up Exercise—Bonus Insights

Observe yourself today and notice if any of your actions, communications, etc. regarding your relationships originate from overcare. Hey, you're not alone. Most of us were raised on overcare. It's time to wean yourself!

> We forget ourselves and our destinies in health,
> and the chief use of temporary sickness is to remind us of these concerns.
>
> — *Emerson*

DAY (5)

Today's Reading

In *The Hidden Power of the Heart*, Chapter 5, "Higher and Lower Heart Frequencies," Sara Paddison offers us a valuable insight from her personal experience on caring and not overcaring for someone who is ill.

> Care is a higher heart band that can easily slip into the lower heart band called overcare. I caught myself slipping into overcare while caring for a very sick friend. I could feel her pain, her worry that she was going to die. In the past, I would have worried and cried with her in sympathy. However, I knew that worry would only drain both of us. Instead, I activated the most sincere care I could feel from my heart and kept sending that quality of care to her. I was able to know when she needed liquid, warmth or a kind word. She became very peaceful and my own energies stayed in balance. At the end of the day, I was serene and she was sincerely grateful.

> When you allow lower heart bands to take over your feelings, they can deplete your system and cause tremendous stress. People operate from the heart some of the time, but often believe they consistently do, when it's really overcare, attachment, sentiment and expectations they are feeling. These frequencies cut off your connection to your higher heart. They can easily lead to thoughts of worry, disappointment and fear. These thoughts then activate more feelings of insecurity, hurt and pain. That's why the heart is often perceived as being so vulnerable.

The best way to determine if you're in overcare is by how you feel. If you are feeling any stress, you know that you've crossed that fine line. Remember, care feels good. Overcare doesn't. Jot down your insights.

_____

_____

_____

Exercise

You can get yourself out of sympathy and into empathy by converting your overcare to compassion. This would be especially true in dealing with people who are close to you—your relationships. Both empathy and compassion come from a wider perspective so you can see more of the picture. Sympathy and overcare are like sitting in a dark room. Turn on the light—from your heart—for a deeper understanding.

From time to time do you find yourself sucked into an energy vortex of sympathy and overcare? Do you have a situation in your life like this? Ask your heart for that wider perspective.

Situation

_____

_____

_____

Heart Intuition Response

_____

_____

_____

_____

We've all had times in our lives when a family member or close friend has been very ill. This can be a tough time for all concerned. Thoughts of worry often pop up during times like these. Since you know now that these thoughts will take you down a dead-end street, try to catch them in the moment and re-route them with feelings of love and care. That will certainly help you feel better—and for all you know, it might even help that person. Try it and see!

Jot down any insights you might have from an experience like dealing with illness. Remember, it is important to always care when someone is ill or having other problems but it is hard not to get into overcare. It's just better for them and for yourself to try and get out of overcare so that your true care can have more effect on the situation.

Follow Up Exercise—Bonus Insights

Overcare is hard to catch. It can be about anyone, anything, at anytime. The only cure is to be operating from your heart intelligence so that you can be self-aware enough to see and eliminate overcare. Care not to overcare and care to catch yourself overcaring. That would be true care for yourself and others. Do you care?

Jot down your observations about the need for more care and less overcare in relationships.

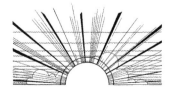

The part can never be well unless the whole is well.

— *Plato*

DAY ①

Today's Reading

In *The Hidden Power of the Heart*, Chapter 6, "The Dimensional Shift," Sara Paddison gives us another perspective on the power of love as the world moves towards actualizing more of it.

> In personal and international relationships of the future, attempts to overpower others will be seen as dysfunctional behavior. Such actions will be recognized as harmful to global balance and peace. Love is inevitable; it is our true essence. We are multi-dimensional beings waking up to our own higher natures. As we love more, we break through old barriers and crystallized patterns. However, going against the flow of the planet's transition into truer love will create overloads of stress. Resistance to change creates inharmonious feedback in the human system, affecting family, business, social and political structures.... Conscious, intelligent love can overcome all resistance. There are solutions, knowledge, understanding, and tools to facilitate....Remember, love conquers all.

> The power of love, or heart power, is qualified power, based on how well energy is managed within a system. Picture the heart as the hub of a wheel of power; the spokes are the mental, emotional, physical and other aspects of our nature. In a family or organization, the spokes are the collective individuals. What is the United States of America but a collection of individuals? It's the same for a city, a gang, a corporation, the world and, yes, the same principle applies to the universe. The universe is a collection of individual energy units. All parts working harmoniously together create wholeness.

We are each a part of the whole—the universe. The head separates. The heart unites. You can become greater than yourself by uniting with love and work harmoniously towards creating the wholeness of the universe.

Jot down your impressions of Sara's profound insights.

_____

_____

_____

_____

_____

Exercise

If you picture the planet, you can view it as a sphere—one continuous unit. Or you can choose to see it as made up of many countries separated by artificial boundaries. Boundaries are man-made. The planet was not created with them, with the exception of natural ones like mountain ranges, rivers, lakes, etc.). The head prefers to view things as separate (an illusion) and draw boundaries.

Perhaps there are areas in your life where you still perceive yourself as separate. This would be true for almost everyone. It could be with the maintenance engineer (because he holds a lesser position), a coworker (because he attended a lesser college), your neighbor (because his skin is a different color), etc. Take a deep, hard look at these areas and ask your heart to help you see a new perspective on the concept of separation.

Areas of Separation

_____

_____

_____

_____

Heart Intuition Response

Follow Up Exercise—Bonus Insights

Today as people cross your path, make a game of greeting them with a smile. In the heart, everyone is family—all part of the whole.

Touch the earth, love the earth, honour the earth, her plains,
her valleys, her hills, and her seas; rest your spirit in her solitary places.

— *Henry Beston*

DAY ②

Today's Reading

In *The Hidden Power of the Heart*, Chapter 21, "Care or Overcare?" Sara Paddison awakens us to the need for love and care for our future and the future of the planet.

The entire world is undergoing tremendous change and growth at this time. As does a teenager going through adolescence, the planet needs a lot of care. Earth was created in the beginning as a planet of love and care. That's obvious to anyone who looks at the beauty of nature. It's a family planet. If we look from the perspective of a caring mother, Mother Earth would want to help her children grow up with as few scratches and scrapes as possible. But there's a fine balance to parenting. In caring for your child, how much do you protect him and how much do you let him explore and make his own mistakes?...A mother wouldn't take away the experience of the scrape because she knows that's how he'll learn, gain his security and become independent. She wants her child to grow up and be responsible for himself.

Mother Earth would rather not lose even one of the souls that are part of her body. But, like any truly caring mother, she would rather they be where they can learn what they need to learn than overcare that they won't be part of her immediate family any longer. It is possible, if enough people move forward in the choice to care, that we can create a network of love and light so finely woven that not one soul need be left behind. The magnetics of such a grid would awaken the hearts and minds of all people to the understanding that to love and care is the only common sense choice.

It looks like it's time to exercise our common sense by loving and caring. It's the best and most efficient thing we can do for ourselves and the planet. Your heart knows that. You just need to convince your head. Jot down your insights about what you have read.

Exercise

Okay, let's get down to the nitty-gritty now. So where could you be more loving and caring in your life? Let's be honest here. And what's stopping you— pride, ego, stubbornness, embarrassment, overcare, etc.? Would you rather stay stuck in your head, holding on to self-limiting concepts which subtly drain your energy or would you finally like to free yourself and find happiness and fulfillment? It's always your choice.

An important step is to identify self-limiting concepts that create separation between you, others and the gift of life itself. The second is to ask your heart for an understanding. And the third is to follow your heart directives. You never know. It might be a lot easier than you think to clean up these areas. And everyone will benefit, especially you. Write them down and go for it!

Areas for more love and care that will create unity and harmony

---

It's our insecurities, fears and lack of understanding that keep us separate from each other. Look for similarities among people, not differences. Once you have discovered the commonalities, then you can appreciate the differences through allowing people to be themselves.

Are there specific individuals or groups of people that you tend to separate from? Write them down. Do a Heart Lock-In today and send heart to the people or groups you feel separated from and then ask your heart to help you find the similarities. Remember, we are all really connected in the heart. It's your head that perceives everyone as separate.

People you perceive as separate   *Similarities*

Follow Up Exercise—Bonus Insights

Really observe yourself today. Just how loving and caring are you and where could you add more love and care? Begin with little things you could do and start doing them. Then you can care more for the "big things," and it will feel more natural. Remember loving and caring nurture the body and soul—and the planet! Before you end your day, write down any experiences you had where you began to feel more connected to others.

A man of humanity is one who, in seeking to establish himself, finds a foothold for others and who, desiring attainment for himself, helps others to attain.

— *Confucius*

DAY ③

Today's Reading

In *Self Empowerment*, Chapter 3, "Care and Overcare," Doc Lew Childre talks about the importance of care in all aspects of life and attributes many of the problems on the planet to a lack of care.

> At this point in time, people as a whole care more for issues, things, money, etc., than they do for each other. Society is learning the hard way that the lack of care and respect for each other causes the ecological and political systems to fall short of balance and efficiency. I'm talking about the lack of care that exists country to country, state to state, town to town, among businesses, within churches, within families and within individuals for themselves.
>
> All areas of relationship are experiencing compounded stress because they have lost contact with the heart frequency of care amidst business and social interactions. Governments and businesses use people as pawns to develop self-centered ambitions, forgetting that care, cooperation and co-creation would produce more harmony, balance and success for the whole.

> The heart's not just some mushy and sentimental doormat. It especially has business bands of common sense and discrimination, meaning: You don't have to lay down and let people take advantage of you without looking out for yourself. If you do that, you end up blaming the negative results on the heart, when your unmanaged head reactions caused the stress feedback. Don't let the head shut off your caring if other people don't respond as you hoped they would. Go back to your heart and find another common sense approach—it could be to simply move on. Just remember, heart intelligence has crisp, clear business discrimination. Use it.

It's important to realize that the heart takes care of business—yours. Don't just rely on it concerning "matters of the heart." To the heart, everything matters! Use its common sense to guide you in all aspects of your life.

Jot down your insights about what you read today.

_____

_____

_____

_____

_____

Exercise

Care in family builds togetherness and cooperation. Care in business builds morale and teamwork. It's the glue that will hold everything together. Even if we think we care, we can always take our care to a deeper level.

Examine both your personal and professional life to see where you could add more care. Ask your heart for insights. It could be the missing ingredient for more efficiency and fulfillment. Take the time to care and then stand back and watch what happens. Sometimes it just mushrooms and grows, adding a sparkle to everyone's day— especially yours. Ask yourself how you can be more caring in your family and business life. Write down what you feel. Remember, global care starts with you.

Additional care to family

_____

_____

_____

_____

_____

Additional care to business

_____

_____

_____

_____

_____

_____

Follow Up Exercise—Bonus Insights

Remember, caregivers have higher levels of Salivary IgA. Take this test: care more throughout the day and see how much better you feel at day's end. That means sincere care—no expectations or hidden agendas, just true care. And give yourself a pat on the back for caring!

Jot down your observations about this day.

_____

_____

_____

_____

_____

_____

If each of us sweeps in front of our own steps, the whole world would be clean.
— Goethe

DAY 4

Today's Reading

Continuing in *Self Empowerment*, Chapter 3, "Care and Overcare," Doc Lew Childre explains how the lack of true care is affecting the ecology of the planet. The remedy, he suggests, is for each of us to clean up our inner ecology.

> ...It's simply that people care too much about the nonessentials and too little about things that count. The planet is toxic with stress because of the lack of true care and the distortions from overcare. This seriously affects the planetary balance as evidenced in the rain forests and the ozone layer. People eventually will realize that distortions in consciousness affect the rhythms of nature. They will recognize the need to clean up the inner-ecology (the giant mental and emotional oil spill). As people clean up their inner ecology, they will intuit more efficient directions to balance the outer ecology.

———— ✦ ————

> The lack of care and harmonious interaction between countries and people has always had an adverse effect on the natural rhythms of the planet. It's just that now the deficit accrued from inefficient thinking and living is releasing a backwash of increased "people stress" into the entire system. The planet is not being punished; it's not a personal thing. It's just a mathematical effect from a cause. Stress is not retribution. It's simply inharmonious incoming energy created by inefficient outgoing energy—a cause and effect kind of thing.

It's amazing how the planet is adversely affected by our lack of care. Cleaning up the planet has to become an inside job. We each have to clean up our own act!

Jot down your insights about today's reading.

_____

_____

_____

_____

Exercise

Caring for people is what counts. If people truly cared about one another, there would be harmony on the planet. That harmony would create its own energy which would further nurture everyone and everything. As people cared more about each other, they would be able to work harmoniously together and create effective solutions for problems and re-establish the "planetary equilibrium."

Can you think of examples of people working together for a common cause? Can you see where egos and hidden agendas are counterproductive? Efficient outcomes are based on individuals who efficiently manage their mental and emotional energies.

Is there a project you're working on in either your personal or business life? Perhaps more care from each individual would streamline the efficiency and effectiveness of the work. Maybe the approach to take is creating cohesiveness among the participants as the primary goal and the project the secondary one. It's certainly worth a try. Sometimes when we put people first, everything else just seems to fall in place. Ask your heart for insights about how to make this project more harmonious and cohesive and jot them down.

_____

_____

_____

_____

Can you think of organizations or movements that were successful in accomplishing their goals? What do you think was the reason for their success? By contrast, identify some groups who had difficulty attaining their goal. What was the reason for their lack of success?

Jot down any insights you were able to gain from these ponderings.

_____

_____

_____

_____

_____

Follow Up Exercise—Bonus Insights

Observe yourself throughout the day. Are you contributing to the toxicity of the planet or are you helping to restore its equilibrium? Remember, the only steps you can sweep are your own.

Before you go to bed tonight, write down any valuable insights you had today while observing yourself and your contributions to the world as a whole.

_____

_____

_____

_____

_____

How should one live? Live welcoming to all.

— Mechtild of Magdeburg

DAY 5

Today's Reading

Once again, continuing in *Self Empowerment*, Chapter 3, "Care and Overcare," Doc Lew Childre helps us to understand how loving and caring can restore the planetary equilibrium.

> From my perspective, the next decade will produce enough stress to cause mass reconsideration of the effects that negative, non-caring thoughts and actions have on our (future) ecosystem....
>
> For many people, harmonious living sounds like a pipe dream or a non-approachable idealism. By harmony, I'm not implying that within a few years everyone will be giving each other foot massages and the shirts off their backs. Still, life can get much better than it is if individuals practice self-responsibility. As people relate more from the heart, the planetary equilibrium can be re-established. Again, it's just math—efficiency outgoing produces more harmony incoming.

> ...You don't have to wait for the rest of the planet to find balance before you can have your peace, fun and quality in life. Practice loving and caring for people more. You enjoy it when it comes your way. It's the way of the heart and can tremendously help clean up the internal stress environment. Planetary equilibrium readily responds to the balance or the lack of balance in the people. As people love each other more, they develop more of a natural tendency to extend that love to the earth and all aspects of creation. Everything is nurtured as it experiences love.

In every moment, we each have a choice to be loving. Making an inefficient choice will not only affect us adversely, but can negatively affect those around us—as well as the planet. The most caring choice is love!

Jot down your insights.

_____

_____

_____

_____

Exercise

We've already identified areas where you could be more caring in family and business. But care doesn't begin and end there. There might be other overlooked areas where you could extend your care. How about friends, neighbors, coworkers, relatives, the grocery clerk, gas station attendant, etc. After doing your Heart Lock-In today, make a list of these people. If they've already been covered in your previous list, that's okay too. Ask your heart how you could be more caring in this area of your life as well. Then the next step is to acknowledge these people when you see them by appreciating and sincerely caring about them. So often we tend to take people like these for granted. They deserve our care, too. They're part of the family of man. In order to restore harmony to the planet, there has to be harmony among people—all people.

Extending Care List

_____

_____

_____

_____

_____

Are you, by any chance, still carrying around any grudges, resentments, judgments, etc.? Remember, they're contributing to the toxic spill on the planet. It's time to clean them up. Besides, why would you want to have that negative energy in your system? It's not healthy for you or the planet. It's time to let go and move on. Ask your heart for insights to help you release these thought patterns and get to a place of peace.

Negative Thought Pattern

_____

_____

_____

Heart Intuition Response

_____

_____

_____

Follow Up Exercise—Bonus Insights

This month a lot has been covered primarily around the understanding of the power of and need for care as well as the drain and inefficiency of overcare. Make a list of the five most important insights you have had this month and then make a commitment to act on them.

1. _____
2. _____
3. _____
4. _____
5. _____

MONTH 5
Balance

> ...we are the masters of our fate, the captains of our souls,
> because we have the power to control our thoughts.
>
> — *Napolean Hill*

DAY ①

📖 *Today's Reading*

In *The Hidden Power of the Heart*, Chapter 23, "Balance: Faster than Light," Sara Paddison talks about people's efficiency in dealing with financial expenditures, but points out how neglectful they can be in handling their energy expenditures.

Because the heart knows which energy expenditures are efficient and non-efficient, its intelligence can manage your personal assets and deficits. When businesses keep financial records, they use a balance sheet—a record of their assets and liabilities—to determine their bottom line. Most of us know we need to balance our checkbooks to keep track of our cash flow. People who play the stock market pay close attention to the various aspects of their portfolio, maneuvering their assets to create capital gains....Much time and energy is put into evaluating finances. If people put even a small percentage of their time towards balancing their energy expenditures from the heart, what would that do for their real bottom line—peace and inner security?

Balance is like standing in the middle of a seesaw and finding how much weight to put on each side so it won't tip over and you can enjoy the ride. Balance applies to all aspect of life—physical, mental, emotional, spiritual. Letting your heart computer weigh the pluses and minuses in each situation is the most efficient means of finding balance....

Have you ever really wanted to do something but found yourself dragging and saying in despair, "I just don't have the energy anymore!" Life is an economy game. Heart intelligence shows you how to both save and invest your energy efficiently.

Your heart can help you find balance in your life and how to expend your energy efficiently. It's the best accountant to manage your energy expenditures and balance your energy deficits, and the price is right. Jot down your insights about the concept of energy efficiency.

_____

_____

_____

Exercise

Balance is one of the keys to happiness and fulfillment. Being aware of when you're out of balance is important. You can be out of balance mentally, emotionally and/or physically. Look at the balance checklists below to see if there are any areas you can identify with. Knowing that these things can upset your balance might help you catch yourself next time so that you won't tip the seesaw of life.

Physical Balance List

❏ not enough rest or sleep
❏ eating on the run
❏ not eating properly
❏ not enough exercise
❏ poor posture (limits breathing capacity)
❏ having that "one for the road"
❏ bingeing on food
❏ watching too much television

If there are areas you can identify with on this list, ask your heart how you can achieve more balance for your physical system. Jot down your insights and do try to follow your heart directives.

_____

_____

_____

Mental-Emotional Balance List

❏ agendas and expectations
❏ attachments
❏ anger
❏ thought loops
❏ overcares
❏ judgments
❏ frustration

If there are areas you can identify with on this list, ask your heart how you can find more balance for your mental and emotional systems. Jot down your insights, and once again, do try to follow your heart directives.

_____

_____

_____

Follow Up Exercise—Bonus Insights

Every day is a balancing act. Oftentimes, we feel like we're walking a tight-rope without a safety net. By now you've learned that you have the greatest safety net of all—your heart! Remember to be conscious of balance through-out the day and keep yourself balanced! Jot down your observations before you end your day.

_____

_____

_____

_____

It is not because things are difficult that we do not dare;
it is because we do not dare that they are difficult.

— *Seneca the Elder*

DAY ②

Today's Reading

Continuing in *The Hidden Power of the Heart*, Chapter 23, Sara Paddison asks us to look at our mental and emotional expenditures at the end of each day to see if they have been productive or non-productive. Keeping an account of our energy investments can help us achieve balance.

> An efficient self-management strategy would be to observe your mental and emotional energy expenditures. If you are serious about wanting a larger return on your energy investments, create a personal balance sheet to see how you spend your precious vital energy, your "vitality." In practicing the HeartMath system, I've often asked my heart computer, "Are my energy expenditures (actions, reactions, thoughts, etc.) productive or non-productive? During the course of my day, have I accumulated more stress or more peace?" Before you go to bed at night, or at some convenient time during your day, try to remember the flow and feeling of your day—its ups and downs and how you felt by the end of it. Truthfully, ask yourself if these feelings added to the quality of your day or detracted from it.

> Though it may seem a bit time-consuming to keep a written record of your energy assets and deficits, it will buy time for you in the long run. As you practice, it gets easier and you'll no longer need to write everything down. You'll be able to recognize assets and deficits just by using your intuition. Within time, you'll see where to simply self-correct right in the moment of the day. Remember, you wake up each morning with a specific amount of mental, emotional and physical energy to spend that day. Efficient choices add to your energy account. Inefficient choices deplete your vitality.

L ife is a matter of efficiency—are you investing your energy efficiently or inefficiently? Every thought, action or behavior is either productive or non-productive. Think about how you feel right now. Then check out your energy account to see if it is balanced. Jot down your insights if you'd like.

_____

_____

_____

_____

_____

Exercise

This is an exercise to keep track of your energy bank account—which energy expenditures are adding to your account and which are depleting it. As you become more efficient with your mental and emotional energy, you begin to see that you are winning at the game of life that day, month or year. Here's your assignment. Think about your day or if it is more appropriate, yesterday.

1. Write down your assets and deficits in two columns, like a banker, taking a clear inventory so you can objectively see your inner world.

2. Note your efficient, fulfilling thoughts and actions in the Assets column— the times when you followed the directions of your heart, or used FREEZE-FRAME, etc.

3. Also spend a little time noting the mental and emotional reactions of irritations, impatience, hurt, pain, disappointment, jealousy, self-doubt, judgment, anger, etc.—all the head reactions that cause Deficits.

Energy Asssets	*Energy Deficits*

If you look at your head and heart reactions at the end of a day, a week or a month, you can see how much and where you are missing or gaining in the quality of life. Using your Energy Efficiency Balance Sheet will focus your energies, clean up your backyard and accelerate you quickly.

Follow Up Exercise—Bonus Insights

Take a few moments during the course of the day and look at your energy bank account. Are you making more withdrawals than deposits? If you're loving, caring, appreciating, etc., you're adding to that bank account.

Life is not a matter of holding good cards, but of playing a poor hand well.
— *Robert Louis Stevenson*

DAY ③

Today's Reading

Reading further in *The Hidden Power of the Heart*, Chapter 23, "Balance: Faster than Light," Sara Paddison helps us to gain an understanding of the role of the heart in achieving balance.

> Balancing is an "understanding game" you play with yourself to find out which choices are best for you at any moment in each area of your life. If you manage your head thoughts and emotions enough to see and understand both sides of any issue—both sides of the seesaw—then the balance point is easily accessed. But your head can fool you without an injection of real wisdom from the heart.
>
> Bringing anything into harmonious proportion increases your overall enjoyment and feeling of well-being. Anything that becomes an addiction is out of balance, whether it's food, alcohol, sex, work or other stimuli. When balanced by your own self-management, you can appreciate stimulation without losing control.

> Passion is a powerfully regenerative energy that is balanced when expressed from the heart. When expressed through the head, passions get out of balance and can run you around the block and them some! It's up to each individual to discover the right balance for their system. Your own heart computer will indicate areas you need to adjust. You may hear the voice of your consciousness inside or have a funny feeling when you begin to do something that will take you out of balance. Stress is a sure sign you're not balanced. As you practice becoming aware of stress, you can then go back to your heart for a read-out on what you might be overdoing or underdoing or missing altogether.

Y ou don't have to be a detective to know when you're out of balance. Stress is your first clue. The bigger stressors are more obvious. It's those subtle, little ones that are more difficult to detect. A good detective starts with the little clues because he knows they lead somewhere. In this case, it's back to the heart! Jot down your insights about what you have read today.

Exercise

Everything in life needs to be balanced. Too much of anything can be detrimental. People can become almost fanatical in their endeavors and overdo just about anything—overexercising, overeating, overworking, oversleeping, etc. Not enough of something can be equally harmful—not enough exercise, not enough food, not enough sleep, etc. Are there areas in your life that could benefit from more balance? Seriously look at a typical week and see where you could add more balance. Ask your heart for guidance.

Areas That Need More Balance

Heart Intuition Response

An area that we often overlook is the balance between work and play. In today's fast-moving society, finding time for play and recreation seems difficult. But it is important for regeneration and rejuvenation. Sometimes taking even a couple of hours on the weekend for something other than household chores can be very refreshing and enables us then to take care of business more easily and efficiently. All work and no play can actually be unhealthful. Trying to make work your play is also helpful. Balance, though, is the key. During your Lock-In today (yes, another friendly reminder to do Lock-Ins regularly), ask your heart to help you find that balance. Jot down your insights about the need for balance between work and play.

_____

_____

_____

Follow Up Exercise—Bonus Insights

Make an effort today to be more sensitive to your inner balance. Try to find a smooth flow through your daily activities. If things start to move too fast or you start to feel stressed, take a few minutes and practice a tool like FREEZE-FRAME or appreciation and find the flow again. If you'd like, before you end your day, write down your insights about how you did at staying in the state of balance.

_____

_____

_____

A matter that becomes clear ceases to concern us.

— Nietzsche

DAY (4)

Today's Reading

In concluding Chapter 23, Sara Paddison once again emphasizes the importance of energy efficiency and makes it perfectly clear that the most efficient way to manage your energies is through the heart.

Remembering to balance your account causes rapid acceleration. HeartMath shows that 1 sincere effort—1 investment in activating heart frequencies— brings a 9 energy return. A great investment! As you come to know the deeper levels of your own heart, you also come to know that life really boils down to an economy game. As your assets increase, fulfillment increases. As you become more efficient with your mental and emotional energies, you realize that you're winning at the game of life that day, month or year.

Through your heart, do your best to find balance in each moment. Then go for deeper, more sincere love and care. For example, when daily life starts to look overwhelming, the first rule in my system is to stay in peace. Then I can find my balance and know what action to take as I follow that flow. I can watch an intricate timing of events where everything seems to fall in place. Since there is no time in reality, balance crunches time into a flow. Everything gets done. You find you are creating your own timing with efficient decisions each moment. As you do your best to balance, it mathematically activates your next level of awareness, so you can enjoy any ride through life and create your next level of fulfillment.... At each step of the way, go back to the heart and balance again.

The point of balance is the heart. It's the foundation on which to build. Activating heart frequencies by loving and caring will balance your system, bringing peace in the moment. It's the best antidote for restoring balance and alleviating stress. Jot down your insights about what Sara has said.

Exercise

Being out of balance mentally and emotionally will affect your physical balance. It all goes back to energy efficiency. One of the steps to achieving balance and efficiency is to be aware of your thoughts and emotions and balance them out in the moment before they deplete your system. Every inefficient thought or emotion can be balanced by an efficient frequency from the heart.

Balance for Your Thoughts and Emotions

Head Frequency	Heart Frequency
frustration and impatience	patience
anger	tolerance and compassion (for self & others)
overcares (worries, doubts, concerns)	care (going back to the original point of care)
judgments	compassion and love
self-judgments	forgiveness (for self & others)
resentments and grudges	appreciation (of what we have)
comparisons	self-security

Next time you find yourself in an inefficient head frequency, switch that frequency to the heart. Your heart can help you become energy efficient. And remember, 1 sincere effort to activate a heart frequency will bring a 9 energy return. Now that's a good investment!

Now that you have been practicing HeartMath for several months, are you able you notice subtle patterns in your mental and emotional reactions? Are they efficient or inefficient? Review your reactions to situations in your life that cause you stress and ask your heart how you can handle them more efficiently and no longer repeat those same behaviors. You now have more heart power from doing this program, and no matter what your patterns are, you have new ability to correct them, if needed, for your fulfillment.

Habitual Mental and Emotional Reactions

Heart Intuition Response

Follow Up Exercise—Bonus Insights
It really feels good when you can catch yourself in the moment reacting inefficiently to a person or a situation and then shift to a heart frequency. By switching to the heart, you'll feel better mentally, emotionally and physically. Make that your intention today! Today in the name of balance, stay extra conscious of building your foundation from the heart.

267

Many could forego heavy meals, a full wardrobe,
a fine house, et cetera; it is the ego they cannot forego.

— *Mohandas Gandhi*

DAY 5

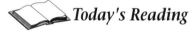 *Today's Reading*

In *Self Empowerment*, Chapter 8, "Ego-Economics," Doc Lew Childre explains the need to balance the ego which has a tendency, on its own, to expend energy inefficiently.

> To experience ego-economics, you don't repress your ego enjoyment; you learn to balance and manage it. Without balance, the ego drive often causes tremendous amounts of inefficient energy expenditure. It can cause you energy deficits as it plunges ahead with unbridled assertion. Your heart intelligence has the capacity to balance and fulfill your ego nature. As you practice managing your attitudes from the heart, you unfold a harmonious synthesis between your ego and the rest of your inner nature.

> Many have believed that you need to annihilate the ego to achieve peace or enlightenment. Let's look at the ego as an important part of your nature, just as the mind and emotions are—when unmanaged, they all create stress feedback and block the flow of light from your spirit. The unmanaged mind can make you miserable. But you don't destroy the mind; you refine and manage it. The emotions can make misery worse, but you don't eliminate the emotional nature; you bring it under management and realize it's a gift. The ego is not bad; it just needs to be balanced and managed like the other aspects of your nature.

I t's all about balance and managing the ego so that it doesn't tip the scales —another aspect of you that your heart can help bring into harmony. What a relief—the ego isn't bad after all. It just needs to get in sync with the heart. Doc has said some interesting things. Jot down your insights about what you have read.

_____

_____

_____

_____

Exercise

Sometimes we feel uncomfortable taking credit for our achievements— thinking that behavior would be inappropriate. Then there are others who openly flaunt their successes. Once again, balance would be the way to go. There is nothing wrong with receiving recognition for your endeavors. However, as the saying goes, "Don't let it go to your head!" Keep it balanced from the heart. That's energy efficiency. It's okay to feel good about your accomplishments. You don't have to feel bad because you excel in an area others don't. Have you repressed your ego because that is what you were taught? Give yourself credit for your accomplishments—from your heart!

Are there areas in your life where you haven't allowed yourself a pat on the back from yourself or others? It's time to accept those pats. Jot down some of your accomplishments and then send love and appreciation to yourself for your successful endeavors. Remember, appreciation is a wise energy investment because it appreciates or grows in value. (Accomplishments can range from overcoming obstacles, landing that big business deal, controlling your temper, cooking a delicious meal, publishing an article, painting a picture, etc. Allow your ego moments of glory!)

Accomplishments

_____

_____

_____

_____

_____

_____

_____

_____

Different egos have different ego appetites and levels of fulfillment. Some people may want a house with a white picket fence; others may prefer not to be tied down and choose to live in a small apartment so they can afford to travel. By following your heart and being true to yourself, you will draw to yourself balanced fulfillment. At the same time, allow others the latitude to be themselves and enjoy their own ego nourishment regardless of whether you agree with it. If you think their choice is unproductive, have compassion and understanding—that's what you'd want for yourself. That would be the most energy-efficient thing to do. Let's be honest—are there people you tend to judge for what you see as a big ego? Ask your heart to help you gain an understanding and get to a place of compassion. Oftentimes it's insecurities that cause the ego to become unbalanced or inflated. Jot down your insights.

_____

_____

_____

_____

_____

Follow Up Exercise—Bonus Insights

This has been a week of studying how you spend your vital, precious mental and emotional energy. Sometimes it's easy to see—you're either energy efficient or energy inefficient. You're either in your heart or not. It's just a matter of remembering and observing. We all improve with practice and so will you. Life's a game and you're getting to be a more efficient player every-day—the HeartMath way. That's a pat for your ego! Write down three important insights you gained this week.

1. _____

   _____

2. _____

   _____

3. _____

   _____

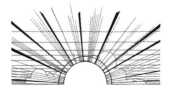

Law rules throughout existence, a Law which is not intelligent but Intelligence.

— *Emerson*

DAY ①

Today's Reading

In *The Hidden Power of the Heart*, Chapter 6, "The Dimensional Shift," Sara Paddison clarifies the meaning of "dimensional shift" and offers an understanding of third dimensional reality—the state of ordinary awareness.

Many business leaders and trend forecasters are saying that the world is going through a paradigm shift. Some are calling it a dimensional shift. A paradigm is a model of how we view reality. A paradigm shift occurs when our fundamental view of reality changes to a new, wider perspective.

A dimensional shift is made of many paradigm shifts unfolding over time. Although science speaks of dimensions just in terms of time and space, a dimension is actually a specific frequency range of perception and intelligence. Each dimension embraces the intelligence of the dimension below it and can be perceived as its own world of energy and form.

Our physical reality, including our dense physical body, exists in the third dimension. Newtonian physics led people to believe that the only "reality" is what we can perceive with our physical senses. Our senses perceive every piece of matter as separate, leading us to conclude that everything is separate. Adopting this paradigm view, many scientists closed their minds to the possibility of another reality. This is an example of third dimensional perception and intelligence.

Third dimensional reality or physical reality views everything as separate. Could this be a limited perception? How lonely everyone would be—isolated particles of matter adrift in the sea of life. That might explain the lack of love and care in the world. It's time to broaden that perspective! Jot down your insights if you'd like.

_____

_____

_____

Exercise

The third dimension is bound by the illusion of limits. It tends to perceive things as good or bad, right or wrong, black or white. It is where you feel that things will never change and where the main focus is on survival, even at the expense of others, rather than hope and a sense of something greater than the current situation.

More than likely there have been times in your life when you've realized or had the feeling that there's more to life than what you perceive with your senses. For example, can you recall when you first fell in love and felt totally at peace and one with the Universe? You loved everyone and everything and felt connected to it all. Can you recollect similar instances and how you felt then? Jot down any insights.

_____

_____

_____

Seeing everything as separate can create more stress. Limiting thoughts of good or bad, black or white don't allow for flexibility or growth. How can you feel hopeful in a separate, "dog eat dog" world? Third dimensional reality is cut off from the heart—the source of nourishment and fulfillment.

It doesn't have to be that way. Is there a situation in your life that seems limited? Ask your heart for a perspective beyond third dimensional reality.

Situation

_____

_____

_____

Heart Intuition Response

_____

_____

_____

Follow Up Exercise—Bonus Insights

Have you ever noticed how good you feel in the great outdoors, or for you city dwellers, in the local park or on the balcony of your apartment over-looking the greenery? There's something about being in nature that enables us to feel more at peace. We feel better (except perhaps for those with aller-gies) and can even feel greater than ourselves. Why is that? Perhaps we aren't really separate. Perhaps everything truly is connected. Today, try to experi-ence feelings of connectedness with life.

The fairest thing we can experience is the mysterious. It is the fundamental emotion which stands at the cradle of true art and true science.

— *Einstein*

DAY ②

Today's Reading

Continuing in Chapter 6, "The Dimensional Shift," Sara Paddison explains the fourth dimension, which perceives from a wider perspective and sees more wholistically.

> The fourth dimension is a range of intelligence and perception that lifts us beyond the ceiling of the third—with thoughts that are more efficient, caring and hopeful. This dimension increases your power for growth and change. Lower fourth dimensional awareness allows you to philosophize and ponder new possibilities and start to work on inefficient patterns. You'd consider the importance of positive thinking, but you wouldn't necessarily act on it.
>
> ...In the lower fourth, you continually create new stuff—hurts, pain, guilt—to be cleared away. Recovery can seem like a never ending process because you aren't getting to the root cause of the problem. The lower fourth involves continually working things out, continually healing, dieting, cleansing, clearing. It goes on, and on, and on....
>
> The higher fourth dimension is where the frequencies of love, care, compassion, forgiveness and inner peace reside...We experience more hope, and hope is a powerful fuel to create momentum for positive change and fulfillment. The higher fourth represents a quantum leap in human consciousness.

> The higher fourth holds magic, majesty, wonder and delight and is a level of awareness available to you any time you choose to experience it. When Christ came to Earth, he brought in new perceptions of love and broke through many mindsets of that time. He created and left

behind an opening into the fourth dimension. This was a powerful transformation for a society that was largely operating in the second dimension—the undeveloped mind. In the higher fourth dimension you see union, you see all people as one.

The higher fourth dimension is definitely the place to be. "...magic, majesty, wonder and delight..." And your heart can take you there. Jot down your insights about what you have read.

_____

_____

Exercise

Okay, it's time to make your own quantum leap. Let's move from lower fourth dimension positive thinking, through mid-fourth working things out, to higher fourth—the frequencies of love, care, compassion, forgiveness and inner peace. From this perspective, everything is connected—you aren't alone. So with this more hopeful attitude, look at any areas of your life where you've been struggling—feeling separate and apart—and now try to view them from a higher fourth perspective—from the heart—and find a more efficient way to deal with them. Do a Lock-In. Just try to feel the frequencies of love, care or appreciation. After you complete your Lock-In, ask your heart to show you an area in your life where you are "still working it out" and how you can shift to a new dimension beyond this struggle.

Situation

_____

_____

Heart Intuition Response

_____

_____

_____

Third dimensional energy is constrictive, restrictive and fearful. It is exemplified by thoughts, feelings and actions of hiding, hoarding, clinging, blaming, etc. Fourth dimensional energy is expansive, open and loving. It is exemplified by thoughts, feelings and behaviors that are caring, compassionate, understanding, etc. Can you see areas of your life where you operate in a third dimensional mode while perhaps in others you are in a fourth dimensional mode? Notice how they both feel and then ask your heart to help you maintain fourth dimensional perspectives in your life. Jot down your insights about when you are perceiving from third dimensional perspectives and from fourth dimensional perspectives.

Third Dimensional Perspectives

Fourth Dimensional Perspectives

Follow Up Exercise—Bonus Insights
As you go through your day, see yourself as a fourth dimensional person and feel your connectedness to everyone and everything. Tap into the wonder and magic of the higher fourth dimension and enjoy the ride!

> We are what we think. All that we are arises with our thoughts.
> With our thoughts we make the world.
> — *Siddhartha Guatama*

DAY ③

Today's Reading

Venturing farther in Chapter 6, "The Dimensional Shift," Sara Paddison offers a clear understanding of the fifth dimension—"a powerful dimension."

By operating from the heart, you build a bridge of awareness from the third to the higher fourth dimension—a bridge that leads to the inner knowingness of the fifth dimension. In the fifth, awareness is guided by intuitive directives that free you from the endless cleansing and recovery of the fourth, and from the self-limiting fears and phobias of the third.

Fifth dimensional intelligence provides streamlined inner efficiency—for you, me and the entire human race. Stress is transformed through the heart. There are no limits. You are responsible for bringing heaven to earth. You perceive and understand everything as light, energy and frequencies, and it's up to you to manage your energies effectively. Actions are neither good nor bad, right nor wrong, but rather energy-efficient and leading to more love, or less energy-efficient and leading to more stress.

Each new dimension embraces the intelligence and awareness of the perspective below it. In the fifth dimension you comprehend the third and fourth dimensional perspectives without being limited by them or judging them. You understand why people think and act the way they do, even though it may not be efficient or in their best interests.

The fifth dimension is about making efficient choices in life—choices that will either create more love or more stress. Perhaps knowing the outcome of these two choices will help us choose more wisely.

Jot down your insights.

_____

_____

_____

Exercise

The fifth is a powerful dimension for creative manifestation and self-empowerment. Can you see areas where you are still making inefficient choices moment-to-moment or day-to-day? You don't have to. With sincere practice, using the amazing power of your heart, you can access the awareness of the fifth dimension. You have to use your heart to get there. From the fifth dimension you can learn to see stress as just an "untransformed opportunity" for more love and empowerment. Just viewing stress from this perspective will take some of the stress out of it. Look at any area of stress in your life and transform it from your heart. Ask your heart for a wider perspective—beyond the self-limitations and illusions of the third and beyond the struggle of the lower fourth. In the fifth dimension you can create your own world and are not a victim anymore.

Is there a situation in your life that you can now view as an "untransformed opportunity" and with help from your heart transform it? Remember, your heart can give you a wider perspective beyond the third and reduce some of your stress. It's well worth a try. Efficiency is the key—efficiently managing your mental and emotional energies—this builds transformative power. Ask your heart for an energy-efficient solution.

Stressful Situation

_____

_____

_____

Heart Intuition Response

_____

_____

_____

_____

Follow Up Exercise—Bonus Insights

Remember to spend some time each day in a Heart Lock-In. If your time is limited, try to find at least five minutes to focus in your heart. This will help you develop your intuition and is a step towards achieving fifth dimensional inner-knowingness and becoming more energy-efficient and self-empowered. Try to find the time to do a Heart Lock-In today.

Fear always springs from ignorance.

— *Emerson*

DAY (4)

Today's Reading

Proceeding once again in Chapter 6, "The Dimensional Shift," Sara Paddison offers us insights into the global paradigm shift.

> This is a challenging time in history. The world is going through a global paradigm shift, moving as a whole from the third to the fourth dimension and taking a quantum leap into the edges of the fifth dimension. You can see signs of this in all the rapid political and social changes that are occurring. The end of communism and the fall of the Berlin Wall are just two examples of changes that occurred much more rapidly than third dimensional awareness could have predicted. Mass consciousness tends to move in waves as old patterns and crystallized structures crumble. The pendulum swings into love, back into fear, into love, back into fear, back and forth. An example of this can be seen in the ethnic wars that broke out in Europe after the iron hand of communism was lifted. For months the countries felt great hope, then the violence began.

> The problem is that third dimensional frequency perspectives see people, structures—everything—as separate from each other, with tremendous duality, antagonism and opposites. So, in this dimension people gain a little hope, then revert back to fear. There are still thick boundaries and strong limitations in the thinking of the world. Mind-sets are so rigid that when amplified by unmanaged emotions, tremendous conflict results. Third dimensional awareness keeps hitting its head on the ceiling of its own limitations. Because it sees with separate eyes, there are many enemies. If you project into the future and can't see a way out of a dilemma, you can become fearful. When fear is present, the consistency of love cannot hold.

Fear is the antagonist to love. Viewing life from the third dimensional perspective of separateness creates these fears. It's the power of the heart which can take us beyond the third. Jot down your insights about what you have read today.

_____

_____

_____

_____

Exercise

Ongoing conflicts are a part of the history of the planet, ranging from conflicts between brothers and families, and extending to those between countries. The heart can provide us with the understanding and higher dimensional perspective to transmute these third dimensional energies to more efficient energy patterns. With increased higher fourth and fifth dimensional awareness, more people will be aligned with promoting wholeness and well-being for all—planetary peace. However, in order to achieve world peace, people will first have to make peace with themselves.

Oftentimes it is our fears or insecurities that cause us to adopt these negative thought patterns that lead to conflict. Love can give us the understanding and wider perspective to move out of these self-limiting third dimensional beliefs.

What are the areas of conflict within yourself or within your life? Now that you have a better understanding of the dimensions and their ramifications, why not try to get to a place of peace and resolution? It's better for you and the whole. Move out of the self-limiting beliefs of the third dimension into the harmony of the higher fourth and fifth. Go deep in your heart and ask for understanding to help you gain this wider perspective.

Conflict

_____

_____

_____

_____

Heart Intuition Response

_____

_____

_____

_____

Follow Up Exercise—Bonus Insights

During the course of your day, ask yourself if your energy expenditures are efficient or inefficient, productive or non-productive. Do your thoughts, feelings and actions come from love or fear? Are you accumulating more peace or more stress? Jot down your observations.

_____

_____

_____

_____

What you do may not seem important, but it is very important that you do it.

— Mohatma Gandhi

DAY 5

Today's Reading

Concluding in Chapter 6, "The Dimensional Shift," Sara Paddison emphasizes the importance of inner peace and how to use the power of the heart to overcome fears and achieve balance and fulfillment.

One of the basic resistances to this higher vibration of peace is human inertia. Many people do not consciously value peace enough to bring about inner change. Some avoid trying to achieve balance and fulfillment because they fear failure. But this fear is not based in reality. It's just a projection of the third dimensional limits they've put on themselves. They allow this fear to control them. Heart intelligence helps you understand your fears then, naturally, they dissipate.

———

As you love people at deeper levels, you make it easier for them to access these heart frequencies. Through the heart, God's intelligence lifts you and speeds you on to a new understanding in the higher dimensions. Stuck in the head without heart contact, the accelerating evolutionary energy only intensifies your inner conflicts and stress. As more people come into deeper contact with the power of the heart, stress will be recognized as an untransformed opportunity for greater empowerment. Heart empowerment, not ideally but actually, can bring in the intelligence to end the conflicts so prevalent in the third dimensional world. In the higher fourth dimension, all opposites cease to be and all that is seen is the One Light. This is not the end of seeing, but it is the end of seeing with the separate eye. It is direct perception that all is energy, not just a theoretical knowing.

The heart is the key to peace—individually and collectively. The head separates; the heart unites. The greater our awareness, the greater our chances for peace—awareness from the heart.

Jot down your insights.

_____

_____

_____

_____

Exercise

According to quantum physics, everything is energy and everything is interconnected and interrelated. This means that we as individuals each have a responsibility to the whole—to the planet. Our thoughts, feelings and actions influence and affect those around us. Each one of us is like a molecule of water in a great ocean. We can help to make that water pure and pristine, or we can muddy it. Either way, we each affect the ocean. As humans, we are no different—each a part of the sea of humanity. And we each have a choice in every moment—do we choose the head or the heart? Are we muddying the water or keeping it pure and pristine?

Look at your life and the contributions you're making to the planet on an energy level—the energy of your thoughts, feelings and actions. Could you be more efficient with your energy? Briefly survey your thoughts, feelings and actions—how you operate in the world—to see what kind of energy contribution you are making to the planet on a daily basis. Then check in with your heart to see how you could be more energy-efficient.

Jot down your insights.

_____

_____

_____

_____

_____

_____

_____

Follow Up Exercise—Bonus Insights

"...love matters more than anything...and nothing else really matters..."
Make sure it matters in your daily life—for your own well-being and the
well-being of the planet. It is the most efficient choice to make. Choose love
and then sit back and enjoy the ride!

Jot down your observations about this week of learning about dimensions.

_____

_____

_____

_____

_____

_____

_____

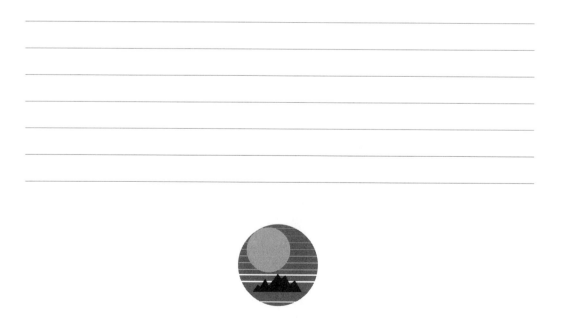

The ineffable joy of forgiving and being forgiven
forms an ecstasy that might well arouse the envy of the gods.
— *Elbert Hubbard*

DAY 1

Today's Reading

In *The Hidden Power of the Heart*, Chapter 19, "Forgiveness," Sara Paddison gives us a valuable perspective on forgiveness—we are the ones who benefit when we forgive!

Forgiveness is one of the ultimate power tools for personal transformation. You do yourself a huge favor when you truly let go and forgive. If you make a deep heart contact with yourself first, then sincerely forgive yourself or someone else, you receive an extremely high return of peace for your effort. Remember that anyone can get off track and make a left-hand turn. Forgiveness is really for you more than them. Often, the people whom you haven't forgiven don't even know it. But your own system does. So do it for yourself rather than waste energy through continual, often subliminal, mental and emotional processing.

———— ❦ ————

Forgiveness can seem hard to do when you've been betrayed or deeply hurt. When you feel justified in not forgiving someone, that resentment stays with you and can gnaw away inside for your whole life. Forgiveness from the head just doesn't work! The hurt lurks in the subconscious and resurfaces once a month, once a day, once a night, and for many people, every day and every night. Even if it comes up only once a year, it's still stewing in your subconscious and draining your spirit. If you find yourself saying, "Well, I've forgiven him, but I don't want him in my face," or, "I forgive you but I don't ever want to see you or talk to you again," you haven't forgiven. If your stomach wrenches or you still have a negative association at the mention of a person's name, you haven't truly forgiven.

L ove is for-giving. You give yourself a great gift when you let go of hurts and resentments from the heart. Releasing blame and forgiving frees you from self-imposed imprisonment. By not forgiving, there is only one person you are really hurting—you! So let go and move on.

Jot down your insights about what you read today.

_____

_____

_____

Exercise

Scientific research has shown that repetitive over-identity with resentment also creates stress on the heart and immune system, often resulting in physical ailments. It can be hard to forgive and let go if the mind "knows what it knows" and believes it's justified in feeling blame. No matter how justified a hurt or resentment may seem, you gain freedom only when you change your own reactions instead of trying to change others.

Let's begin the process of forgiving by forgiving yourself for something you might have done years ago or as recently as yesterday. The negative effects are still felt in your system regardless of when the event occurred. (Of course, the longer they've been in your system, the more opportunity they have for causing damage.) Remember, anyone can get off track and make a mistake— even you.

To forgive, you begin by first making deep heart contact with yourself. Send sincere care and compassion to yourself. It is out of care for yourself that you are able to take responsibility to re-balance your mental and emotional disturbances and create inner harmony. FREEZE-FRAME all thoughts and feelings of blame or hurt in the heart and surrender your mind to your heart. This gives your heart intuition a chance to tell your mind to release and let go. As you sincerely feel forgiveness for the people involved and for yourself, you release your identity with that pattern. You realize that the past is not going to undo itself. Your heart intelligence then transforms those past frequencies into new perspectives and understanding. You receive an extremely high return of peace for your effort. Don't be impatient or expect to see the total picture right away. Just do it over and over again until you feel free. Try this now and make an effort, from the heart, to forgive yourself.

Jot down your insights from this practice of forgiveness.

_____

_____

_____

_____

Follow Up Exercise—Bonus Insights

During the course of your day, if any unresolved feelings, insecurities or judgments pop up, remember to FREEZE-FRAME and surrender your mind to your heart. You would want others to forgive you; so why not treat yourself the same way—lovingly?

Jot down your observations before you end your day.

_____

_____

_____

_____

A man who studieth revenge keeps his own wounds green.

— Francis Bacon

DAY 2

Today's Reading

Continuing in Chapter 19, "Forgiveness," Sara Paddison explains how important it is to achieve a deep level of understanding from the heart in order to forgive.

Sometimes we react with anger or hate and know it's just momentary. But if feelings of anger, betrayal and hate linger and constantly replay in your mind, their frequency becomes engraved in your hologram. It then keeps resurfacing as a deep-rooted, unresolved problem. You can't completely forgive and erase these deeply etched patterns until you see all the perspectives of the grid and understand them. But you won't understand them until you make sincere efforts to forgive. It's a catch-22. That's why total forgiveness of deep patterns takes time.

Your heart will keep bringing up to conscious awareness old unforgiven feelings and memories for you to forgive, release and let go. As you sincerely try to forgive, it helps to remember that mentally and emotionally processing an unforgiven event drains you, just like a car battery gets drained when the door is left open. Resentment maintains a constant, slow leak that can age you prematurely. Regardless of what another person did or didn't do, don't imprison yourself mentally or emotionally. Life goes on. Sincere forgiveness from the heart will release you and release the heart of the person you were hating, whether they are aware of it or not.

Forgiving someone else releases you from the blame and resentments that are festering inside and slowly draining your system. Which feels better—holding on to those negative thought patterns or letting go and being at peace? Besides, can you truthfully think of any benefits you gain from holding on?

Jot down your insights.

_____

_____

_____

_____

_____

Exercise

If you still have a negative association or hurt feeling at the mention of someone's name, you haven't totally forgiven them. Remember, true forgiveness erases all negative associations and all blame from your holographic heart. It is the ultimate clean-out. You can't completely erase a deep-rooted pattern until you see it from all the different sides. But you can't see all the sides until you make sincere efforts to surrender the mind to the heart and forgive. If you realize that you're the primary one who will benefit, then you'll have more heart commitment to complete the act of forgiveness at the heart level.

Is there someone you still haven't forgiven? Is it worth holding on to those hurt feelings or resentments? How much longer do you want to keep carrying around that ball and chain? Why not make a sincere effort from your heart to release those negative frequencies and replace them with a heart perspective? Perhaps with understanding from the heart, it won't be such a big deal to let go. Ask your heart to help you. Remember, it may take more than one attempt to release something that's been deeply ingrained in your system, down to the cellular level. Sincerely feeling the heart frequency of forgiveness can release blame from your system and bring new understanding. It takes continuity of sincere heart commitment to overcome identity with hurts or resentments.

Do a Heart Lock-In and ask your heart to help you gain an understanding of the situation so that you can be free of the burden you are still carrying. It truly is a step in your own best interest, a step towards more peace and feeling good, and you're doing it for yourself, not the other person! Jot down your insights.

_____

_____

_____

_____

_____

_____

_____

_____

_____

Follow Up Exercise—Bonus Insights

Remember, only your heart can free you from the imprisonment of negative frequencies. Being in prison isn't any fun. But who put you there? Did the other person imprison you or did you imprison yourself because you keep choosing to feel hurt or resentful? Well, if you put yourself there, it stands to reason you can release yourself. You're holding the key—forgiveness. Use it!

Man who waits for roast duck to fly into mouth must wait very, very long time.

— *Chinese proverb*

DAY ③

Today's Reading

Reading further in Chapter 19, "Forgiveness," we gain an understanding of the power of forgiveness and the ramifications it has for others as well as ourselves.

> As you practice forgiveness, your heart wisdom might say, "I forgive him. He really didn't realize what he was doing," or, "He might have been doing the best he knew how," or, "I've made mistakes in my life, too. I sure hope people forgave me. I don't want them to be harboring resentment and hate for me." As you forgive others, it helps erase any negative holographic patterns they may hold about you as well. Because we're all interconnected in the heart, forgiveness helps to re-create a harmonious flow between yourself and everyone.

> Sincere forgiveness isn't colored with expectations that the other person apologize or change. Don't worry whether or not they finally understand you. Love them and release them. Life feeds back truth to people in its own way and its own time— just like it does for you and me.

Waiting for someone to apologize or change means that we haven't forgiven them. Besides, that's the head still waiting. Standing on principle will leave you there—standing and waiting for a very long time. The heart doesn't need to wait for anyone—except you. It can forgive without expectations or agendas. When you get tired of standing and waiting, sit down and go to your heart!

A lot has been said in these few paragraphs. Jot down your insights if you'd like.

Exercise

Make a list of all the people, organizations, issues or anything you still hold judgment, resentment, hurt or anger against (even yourself). If more memories pop up later, add those to your list. Make a sincere effort from your heart to release those negative frequencies and replace them with heart perspectives. Do this until you feel clean and free from these issues.

Forgiveness List

1. _____
2. _____
3. _____
4. _____
5. _____
6. _____
7. _____
8. _____
9. _____
10. _____

Follow Up Exercise—Bonus Insights

During the day, if negative thoughts pop up from your list, keep sending the sincere heart frequency of forgiveness to allow intuition to come to you. Be patient with yourself. The answer may not come in the moment. True forgiveness takes time.

Jot down your observations.

_____

_____

_____

_____

_____

Freedom is the greatest fruit of self-sufficiency.

— *Epicurus*

DAY ④

Today's Reading

Proceeding in Chapter 19, "Forgiveness," Sara Paddison explains how forgiving can help us achieve a feeling of freedom.

> Most of us still harbor resentments. The quickest way out is to make sincere efforts to release those negative frequencies from your system. Replace them with the sincere heart frequency of forgiveness. Do it over and over again until you feel free. You'll know forgiveness is complete when you have a new perception that's not colored by negative associations. Old whisper feelings might occasionally creep in, but your thoughts remind you, "No, I've forgiven him." Just keep releasing and letting go. Your heart will be at peace and you'll have a light, clean feeling once the program is totally erased from your hologram. Until you feel this freedom, keep activating the power tool of forgiveness.

> In the heart, people do understand the importance of forgiveness. They know they want to forgive, but it's frustrating when the hurt doesn't go away. Don't look at yourself as a failure if old resentments resurface with a vengeance and take you back into negative thought loops. View this as your system attempting to flush out the old program. Just tell yourself, "That's a deficit." Be seriously sincere with yourself. Don't give up. FREEZE-FRAME, go back to your heart intelligence, listen for your inner wisdom and, again, feel forgiveness. Each time you do that, you create an asset for yourself. But if you refuel old hostilities, anger, guilt or pain, you just keep on creating deficits.

Patience and sincerity of effort are the keys to forgiveness. Remember, you're erasing patterns that are etched in your cellular memory. That's major house cleaning. It takes time to dust off each one of those little cells and get them to sparkle again. But you'll notice the difference when you're done because you'll actually feel that sparkle.

Jot down your insights if you'd like.

_____

_____

_____

Exercise

In some instances, people have been holding on to resentments and grudges for so long that they've almost forgotten why. Families that carry on those family feuds from generation to generation might not even know why they are still feuding. In any case, if you're still holding on to something from the past, chances are that the person you're holding these negative feelings about might have changed and may act differently under those same circumstances today. After all, you've changed, so perhaps they have, too. In other instances, where you're stuck, you may not have all the facts or may be operating under misinformation. All the more reason to let go and forgive. Besides, it pays to give people the benefit of the doubt. Isn't that the way you would want to be treated?

So take a look at that list of resentments and grudges you made yesterday, do a Heart Lock-In and make another effort to free yourself from them once and for all. It's the energy-efficient thing to do. It's really not worth the wear and tear on your system to keep holding on. Ask your heart to give you a deeper understanding of these situations so that you can sincerely forgive and move on. Remember, you are the one who benefits by forgiving!

Write down your insights.

_____

_____

_____

_____

_____

Follow Up Exercise—Bonus Insights

During the course of your day, opportunities may present themselves where you once again have the choice to feel resentful or hurt. These are "untransformed opportunities for empowerment." Allow your heart to help you forgive in the moment and surrender to the wisdom of your heart. Don't go down that road of hurts and resentments, because it can be an arduous trip with a lot of unnecessary baggage, and the return trip might take even longer. Write down your observations.

_____

_____

_____

_____

_____

_____

They have a right to censure that have a heart to help.
— *William Penn*

DAY 5

Today's Reading

Concluding in Chapter 19, "Forgiveness," Sara Paddison helps us to realize that the real culprit in any situation is our response to it!

> Personal freedom is knowing how to use heart intelligence to create more internal power. With power, you can exercise your options. It's only your willing permission that justifies a hurt feeling. You hurt yourself far more by holding onto them than by whatever happened to you in the first place. Build your power to forgive. It's not who hurts us or what happens to us, but our response that entraps us, taking away our real freedom. You'll feel a clean heart connection with yourself and others, once you've totally forgiven.

> As you develop your heart and internal power by forgiving, managing any tough situation gets easier....

> Most people blame the outer trappings of life, especially other people, for their woes. This robs them of real freedom and totally saps their power. It's forgiving and releasing those inner entrapments that brings us lasting freedom and empowerment.

Blaming others is a position of weakness. Real freedom and strength come from making efficient responses and choices from the heart, unencumbered by what others say or do or don't say or do. Why give others the power to control how you feel? That's like being dragged around by a pack of wild stallions. Grab the reins and take control of your feelings from the heart.

Jot down your insights if you'd like.

_____

_____

_____

Exercise

The more you develop your inner security from your heart, the less you will allow yourself to blame and resent others. Realize that any of these negative thoughts or feelings you might be harboring are from a time when you weren't as aware as you are now. You did the best you could in those days, but now you can do even better. Besides, in the overall scheme of things, how important is it to be carrying around leftover baggage from years ago or even minutes ago? So don't allow whatever your brother, sister, parent, friend, spouse, etc. did way back when or even yesterday to affect who you are today and cause even the tiniest energy drain in your system. It's time to plug up all those leaks. You'll feel a clean connection with yourself and others once you've totally forgiven all. And don't forget to forgive yourself in the process for having held on to the past.

If there are still some hurts and resentments hanging around or even any residues from them, ask your heart again to help you gain a deeper understanding so that you can forgive once and for all. Allow yourself more room to attract good in your life by clearing out the debris. Since everything is energy and interconnected, by holding on to negative thoughts and feelings, not only are you constricting your energy, but you are diminishing your ability to attract more good. Remember, like attracts like. How attractive are you at the moment? Forgiving will make you very attractive on many levels.

Review the list you made of people, situations, etc., you made earlier in the week. Have you made some progress on forgiving? Take some time now, do a Heart Lock-In, and use the power of your heart to help dissolve any leftover negative feelings you may have.

Write down your insights.

_____

_____

_____

_____

_____

Follow Up Exercise—Bonus Insights

This may have been a tough week of heart practice. Forgiveness can be hard and one of the last things we often get around to doing but it is powerful and opens the door to new freedom. Think of forgiveness like cleaning out your closets—throwing out or giving away all those old clothes that no longer fit or aren't appropriate. Then you'll have room for new. It feels good to do that. So does forgiveness! Jot down your observations about your week.

_____

_____

_____

_____

_____

_____

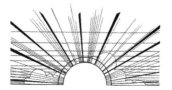

You can't cross the sea merely by staring at the water.
— *Rabinolranath Tagore*

DAY 1

Today's Reading

In *The Hidden Power of the Heart*, Chapter 7, "Heart Power Tools," Sara Paddison offers us an understanding of the power of sincerity—"a generator for all the power tools," especially love.

> Sincerity is a higher heart frequency band that acts like a generator for all the power tools. It has tremendous leverage. Plug into deeper sincerity and you boost the power of whatever tool you use. Sincere love keeps widening your intuition by creating alignment with your higher self. As you love sincerely, you draw in that wider perspective of higher intelligence which gives you more understanding in your relationships, in work and play....Sincere love radiates heart power into density where you can effect change. At the same time, it keeps the sense of fulfillment growing and expanding. Real practiced love is what evolution is about.

> ...Love is the power that connects and completes. Practicing love is not a new idea, but it's an idea that hasn't been fully understood. Through practicing love, you develop greater awareness and understand more programs from your heart computer that you can implement in life.
>
> Love isn't always soft and gentle. It can be explosive and energizing. It can have a bottom line, business-like quality to it. Because it connects all, love creates communion, resonance and deeper communication....
>
> Real love is caring, forgiving, appreciative and compassionate. It transcends the limitations and fences we create in the name of love. It nourishes, embraces, fulfills and rewards.

Everything you do becomes more powerful when you get more sincere about it. This definitely includes the power of your love. All of the things you have learned so far in this program will come to life in a whole new way through the power of your sincerity. Jot down your insights if you'd like.

_____

_____

_____

Exercise

Love is not automatic. It takes conscious practice and awareness, just like playing the piano or golf. However, you have ample opportunities to practice. Everyone you meet can be your practice session—each member of your family, the grocery clerk, coworkers, gas station attendant, etc. Remember, thinking that you're loving is different from sincerely feeling love in your heart and consciously sending it to whomever crosses your path. You can send love to those at a meeting you're attending, your dinner companions, to all those cars stuck in the traffic jam with you or to the person you're speaking with on the phone. There is no specific time or place to send love. The time is now—anywhere, anyplace and to anyone.

"The more that people practice real love, the better chance the world has to dissolve its social problems and recreate a society that can take care of all its people." You're an important part of that equation. And now you have the awareness and understanding to be a part of the answer. Begin by making a list of the people you most frequently interact with during the course of your day. Then start your engine and begin sincerely sending love. You're giving yourself a gift as well as others. Notice how it feels when you're sending love. You can generate those same good feelings anytime you are sincerely sending love. Jot down any insights that might pop up.

303

People With Whom You Most Frequently Interact

Insights

Follow Up Exercise—Bonus Insights

The trick here is to remember this little exercise you just did and put it into real practice when you encounter the people on your list—just send sincere love. You can become quite a heart power generator. It's fun to do because no one knows you're doing it. However, some might notice something a little different about you—a new hairdo, a new color on you, etc. A new attitude perhaps and a wonderful heart would be more accurate! Try this today and jot down your observations.

> I should say sincerity, a deep, great, genuine sincerity,
> is the first characteristic of all men in any way heroic.
>
> — *Thomas Carlyle*

DAY 2

Today's Reading

In *The Hidden Power of the Heart*, Chapter 20, "The Magnetics of Appreciation," Sara Paddison emphasizes the value of appreciation—especially when done with sincerity.

Appreciating something positive in a negative event sends a signal to the heart that magnetizes balanced understanding. Why not remember the positives? They're the fuel for your self-empowerment. It doesn't really matter what you appreciate—as long as it's sincere. The activation of this particular heart frequency is what counts. Appreciate that you have food to eat, a job, your health, a place to sleep instead of the sidewalks and all the positives you take for granted. Create an attitude of gratitude and you'll magnetize more rewarding experiences.

The rewards of appreciation are tremendously increased as you practice with deeper levels of sincerity. If you practice appreciating the little things in life, then when bigger problems or situations arise, you find you have an easier time dealing with them. Appreciation is simply a magnificent feeling in the heart that becomes the compass to find more good. It's the fast track to finding balance and fulfillment.

Appreciation is a powerful tool—it's a magnetic frequency that attracts more good to you. Can you imagine increasing its power just by adding sincerity? It's the difference between driving your car on low grade fuel or going for the higher octane. You'll get a better ride with higher octane, so fill your tank with sincerity. Jot down your insights.

_____

_____

_____

Exercise

There's mental appreciation (making a list and checking it twice) and then there's heartfelt appreciation. The latter is obviously more sincere. When you are actively appreciating something, make sure you can feel that feeling in your heart. Don't just think appreciation (although it's a good place to start), sincerely feel it. Then you're really appreciating and enjoying that heart frequency which can magnetize more fulfillment to you.

Let's begin by making a list of the people, places and things you appreciate most in your life. You've done this before in a previous month but this time go deep in your heart and try to access the core heart frequency of sincerity. A sincere appreciation list could go on forever. Actually, you could add to your list everyday. There's no end to appreciation—only a beginning. Spend ten minutes in your Lock-In sending appreciation to the items on your list. Jot down any insights that might pop up.

Appreciation List

1. _____
2. _____
3. _____
4. _____
5. _____
6. _____
7. _____
8. _____

9. _____

10. _____

11. _____

12. _____

Heart Intuition Response

_____

_____

_____

Follow Up Exercise—Bonus Insights

Take time during the day to sincerely appreciate everyone and everything from the time you wake up—appreciate the fact that you woke up, that you have a warm bed and a roof over your head, that you can get up and have someplace to go, that you have indoor plumbing, a refrigerator, food in the refrigerator, etc., etc. Remember, appreciation appreciates!

Jot down your observations about your day of sincere appreciation.

_____

_____

_____

_____

_____

_____

What is uttered from the heart alone
Will win the hearts of others to your own.

— Goethe

DAY ③

Today's Reading

In *Self Empowerment*, Chapter 10, "Summary: Important Points to Remember and Practice," Doc Lew Childre impresses upon us the importance of care. It creates the family frequency, a missing ingredient for peace on the planet.

> Remember the family concept—a more sincere care for all people—at home, in business, in social and political issues—and especially for yourself. Relating to people from the heart creates the family frequency which in turn creates harmony in your environment. The word "family" has love, care, warmth, compassion, forgiveness, non-judgment and cooperation tucked within its meaning. Just like you, other people have their own mind-sets and ceilings to break through. If you make more sincere efforts to care at deeper levels, that will make it easier for everyone to let go of draining attitudes and crystallized mind patterns.

> Care is a major ingredient in the recipe for peace within yourself, your community and the planet. If you feel that you already care, then go deeper, care more and find the next level. Care is enlightening and leads to personal fulfillment if you would dare to believe there is such as that. There is! Cash in on the family frequency by extending your care and sincerity to larger numbers of people and experience the true profits of quality in life.

Caring for others brings you peace and fulfillment, especially if it is sincere care, not just an on-the-surface gesture. Definitely a win-win situation. Care to find out! Extend your care to as many people as possible with as much sincerity as you can and you'll reap the rewards.

Jot down your insights about what you have read today.

_____

_____

_____

Exercise

Sometimes we show our care with big things—on birthdays and special occasions—with expensive gifts, elaborate surprises, etc. How about making every day a special occasion and showing your care with little things—a smile, a word of encouragement or a knowing wink, an offer to take out the trash, an unexpected phone call to someone, an effort to listen more sincerely when someone speaks with you, etc., etc.

Are there areas in your life where you could care more sincerely, with certain people or in specific situations? Make a list of them and then spend ten minutes in your Lock-In sending care to the items on your list. Jot down any insights that might pop up.

Care List

1. _____
2. _____
3. _____
4. _____
5. _____
6. _____
7. _____
8. _____
9. _____
10. _____

Insights

_____

_____

_____

Follow Up Exercise—Bonus Insights

Today, see how many people you can send care to during the course of your day. Why not keep a tally list? The idea here is to care about people—all people—sincerely care. Remember, you're giving your immune system a boost when you care (just like professional caregivers) and who knows what kind of boost you're giving to others by caring. It really doesn't matter if you're an amateur or professional caregiver. What matters is that you care, 'cause in your heart, you're no amateur! List the people, situations, etc. that you applied sincere care to today.

1. _____
2. _____
3. _____
4. _____
5. _____
6. _____
7. _____

Sincerity is the highest compliment you can pay.

— *Emerson*

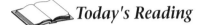

DAY **4**

Today's Reading

In *The Hidden Power of the Heart,* Chapter 8, "Tools for Rapid Self-Adjustment," Sara Paddison explains the role of sincerity when activating the power tool FREEZE-FRAME.

> With FREEZE-FRAME you create a momentary pause so you can just be still and collect yourself in the heart. Calm your head chatter and emotional reactions, then shift the energies to the heart. It takes practice, but the practice has a big return. Freeze-Framing gives you a break from inefficient mental and emotional reactions. Then you can choose to self-adjust, saving energy and building power in your system—your own power.

Freeze-Framing works better when you remember to activate a positive heart frequency. As you put your movie on pause, make a sincere effort to feel something in your heart, such as love, care or compassion. This sets the stage for your heart intuition to come in. It's no different than fine-tuning your radio dial to get a clear station and tuning out the static. You may not always be able to feel a deeper heart feeling right away, but stay focused in the heart. The sincerity of your effort can reconnect you to your heart current and start the juices flowing. To plug in, think of someone you love or remember what feels good, maybe a fulfilling experience. Feelings help you remember. You become sensitive to the difference between head reactions and heart feelings—they really do feel different. Remembering this difference helps you go back to the heart more often—it feels better.

S incerity is an access code to plug you into your heart computer and connect you with your inner wisdom. You can make that connection anytime—with sincerity. Write down your insights about what you have read today.

_____

_____

_____

_____

_____

Exercise

If you've been saying to yourself, "Sometimes FREEZE-FRAME works and sometimes it doesn't," perhaps what's missing is the sincerity of intent and effort, and maybe an extra dose of sincere patience. There's a big difference between Freeze-Framing from the head and thinking about appreciation or love, etc. and Freeze-Framing from the heart where you sincerely feel those feelings of love, care, appreciation, etc. With practice, you will become more aware of the difference. Generating feelings from the heart always feels good. Adding sincerity deepens and enriches your experience of engaging the heart.

So let's practice FREEZE-FRAME—with sincerity. Is there a current situation about which you would like more clarity or answers? FREEZE-FRAME now with sincerity and then ask your heart for understanding.

Situation

_____

_____

_____

_____

FREEZE-FRAME Response

Follow Up Exercise—Bonus Insights

If something comes up today where you need clarity or perhaps even a dose of inspiration or a dash of creativity, remember to FREEZE-FRAME with sincerity. That's the recipe for success. Your true source of inspiration, creativity and answers, as you are well aware by now, is your heart!

To listen closely and reply well is the highest perfection
we are able to attain in the art of conversation.

— *La Rochefoucauld*

DAY 5

Today's Reading

In *Self Empowerment*, Chapter 2, "The Head and the Heart," Doc Lew Childre stresses the importance of sincerity in communication.

> When communication is approached from the heart, you experience sincerity and resonance. Without the heart engaged, communication can be dry and dull—and you can't wait to get away for a break. Have you ever noticed workplaces where people seem to co-exist in a mechanical, robotic way, without much sincerity or care in their communications? It's like being in a sleepwalking environment. The absence of heart energy sterilizes an environment.

> The heart is not just for bailing you out of problems. It's especially good for preventing problems. It's a source of strength and commitment, adding quality and buoyancy to your relationships or activities. You can notice the difference in the quality of a lecture or a talk when it is given from the heart with sincerity. People tell each other to play and sing from the heart. This brings another level of obvious quality and texture to their performance.

People pay attention and listen when there's sincerity in the conversation. Sincerity from the speaker opens your heart to listen. By the same token, when you speak with sincerity, you're probably deep heart listening to yourself, and others will be drawn to listen more deeply too!
Jot down your insights if you'd like.

_____

_____

_____

_____

_____

_____

Exercise

If you want to improve your communications, and turn monologues into dialogues, speak sincerely from your heart. Then the words will flow more smoothly, you'll stand a better chance of feeling heard and the other person will more readily listen. Sincerity will enhance all conversations.

The other half of that coin is to sincerely listen when someone speaks with you. They will appreciate that you are fully present in the moment. That's a gift that so many lack in their lives and you can give it to them each time you sincerely listen from the heart.

Sincerity is also a key element in written communication. If you're going to take the time to write something, make it count and write it with sincerity. Do a quick FREEZE-FRAME—get into your heart—and then write from your heart. Freeze-Framing will give you clarity and inspiration. It will be easier for your reader to feel your message when you take the time to write with sincerity. Why not start now? Is there someone you would like to write a note to, someone from the past or the present? (And you don't necessarily even have to present it to them.) FREEZE-FRAME and then from that place in your heart, sincerely write your message.

Follow Up Exercise—Bonus Insights

Today, practice being sincere in all your communications—verbal and written. Notice the difference it makes and how you feel when you communicate with sincerity. Notice how others respond as well. Sincerity in

315

communication is like adding spices to food. Your conversations will become more flavorful.

This month you have covered a lot of important subjects. Write down the five most important insights you gained from this month's study.

1. _____
   _____
   _____

2. _____
   _____
   _____

3. _____
   _____
   _____

4. _____
   _____
   _____

5. _____
   _____
   _____

MONTH 6
Co-creating Reality

WEEK 1
DNA Blueprints

WEEK 2
Holographic
Awareness

WEEK 3
Pump Up the
Power Tools

WEEK 4
A Hopeful Self

As a man thinketh so is he, and as a man chooseth so is he.

— *Emerson*

DAY ①

Today's Reading

In *The Hidden Power of the Heart,* Chapter 16, "DNA Blueprints," Sara Paddison helps us to understand how we can fulfill our DNA blueprint.

> Your holographic heart crystals imprint their electrical patterns and programs in your DNA. As you activate new heart programs, they are communicated directly to your DNA. Like the heart crystals, the DNA structure has the core frequency of "love" as its bottom line frequency grid. The human body is composed of intricate and interwoven frequencies that are biological patterns imprinted in the DNA. The DNA takes responsibility for creation. Historically, for the first time, as we move into the higher dimensional awareness, the entire human family will emerge into a totally new cycle of creation....You must use your highest intelligence as your guide. This type of energy management leads to making consistently efficient decisions that are fulfilling. They keep you on your highest blueprint.

> In day-to-day life, inefficient choices aren't wrong since there is no wrong in evolution. They just take you around the block on a longer journey than necessary to reach your destination and fulfill your DNA blueprint. It takes even longer if you add self-judgment, overcare or guilt. We've all done this, so it's no big deal—it's just not efficient and not very fun.

The heart can guide us efficiently to fulfillment. Inefficient choices can delay us in reaching our destination. We all know that the shortest distance between two points is a straight line. In this case, it's the heart.

Sara's writings offer food for thought. Jot down your insights if you'd like.

_____

_____

_____

Exercise

Can you recall a time in your life when you knew you didn't make an effi-cient choice? Ultimately you ended up where you needed to be. You just went the long way. Sometimes that delay can cost minutes, sometimes years. Here is a typical example. How many of us have made a career choice based on practicality and well-meaning advice from parents, friends, etc. only to discover years later it wasn't really what we wanted to do with our life? There was no fulfillment or meaning in that particular career path, no mat-ter how practical it was. We were following the logic of the head and not the wisdom or passion of the heart. Later in life, however, after many years of frustration, we might decide to return to school and study what we are best suited for and then fulfillment finds us. What enabled us to change our path? How did we realize that the first career choice wasn't truly for us? Inefficient choices eventually feel bad or wrong and create stress—inharmo-nious electrical feedback in our system. It doesn't mean people are wrong or bad. It just means we don't always start out following our heart.

Take a little trip down memory lane to see if there have been times when you took the long way to your destination. How did you feel when it was happen-ing? What were the clues that helped you to realize that you were off course? Complete the following exercise and be sure to jot down your insights.

Situation

_____

_____

_____

Clues

_____

_____

_____

Feelings

_____

_____

_____

Insights

_____

_____

_____

Follow Up Exercise—Bonus Insights

Realize that you create your own reality by the choices you make. Do you create peace or stress? Today, allow your heart to help you make your decisions so that you can travel the path to peace and fulfillment, and "make your own beautiful footprints in the snow."

Nothing is more difficult, and therefore more precious, than to be able to decide.

— *Napoleon I*

 *Today's Reading*

In *The Hidden Power of the Heart*, Chapter 16, "DNA Blueprints," Sara Paddison offers an explanation of the term "blueprint" and helps us to understand how we can best follow our blueprint.

> The best way to understand your blueprint is to imagine a city map. You have to navigate the city with all its one-way streets, left and right-hand turns, traffic jams, and detours. In this city, each time you take a left-hand turn it drains your energy because it's not the most efficient way to get you where you want to go. So when you turn left, you get stress feedback in your feeling world in the form of tension, anxiety, repression and guilt. This is not to punish you; it has a purpose. It's a signal to help you change your course to get back on the right track— in the universal flow....You get into a bottleneck because you aren't practicing what you know you should be doing. Detours are like side trips—life geometries that bring you expansion in often unexpected areas to help you learn and grow.

> When you make a "left-hand turn" in life, your heart computer will try to help you get back on track. It will try to help you make a right-hand turn, then another right, and another right, to get you back around the block to where you were going in the first place. Left-hand turns can happen in the smallest situations of life or the biggest....Left-hand turns take longer and are just more work for yourself. Right-hand turns are the product of listening to and following your heart computer—living through the spirit.

When you come to an intersection and aren't sure whether to make a right turn or a left, there's only one way to find out. You've got your own built-in compass. You just have to remember to use it!

Jot down your insights about what you have just read.

_____

_____

_____

Exercise

Left-hand turns are not fun. Yet so often we find ourselves making them. Sometimes we're not even aware that we've made them until we feel the stress in our system or get the sense that something doesn't feel quite right. Paying attention to these feelings is important and will help us get to where we really need to go.

And then there are right-hand turns. You know when you've made one because it feels good. It feels right. Everything clicks. Yes! And how did you make that efficient choice? Was it a feeling—a heart-prompting—perhaps your intuition? Maybe you really were following your heart. Recall one of these times. How did you make that decision? What were the clues that told you it was right or efficient? And how did you feel at the time? Complete the following exercise and perhaps it will offer you some insights on how you can follow your blueprint more often and continue to make efficient choices in life.

Situation

_____

_____

_____

Clues

_____

_____

_____

Feelings

_____

_____

_____

Insights

_____

_____

_____

Follow Up Exercise—Bonus Insights

Before you make any decision today, go to your heart and see how that decision feels. Try it on for size. If you're not sure how it feels, do a FREEZE-FRAME and ask your heart for guidance and understanding. You'll save time and energy in the long run by taking these steps first. It's just a matter of becoming an efficient player in the game of life. Jot down your observations before ending your day.

_____

_____

_____

Heaven is under our feet as well as over our heads.

— Thoreau

DAY ③

Today's Reading

In *The Hidden Power of the Heart,* Chapter 16, "DNA Blueprints," Sara Paddison explains how making decisions from the heart helps us create "heaven on earth."

> Your little, everyday choices really do count in the unfoldment of your blueprint. If you're not sure which way to go in making decisions, stay in the heart and love, radiate heart energy until your heart computer kicks in with a read-out. You will increasingly make choices that activate your higher frequencies. That's creating heaven on earth for yourself through "care." It means taking the time to go to your higher intelligence for direction. With practice, it doesn't take much time, and direction comes as quick, spontaneous intuition.

> The most efficient way to understand the universal principles is to understand your own self in day-to-day life. The puzzle pieces or events in a day are your life geometries for experiencing and expanding awareness. Making right-hand turns and following your highest blueprint will lead you to your mission in life and activate your passion to be all you can be. It builds real self-esteem that lasts. Those who make continual efforts to self-manage their energies from the heart over the next ten years will have increased fun and fulfillment in life. Those who continue to operate mostly from head bands will experience increased stress—head processors feeding back on themselves.

Finding fulfillment in life and enjoying "life after birth" boils down to the choices we make in the moment. Heart-based choices feel good and will guide us to make right-hand turns which lead to more fun and fulfillment.

Jot down your insights.

_____

_____

_____

_____

_____

Exercise

Right-hand turns are a product of listening to and following your heart directives. To stay on your highest soul blueprint if you're not sure which way to go, FREEZE-FRAME and go to neutral, stay in the heart, and activate love or appreciation until your heart intelligence gives you a clear read-out. That's taking care of yourself and will help you put the puzzle pieces of your lifeêügether. The puzzle pieces or events in life are life geometries for learning and growing. The math of your heart will bring you effective solutions if you listen to it.

Is there a decision that you are currently having difficulty making? Why not FREEZE-FRAME now and find out which way to go? Avoiding left-hand turns saves time and energy. The best short-cut to get you where you need to go is through the heart.

Situation

_____

_____

_____

_____

_____

Heart Intuition Response

_____

_____

_____

_____

Follow Up Exercise—Bonus Insights

Remember, you create your own reality by the choices you make in the moment. Today, go for more moments of creating "heaven on earth." It's your choice. Efficient decisions from the heart will take you there.

Jot down your observations from this day of practice.

_____

_____

_____

_____

_____

_____

Life is a game, but you must be present to win.

— *Unknown*

DAY 4

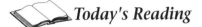 *Today's Reading*

In *The Hidden Power of the Heart*, Chapter 16, "DNA Blueprints," Sara Paddison explains how operating from the heart enables us to create more peace for ourselves.

> The next decade will accelerate the polarization of people's choices, either to go back to the heart to bail out or remain imprisoned in the stress they are creating. The incoming frequencies are loving, but neutral. It is you who qualifies what the energy does inside you by operating from the heart or the head. You accumulate assets or deficits in your energy system relative to the peace or the stress you have. As you observe your overall level of peace, you can determine the real quality of your life. It's simple math.

———

> Love is the energy of expansion, the vital current of creation. The thoughts you create generate the patterns that shape your environment. With planetary acceleration of energies, people's stressful thoughts will create patterns so they either break down on some level (the inner Armageddon) or wake up and realize they have to go back to the heart....But in the new ratio of intelligence entering the planetary system today, you receive back more light and love than you put out—in a ratio of 9:1. It's like extremely high interest on your bank account —your energy management account. This is the power of the higher dimensional energy equation accelerating the planet.

Efficient management of your thoughts will help you create a harmonious environment for yourself. Making life a joint venture between head and heart pays big dividends, bigger than any other capital venture you could enter. And it's not a risky investment! It's solid from the heart.

Jot down your insights if you'd like.

_____

_____

_____

Exercise

It's making that 1 effort that will bring you the 9 energy return on your investment. All it takes is one sincere effort to activate a heart frequency—love, care, compassion, forgiveness, appreciation—and you're making an efficient choice in the moment. The 9 might not always arrive in the payback you expect, but you will accumulate energy assets for yourself by doing your "1"! Plus you'll feel good in the process and it sure is a lot better than generating energy deficits. Since you create your reality either way, why not choose the heart's way?

Why not keep a tally sheet today of all the times you did a "1" —when you made that extra effort to go to your heart and activate a heart frequency? Note how you feel throughout the day when you sincerely engage your heart. Then see how you feel at the end of the day. Chances are you'll be feeling pretty good.

Doing Your "1" Tally Sheet

*Situation #1*_____

*Heart Frequency Activated*_____

*How You Felt*_____

_____

*Situation #2*_____

*Heart Frequency Activated*_____

*How You Felt*_____

_____

*Situation #3*_____

*Heart Frequency Activated*_____

*How You Felt*_____

_____

*Situation #4*_____

*Heart Frequency Activated*_____

*How You Felt*_____

_____

So how do you create more fun and fulfillment? Just keep doing your "1" and you'll soon find out! Enjoy your "9's". By the way, you don't need to keep looking for them. They will find you!

Follow Up Exercise—Bonus Insights

You create your own reality whether you're asleep or awake in life. Making conscious choices and consciously choosing the heart will unfold your highest blueprint. Today, practice being awake in the moment so at least you'll be aware of what you're creating. It's the best way to win at the game of life. Go for those right-hand turns!

> To be what we are, and to become what we are
> capable of becoming is the only end in life.
>
> — *Baruch Spinoza*

DAY 5

Today's Reading

In *The Hidden Power of the Heart*, Chapter 15, "Holographic Awareness," Sara Paddison explains how love and appreciation can increase the heart's coherent and harmonious electrical patterns leading to greater efficiency. She explains that this has been documented by a joint research project in which the Institute of HeartMath was involved.

> The research also revealed that heart electricities are shown to be coherent when an individual is highly focused on loving or appreciating someone or something. It is well known by doctors and researchers that heart electricity is the dominant force in the human system. When the heart is radiating coherent energy patterns, it causes the electricities of the brain and its sub-center (the head) to phase-lock with the heart patterns, creating greater efficiency. This research has shown a direct correlation between the frequency signature of cardiac electricity and positive mental and emotional states. The geometric ratios, as seen in the rhythm, amplitude and frequency modulation of heart electricities, also appear harmonically linked to the physical cellular system, the immune system and DNA structure.

> The principle of energy interference among waves of any type (sound, light, water, etc.) is that order (or constructive interference) self-replicates, while disorder (or destructive interference) self-destructs. Simply put, this means you can boost a wave's amplitude by attuning to its frequency, or you can disrupt a wave by introducing a dissonant frequency. Heart perspective brings waves into focus. The points of resonant convergence are where lines of energy and intention meet.

The results of the joint research project showed that coherent emotional waves, like love, are self-regenerating, teachable and easily accessible with practice.

We have a choice in every moment to create electrical coherence throughout our system by engaging our heart through feelings of love, appreciation, care, etc. We affect our physiology by our choices and enable it either to regenerate or create more disorder. Jot down your insights to obtain a deeper understanding about what you have just read.

_____

_____

_____

_____

_____

Exercise

Let's look at what can be a typical day for so many. Nothing seems to fall into place, everything is out of sync and things go from bad to worse. Perhaps it started when you couldn't find your keys in the morning. Then by the time you found them, your coffee was cold. And, of course, by now you had completely forgotten that you needed to get gas on your way to work. By the time you got to work, you were so frazzled you couldn't think straight. And then there was that important meeting for which you were obviously late, etc., etc. Your imagination can piece together the rest of the day and not a peaceful one at that.

This scenario depicts typical events—little things that can go wrong in your day—but what needs to be atypical is your reaction to them. It's not the events themselves that are the culprits. It's your reaction to them. Do you allow incidents like these to dictate how you feel or are you the master of the moment and keep going to your heart and FREEZE-FRAME when necessary? If you let your reactions get the best of you, you're setting up a cascade of negative emotions that will not only ruin your day but negatively affect your physiology. Is this the reality you choose to create for yourself?

On the other hand, had you consulted your heart along the way, you wouldn't have caused as much wear and tear on your system and would have been able to approach the day from another perspective. You see, since everything is energy and everything is interconnected, and like attracts like, you are programming the events of your day or perhaps of your life.

Can you recall a somewhat similar day? Let's go back to those stressful moments and see how you might have handled them differently by going to your heart and choosing a heart frequency.

Event #1 _____

Head Reaction _____

Heart Response _____

Event #2 _____

Head Reaction _____

Heart Response _____

Event #3 _____

Head Reaction _____

Heart Response _____

Event #4 _____

Head Reaction _____

Heart Response _____

Event #5 _____

Head Reaction _____

Heart Response _____

Event #6 _____

Head Reaction _____

Heart Response _____

Follow Up Exercise—Bonus Insights

Heart coherence is the key to health and harmony, and creating a fulfilling reality. During the day, stop to check in with yourself and observe whether or not you are generating coherent frequencies throughout your system. You will be able to tell by the way you feel. Remember, you are creating your reality in every moment. You have the choice of choosing the heart and letting your highest DNA blueprint unfold. This week's subject matter has been at least interesting and probably expansive. Write down the three most important things you learned this week.

1. _____

_____

2. _____

_____

3. _____

_____

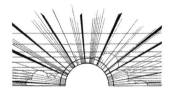

The art of achievement is the art of making life—your life—a masterpiece.

— *Unknown*

DAY 1

Today's Reading

In *The Hidden Power of the Heart*, Chapter 15, "Holographic Awareness," Sara Paddison introduces us to the concept of holograms—integral to creating our reality.

> The basic holographic principle is that every part contains the whole. In holography, every piece of a holographic picture contains the entire picture. In the now famous experiment called, "The Phantom Leaf Effect," an electrophotograph of an amputated leaf revealed a picture of an intact, whole leaf. The amputated portion still appeared in the photo of the leaf, even though the missing leaf fragment had been destroyed....The piece that was cut out left the information of the whole electrically recorded in a non-physical field!

> Every tiny cell in your body contains an identical copy of your master DNA blueprint...Like the phantom leaf, your master DNA blueprint is holographically mirrored in every cell of your body. When you hold a tiny acorn in your hand you know it contains the entire blueprint for a huge oak tree. You also know that when a sperm and ovum come together, they contain the entire blueprint of an adult human. Imagine every cell in your body also containing the frequency blueprint of the whole universe. Only through the heart can you access these higher dimensional perceptions of universal frequency structures. The bioenergetic field of the physical body is a holographic energy template with encoded information of All.

There is no denying that we are a part of the whole. It is encoded in our DNA, which we can access through our hearts. Tapping into that potential enables us to co-create with the Universe. We may be mere mortals, but we have tremendous power through the heart to create our own masterpiece! Jot down your insights about this information.

_____

_____

_____

Exercise

Holographic awareness is learning to consciously co-create with your DNA to create the highest possible outcome. In the higher dimensions, the future is composed of different crystallizing possibilities. The perceptions you identify with play a significant role in which of these crystallizing possibilities will manifest. Most of us are unconscious participants in the patterns and frequencies of our holographic DNA blueprint. But in becoming heart conscious, you activate new possibilities. In other words, the future is plastic and can be changed.

Let's begin molding that plastic now. Look at an event in your life that may be posing a dilemma. You have two choices as you know by now: head or heart. Your choice will not only determine the outcome of that event, but it will also create a sequence of events to follow, contingent on your decision: head or heart. Knowing that the scene can play out either way, FREEZE-FRAME and ask your heart to help you achieve the most efficient outcome. In other words, select the hologram that will unfold your highest blueprint.

Situation

_____

_____

_____

FREEZE-FRAME Response

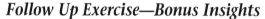

Can you see where your heart response encompasses the bottom line frequency of love and caring for the whole? In other words, the choice would be for your highest and best. And since you are a part of the whole, the solution would be beneficial for all. Jot down your insights from this exercise.

Follow Up Exercise—Bonus Insights

Remember, you are creating the 3D movie of your life by the choices you make. Is today going to be one of those movies you really enjoy or is it going to receive bad reviews and be hidden away in the closet? Take time during the day to actually watch the movie and, if necessary, change the script along the way.

> Your attitude tells the world what you expect from life,
> and whether or not you will achieve it.
>
> — *Unknown*

DAY ②

Today's Reading

In *The Hidden Power of the Heart*, Chapter 15, "Holographic Awareness," Sara Paddison explains how perspective determines our reality—in the hall of mirrors of life.

Holograms are really like a hall of mirrors. It's whatever perspective you want to see, whatever angle you look at in the mirror, that determines your reality. Stopping head thoughts to gain a wider perspective of the moment is the choice of creation. Only through the heart can one see the holographic movie objectively. When your heart directs you to leap into another holodome, do it and surrender to the new movie. Participate in it and experience it fully. That activates your next heart-directed program, and the next, and you move on in your highest blueprint in the universal flow.

In the movie you are living today, are you choosing a heart perspective or a head perspective? Depending on your choice, you will write different sequences for your day and the consequences will be different— activitating different holographic filmstrips. The highest intelligence has "streetsense" in the choices it makes, streetsense being the common sense of the heart which integrates and aligns higher fourth dimensional perceptions into the 3-D world here and now. Streetsense contains complexity broken down into simple understanding. It's a practical, balanced and efficient approach to a life situation that simply "makes sense." Streetsense is the road to clear perception about what is.

Streetsense and *makes sense* are the common sense of the heart. It stands to reason that the highest intelligence would have that bottom line sense of truth. It adds up—simple math—HeartMath.

These are important concepts. Jot down your insights if you'd like.

_____

_____

_____

Exercise

Streetsense is simple and basic common sense accessible by all. Wouldn't it have to be that way, if everyone is part of the whole and it's all about caring for the whole? That's the beauty of the system. Everyone has a heart, so everyone can access their heart intelligence. The key is remembering to use it. That one simple step can change your holographic reality in the moment and give you a different perception of life, just by looking into that mirror from a different angle. It can save you frustration, aggravation, time, stress, and wear and tear on your system. It can lead to fun and fulfillment—a more enjoyable movie of life. Learn to rely on your heart in all situations—big or small—and co-create a fulfilling reality.

Can you see where you have made choices that lacked *streetsense* and did not contribute to your well-being or happiness? Perhaps you can change that hologram by making more efficient choices now. And if you can't change that hologram, at least you can change your attitude towards it and find something to appreciate about it. Perhaps by adopting a wider perspective you will be able to create a more fulfilling reality in the future and attract more good to you.

Is there a current situation that could benefit from an infusion of heart energy? Why not look at it from a wider perspective? Ask your heart to guide you into a more fulfilling hologram. Do a Lock-In and listen to your heart. Write down what it says.

Situation

_____

_____

_____

Heart Intuition Response

_____

_____

_____

Follow Up Exercise—Bonus Insights

During your daily activities today, check out your decisions from the heart to make sure they "make sense." Let the common sense of your heart guide you to create a fulfilling holographic movie. That would be *streetsense*.

Jot down your observations about your day of focusing on *streetsense*.

_____

_____

_____

_____

Your rewards in life are always in direct proportion to your contribution.
— *Unknown*

DAY ③

Today's Reading

Resuming in *The Hidden Power of the Heart*, Chapter 15, "Holographic Awareness," Sara Paddison offers us her personal insight into changing our future by following heart directives.

> From my experience in the holographic heart, the future is indeed plastic and can be changed. I see it as composed of "crystallizing possibilities." Since everything is really interconnected, it's possible to tune in and choose a different holographic frequency pattern and change your future. You are simply doing that when you follow your heart directives rather than your same old head programs.

> Your perspective at any given moment plays a significant part in creating the quality of your future. We are like artists, sculpting our destiny as we go. Most of us are unconscious participants in the patterns and frequencies of our holographic blueprint. But in becoming heart conscious, we activate new crystallizing possibilities that put us on the highest blueprint possible—God's plan for us.

> ...The frequencies of the past and present unite to form a configuration of magnetics that draws a specific holographic pattern into your present. Some of the strongest crystallizing possibilities of your holographic blueprint can be seen in major life events such as marriages, accidents, death and enlightenment experiences.

Becoming "heart conscious" enables us to create a quality future. The choice we make in every moment will determine what the next moment will bring. Our future is happening now. Being "heart conscious" enables us to create a more fulfilling one.

Jot down your insights if you'd like.

_____

_____

_____

_____

Exercise

Begin reshaping your future now by being in your heart this moment. Select a heart frequency—love, care, compassion, appreciation, forgiveness—to attract more quality moments to you. Since your DNA blueprint is aligned with the core frequency of love, your highest evolutionary path would be that of love. By going deeper in the heart and being in the heart of the moment, you can make choices that will put you on your highest DNA blueprint for fulfillment. You can begin now. No matter what happens next, be in your heart as life unfolds. How you react, respond or make a decision will determine how successive moments will unfold. Go for the gold—from your heart. So, in the next moment, if the phone rings or someone comes in to talk to you or if you're alone, be in the heart of the moment and make the moment richer. Remember, the choice you make in the moment will affect what is to follow. Make the moment count by being in your heart. No matter what happens, you can always go to appreciation. Something fun and exciting may be waiting around the next moment for you. Or perhaps there is a challenge presenting itself for your growth. It's your hologram, so why not create a movie you'll enjoy? Jot down your observations and any insights from this experience that is about to unfold.

Experience

_____

_____

_____

_____

Response

_____

_____

_____

_____

Insights

_____

_____

_____

_____

Follow Up Exercise—Bonus Insights

Today be heart conscious as you move through life and approach each
moment from a heart perspective. As you sit in the director's chair, directing
your movie of life, activate heart frequencies and enjoy the scenes as they
unfold. Remember, it's your movie! You can make it a drama, tragedy or
comedy. Even though the scenes may present themselves to you, it's your
response to them that will determine the kind of movie you are making.

If you cannot get rid of the family skeletons, you may as well make them dance.
— George Bernard Shaw

DAY ④

Today's Reading

Continuing in *The Hidden Power of the Heart*, Chapter 15, "Holographic Awareness," Sara Paddison stresses the importance of bringing our lives into harmony and balance to avoid having to learn through misfortune.

> Nature always seeks a balance, so the future patterns people magnetize are their system's effort to create balance. Disasters can teach us profound lessons that result in more understanding. Some people love and respect nature and learn balance from her harmony. As we learn to harmonize our lives, we help balance the holographic patterns in Mother Nature which humanity is part of. Perhaps then, Mother Nature wouldn't need to teach us to care for each other through storms and earthquakes. At least we can know she loves us enough to care that we learn one way or another. Each person still has choice. If you don't go to your heart and learn from a misfortune, you could magnetize similar frequencies to yourself (possibly another misfortune). When you use heart intelligence in life, you rearrange your future frequencies and often can avoid disasters.

> From my experience, a fifth dimensional hololeap is possible when you view your filmstrip and then have the intelligence to erase or re-model part of your character. You can actually walk into the holographic heart and re-enact that part in the play. In other words, you give yourself a fresh start by going into your past and making a different choice. It's like taking out a particular computer chip, an old program, by altering the basic frequency. You come back to your everyday world, but with less baggage and a fresh perspective. Hololeaps could be considered a form of time travel.

I magine cleaning up the past in the present to create a better future. Hololeaps enable us to do just that. It will also help us avoid collecting any skeletons in our closet! Jot down your insights.

Exercise

Many of us have moments in the past that we still feel uncomfortable about and would like to forget—those skeletons rattling around in the closets. Even though it is consoling to know that we were doing the best we could at the time, and if other people were involved, that would apply to them, too. However, those feelings still keep popping up. Fortunately, we can go back into our holographic heart and, in a sense, change that movie. From a wider heart perspective we can gain a deeper understanding of the situation and clean up those uncomfortable feelings.

Dig around in your closet and find an uncomfortable situation and re-write the script with understanding from your heart. You can make that hololeap and feel a whole lot better.

Past Situation

Heart Intuition Response / New Hologram

Could you feel a shift occur within you from doing this exercise? How do you feel now about that situation you just re-wrote? It's amazing what you can accomplish from the heart. Jot down any insights you gained from this experience.

_____

_____

_____

_____

Follow Up Exercise—Bonus Insights

You won't have to clean up the past in the future if you stay in the heart of the moment now. Consciously create your reality by making fulfilling choices based on love and care. That would be your highest blueprint. Remember, you are co-creating everyday, consciously or unconsciously. Why not go for the gusto and be in the heart of the moment?

Jot down your observations at the end of your day.

_____

_____

_____

_____

_____

_____

Today is the first day of the rest of your life.

— Unknown

DAY 5

Today's Reading

Concluding in *The Hidden Power of the Heart*, Chapter 15, "Holographic Awareness," Sara Paddison offers us an understanding of the importance of being in the now.

> Future events often cast a cloud's shadow in our present thoughts and in our daydreams of old memories....I find the best way to prepare for future moments, or to stabilize any unwanted past moment, is to be fully in my present moment, now. To be in the now is a state of mind that doesn't stagnate in the past or the future. Living in the moment is living in the spirit—with buoyancy and sparkle—the spirit being the essence of life.

> Practically speaking, let's say you're eating a hamburger on Tuesday while thinking of a steak dinner you're going to have next Friday. It's likely you are not enjoying the hamburger to its full potential. Being in the moment involves giving maximum appreciation and love to your present experience. This widens the doorway to the potential of the *Now*....

So how do you practically apply holography to the real world of this moment? When you see old patterns of fear arise, that's when you need to go to your heart intelligence for a wider perspective. Your next thoughts, feelings and actions will determine how the next hour and often the rest of your day unfolds. Your little choices really do count.

We are really captains of our ship. Our choices determine whether or not it will be smooth sailing or choppy water. And should we find ourselves in choppy water, how well we navigate depends on how much we rely on our inner compass, for it will assure us safe passage. Jot down your insights if you'd like.

Exercise

In your daily activities, are there repetitive situations where you've been through this so many times before and want to create a new hologram? You told yourself you would never do that again and yet here you are doing it. Then why not change that hologram now? Go to your heart and ask your heart for a deeper understanding of the situation and then ask what would be the best way to proceed. Sometimes you will be surprised by the answers your heart will reveal. You will receive answers that you would never have thought of or been able to figure out from your head alone. And it's so convenient. You don't have to make an appointment and you don't have to pay a fee. So change that hologram now by Freeze-Framing and taking that hololeap!

Repetitive Situation

FREEZE-FRAME Response

Are you in the now, now? So often we find ourselves lingering in the past or wandering aimlessly in the future and missing the now. Now would be a good time to get into the now. Let the potential of the now unfold by appreciating and loving all that you are experiencing this moment. That will set up the dynamic for the next now and the one after that. The best way to experience the now is from the heart. Let your now become "Wow!" Spend five minutes in a Lock-In appreciating. That will be a good investment in your energy bank account and a fulfilling hologram. Jot down your insights from this experience.

Follow Up Exercise—Bonus Insights

During your daily activities, practice being in the now and increase your ability to stay in the heart and love in the moment. Choose the heart hologram and become it. Remember, this moment will never come again, so live it to the fullest. Let this be the first moment of the rest of your life!

This week you have been learning about holographically creating your reality. Write down a sentence or two about what you have learned this week.

Practice is nine-tenths.

— Emerson

DAY ①

Today's Reading

In *The Hidden Power of the Heart*, Chapter 7, "Heart Power Tools," Sara Paddison tells us how we can transform our lives by using the heart power tools.

> What would it be like to have fulfilling feelings of love and care flowing through your system most of the time? If you could buy tools to help you feel more love, would you? What if the instructions that went with the tools were to practice regularly, as you'd do to learn golf, a dance routine or a new video game? Whether your goal is less stress, deeper love or balance and fulfillment, using even one or two of the heart power tools consistently can transform your life.

> By activating the fundamental core heart frequency bands in your system, the tools connect you with your heart power. Your sensitivity increases, communication becomes clear, understanding develops, and perspective widens. Consistent practice can bring results, often within a few days. Using any one of the tools is profitable and yields high dividends....
>
> These tools are for all people—regardless of age, sex, awareness, race, color or religion. They are gifts for the evolution of mankind. Some of them may sound like "old hat," like you've heard them before—and you have. But they have tremendous power, which has largely gone unused. They draw upon the intelligence of your own heart to activate higher heart frequencies of love, care, compassion, appreciation and forgiveness.

I magine achieving results with just a few days of sincere and consistent practice! These are powerful tools capable of bringing you peace and fulfillment. There's only one catch—you have to use them! Jot down your insights about what you have read.

_____

_____

Exercise

The first step to pump up the power tools is to remember to use them. And when you do remember, be sure to use the tool you have selected with sincerity—the generator for all power tools. We're going to begin pumping up today with appreciation.

As you know, appreciation is a magnetic frequency that will attract more good to you. That's power! To pump up appreciation, look for the little things you might still take for granted—like living in the 20th century. When was the last time you had to rub two sticks together to cook your dinner? Or perhaps you need to appreciate the person who cooked your dinner—your significant other, a good friend, the chef in the restaurant or maybe yourself. Then how about all those people who made your dinner possible—the farmer, the trucker, the produce man at the market, etc.? The list could go on and on.

Just for the fun of it, make a list of some of the "little things" you may overlook during a typical day. That will give you an idea of how much you can be grateful for. Take some time to go to your heart and feel appreciation as you make that fun list of overlooked little things to appreciate in your day. An attitude of gratitude would be the way to go.

Appreciation List

_____

_____

_____

_____

_____

_____

_____

_____

_____

_____

_____

_____

_____

Did any insights pop in while you were sincerely appreciating? Jot them down, too, and appreciate them. There's always more to appreciate.

_____

_____

_____

Follow Up Exercise—Bonus Insights

Today, adopt that attitude of gratitude as you move through your day. No matter what happens, truly appreciate it, big or little, fun or challenging. It will add more sparkle to your day. That's really pumping up appreciation.

When you love someone all your saved-up wishes start coming out.

— *Elizabeth Bowen*

DAY **2**

Today's Reading

Continuing in *The Hidden Power of the Heart*, Chapter 7, "Heart Power Tools," Sara Paddison helps us to understand that the energy we radiate out comes back, so that we actually accumulate love.

> How can love be a tool? To use love as a power tool, simply focus your attention on your heart center, activate your own love for someone and radiate that love frequency. As energy goes out, it comes back. As your love goes out, it comes back—adding to deeper feelings of love within you and in your interactions with people. As you continue to send out love, the energy returns to you in a regenerating spiral. Your system accumulates the energy of love, just like it accumulates stress. As love accumulates, it keeps your system in balance and harmony. Love is the tool, and more love is the end product.

> Love is empowering. Many people who thought they were already loving are astonished at the change they experience when they sincerely use love as a tool. Their comments are almost evangelistic, revealing a new understanding of the regenerative nature of this hidden power of the heart. As they focus their energy in the heart, then radiate love, they are amazed at the new textures of love they experience. The difference between how they felt before using love as a tool, and after, is astounding to them. It feels like coming home. They have more contact with their real spirit...

Consciously and sincerely using love as a power tool will enrich the quality of your life. It will enable you to really enjoy the ride. You can always love deeper and more. That's pumping up the power of love. Jot down you insights if you'd like.

_____

_____

_____

_____

_____

_____

_____

_____

Exercise

The only way you can fully understand and appreciate the power of love is by loving. Just love people. All people! Just for fun, today, think of the most loving person you are aware of and feel yourself moving through the day with that person. Just love everyone and everything. And not in a mushy, sentimental way—but in a caring, compassionate, non-judgmental way. Remember, nature doesn't judge. It loves and allows. So try a day of just loving. Have fun doing little deeds of kindness along the way. That would be loving. Remember, we're all connected in the heart. It's the head that separates. The heart unites. So pump up the power of love.

At the end of the day, record how you felt throughout the day and how you feel at the end of the day. Jot down any insights you had from this experience. Was your day fulfilling, satisfying, light-hearted? Was it a tough day with lots of challenges? Were you loving? You might want to try it again tomorrow. You can never have too much practice!

Feelings

_____

_____

_____

_____

_____

_____

_____

_____

Insights

_____

_____

_____

_____

_____

_____

Follow Up Exercise—Bonus Insights

Continue to observe yourself today as you use the power of love. Note areas where you could still be more loving and perhaps where you could add another level of sincerity. Just keep practicing. Love those people!

Love is, above all, the gift of oneself.

— *Jean Anouilh*

DAY ③

Today's Reading

Reading further in *The Hidden Power of the Heart*, Chapter 7, "Heart Power Tools," Sara Paddison shares with us the remarkable power of love on health as documented by a hospital study.

> "Love" is not some sweet, Pollyanna, goody-two-shoes frequency band. The words "love," "care," and "appreciation" are like little word cages for wise, powerful energies. As science proves that "love" is an intelligence unto itself, then researchers will more objectively respect its wide range of potentials. Physics has demonstrated that once two particles touch, they have a permanent connection that goes beyond time and space. Studies are already taking place on the effects of love in relationship to healing. Cardiologist Randolph Byrd recently conducted a ten-month scientific study with coronary patients at San Francisco General Hospital on the effects of love and prayer in healing. He applied the most rigid criteria possible for clinical medical studies. The results were remarkable. Significantly fewer drugs and surgical procedures were required for those patients who received conscious love and prayer than for those in the control group who didn't receive this help.

> There is a difference between consciously directing your life with the energies of love, care and appreciation flowing through your system, and just letting them be there as the mood arises. It's like the difference between using a Makita power drill and a regular screw driver to build a house. As you practice with focused attention, you become much more efficient and knowledgeable in directing these energies. Love is the most powerful core heart frequency of all, and, yes, it is the real hope for the world. Love encompasses all the other power tools and is the first and most important tool.

Love is the most powerful heart frequency. Are you aware of its power? You have a resource that can change your life and you can access it anytime and anywhere. But these are just words on a page unless you know intuitively and experientially. Jot down your insights about what you read today.

_____

_____

_____

Exercise

Some people begrudgingly say, "O.K., so I'll care, or love or forgive"—thinking they're doing it for the other person. And yes, the other person will benefit, but who benefits most? By now you know—it's you! That's right. Any of these powerful heart frequencies are regenerative and balance and harmonize your system and, of course, bring you peace. Remember, the benefits are contingent upon the sincerity of your efforts. Love will actually make your life easier. If your primary thought is love, you are creating a hologram for yourself that will attract more love and a smoother flow.

Now all this may not happen overnight. However, you have been practicing HeartMath for almost six months, so you are more conscious of where you are—head or heart. By now you are having more continuous moments of peace and fulfillment. To further help you remember to practice going to your heart, you might consider little "post-it" notes placed in strategic locations— the bathroom mirror, the refrigerator, your computer, etc. Some people with alarm watches set them to go off on the hour as a reminder to check in with themselves to see if they're in their heart. Any reminder is better than no reminder.

So be heart conscious and awake. Don't snooze on the road to life because you're liable to take a detour and miss all those opportunities to love, regenerate your system and find more peace, joy and fulfillment.

Are there still some areas where you could love more? Ask your heart to help you identify them and how you can pump up your love (Do a Heart Lock-In if you can). Jot down your insights.

Areas for More Love

_____

_____

_____

_____

_____

Insights

_____

_____

_____

_____

Follow Up Exercise—Bonus Insights

Today is a day to simply practice remembering, so follow yourself around like a shadow and give yourself a little tap on the shoulder when you're not loving and a big pat on the back when you are. It's fun to find yourself in the heart!

What value has compassion that does not take its object in its arms?
— Antoine de Saint-Exupery

DAY **4**

Today's Reading

In *The Hidden Power of the Heart*, Chapter 12, "Uncovering Compassion," Sara Paddison explains how compassion is born from care and "a passion to understand and help others."

> Compassion is care with passion. Passion is a neutral energy that adds to and amplifies your care. When you care and have a passion to understand and help others, you have compassion. You can see passionate care in people like Mother Theresa. Something burns inside their hearts in endless service to the sick, the destitute and those whom society has forgotten. You can see compassion in the eyes of a kind teacher, whose heart goes out to a troubled child. You can find it in a wise judge who looks deep into the heart of the accused with a clarity that transcends the letter of the law.

> Compassion digs for the quality of deep understanding. Isn't our judicial system founded on the premise that all are innocent until proven guilty? That's the bottom line of compassion, although many forget it in the heat of today's social problems. Unless you love people, you can never understand them. When you love enough to put yourself in someone else's shoes, you discover compassion. True love and compassion release other people to be themselves because they finally feel understood. Care and compassion are heart frequencies that are activated by a sincere attitude of wanting to help. They are power tools that, if used, strengthen your connection with your own heart and your ability to love.

How can you have compassion without love and care? You can't. However, a sincere desire to help and understand will enable you to be compassionate and allow your love and care to blossom and grow. Jot down your insights to more deeply understand what you have read.

_____

_____

_____

Exercise

Don't confuse compassion with sympathy. There's a big difference. Sympathy has pity in it which doesn't feel good. No one wants to be pitied. It also leads to more self-pity for the person with whom you are commiserating. Empathy and compassion, on the other hand, seek understanding and desire to help. They also enable the other person to begin "moving on." "Using your heart intelligence, you can walk in someone else's shoes without walking off the cliff with them."

Identify the traits or qualities you would ascribe to a compassionate person. Then see how many of them apply to you. Think of the most compassionate person you know as you make your list.

_____

_____

_____

_____

_____

We can pump up the compassion for ourselves, as well as to others. Is there an area where you need to be more compassionate towards yourself? Ask your heart for insights. Remember, you'd be compassionate to someone else in the same situation. So why not treat yourself compassionately?

Area of More Self-Compassion

_____

_____

_____

Insights

_____

_____

_____

_____

Follow Up Exercise—Bonus Insights

Be compassionate today to those who could benefit from an extra dose of care and understanding. It's an opportunity for you to be in your heart and a chance for the other person to feel heard and understood. It's a gift for both of you.

Before you end your day, write down your observations of this day of compassion.

_____

_____

_____

_____

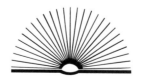

With love and patience, nothing is impossible.

— *Daisaku Ikeda*

DAY 5

Today's Reading

In *The Hidden Power of the Heart,* Chapter 6, "The Dimensional Shift," Sara Paddison explains how true care is just that—care without the overcare generated from third and lower fourth dimensional thinking.

Love can become so coated with negative attitudes from third and lower fourth dimensional energies, that it turns into a deficit instead of an asset to yourself and others. It's important to remember that in the higher fourth dimension you truly do feel care about the world, the environment, the educational system, the people, the laws and so forth. But you don't slip into the anxiety of overcare because you know that will drain you and make your caring less effective. True care has wisdom and discernment. It is love in the active modality—the higher heart and mind joined together.

⸺

The fifth dimensional thought patterns of care are energy-efficient and on a mission—carrying out your purpose. You realize life is a game you play with your own self. In the fifth dimension, you are creating your own universe, so in truly caring you want to run your system as efficiently as possible. The voice of your heart would be loud and clear; your spirit would be speaking. And if you were waking up to who you are, getting to know your complete self, you would follow your spirit, which is made of light. You would put your knowingness into action, creating as you go. In this dimension of light and love, the universe rearranges itself to accommodate your picture of reality.

In the fifth dimension, care is energy-efficient. It's all about you playing the game of life—with yourself—so that you create your own reality. In other words, it's all up to you! Not only is the ball in your court, you get to choose the court and the other players. If you want your team to win, make efficient choices—from your heart.

This is powerful information. Jot down your insights if you'd like.

_____

_____

_____

Exercise

Each time you make a choice that increases love, care, appreciation, compassion or forgiveness, you increase your heart power. Each time you make 1 effort to go to your heart and use a power tool, you receive a payback equivalent to a 9 in return for that 1 effort. Pump up the power tools by being more sincere, more coherent and more intent on activating heart intelligence. Watch the return on your investment increase.

Once you begin to sincerely practice caring, it becomes automatic or natural to always care—to lend a helping hand, to be totally present when someone speaks, to let the person in a rush get in line in front of you, etc.

How does your care measure up? Do you need to pump it up another notch? Rate your care (5 = care a lot; 1 = not enough) in the following areas to see where you could add more care. And if your care is there, then pat yourself on the back.

Care

At Home
With significant other or roommates   _____

With helping around the house   _____

In communications   _____

At Work
With coworkers   _____

Pulling your own weight   _____

Finishing tasks in a timely manner   _____

Being responsible   _____

Follow Up Exercise—Bonus Insights
You do care—that's clear or you wouldn't be doing this program. Just be conscious and caring throughout the day. By now you know that the best way to take care of yourself is by caring for others! Jot down a few insights about this last week.

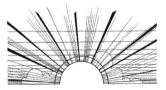

> The best and most beautiful things in the world cannot be seen,
> nor touched...but are felt in the heart.
>
> — *Helen Keller*

DAY ①

Today's Reading

In *The Hidden Power of the Heart*, Chapter 25, "Fulfillment," Sara Paddison again reminds us, from her own experiences, of the power of our heart.

It is my hope that in your journey through this book, you've gained more understanding of what is hidden in the heart or even experienced a feeling of your own heart power. At least, maybe, you have more insight into the math of the real potency you have inside. What a magnificent force within that can facilitate change, eliminate stress and empower us to live our lives to our fullest potential! The only secret for uncovering this power is learning to live from the heart. If I hadn't experienced, and practiced and practiced, I would never have been able to express how dynamically the heart power tools work. Still, to this day, I use the tools to sharpen my skills. The biggest difference now is it doesn't take so long to adjust my frequency and stress is easily released. I remember the adjustments I make, then if a similar stress arises, I know what to do. I can see the math a bit quicker, and don't have so many mind-sets about "knowing what I know" on any subject. I still practice listening more deeply to my friends.

Life still isn't perfect, but 90% of the time life's great—and the other 10% of the time life's good. I constantly remind myself to tune in with divinity, my heart intelligence. I sincerely ask questions like, "How would God look at all this?" and "What would God do?" That's the best I know to do—sincerely ask my own heart intelligence. When I want to know what the future has in store, I remember my ten-year old's simple way of looking at things. He would say, "Mom, are you in your heart? It doesn't look like it to me. You need to get back in your heart." Life in the heart is fun and adventurous. Life out of the heart is not much fun. So adjust and go back to the heart.

Fun and adventure are as far away as your heart. You can get there in a moment. Don't miss the moment. Jot down your insights.

_____

_____

_____

_____

Exercise

By now you are aware that you are responsible for yourself—your thoughts, feelings and actions. You are also responsible for your own happiness, since you create your own reality. The reality of hope is in your heart and is re-kindled every time you connect with it. Separation from the heart can lead to feelings of loneliness, sadness, despair and hopelessness. By following your heart directives you can become more hopeful. Hope is the eternal fire of the spirit. It is, therefore, your source of inspiration because it infuses you with spirit.

Appreciation is also a powerful tool to give you hope. There is always something to appreciate, even if it's just that things could be worse. By making an appreciation list from time to time, you can renew your hope and feel grateful for what you do have.

Is there an aspect of your life that could benefit from an infusion of spirit and more hope? Ask your heart for guidance. Jot down what your heart intelligence says.

_____

_____

_____

_____

_____

_____

_____

Perhaps you are presently feeling more hopeful as a result of practicing the HeartMath tools. Has your perspective changed over the last six months? Jot down two of your most important changes in perception.

1. _____

   _____

   _____

2. _____

   _____

   _____

Follow Up Exercise—Bonus Insights

If you ever feel a little low or uninspired, let your heart pick you back up. Allow it to infuse you with spirit, and get back into the "spirit" of things—feeling more "spirited"—because your heart can lift your spirits.

In the depths of winter, I finally learned there was an invincible summer.

— *Albert Camus*

DAY 2

Today's Reading

In *The Hidden Power of the Heart*, Chapter 25, "Fulfillment," Sara Paddison shares with us the signs of global hope as fences come down around the world.

> There are signs of hope, even amidst the stress and distortion in the world. The iron curtain was an imposing barrier. It's come down. Yes, some ethnic groups are still squabbling over the spoils of victory. But they are also releasing the pent-up frustrations of many years and will eventually understand each other. A fence came down when two influential rival gangs saw each other as brothers instead of arch-enemies. A fence came down between science and religion with the new discoveries showing intelligent order at the beginning of creation. In the future, I do see people taking all their fences down.

> Within the template of the future would be a "World Understanding" based on truth being validated by one's own heart. The foundation, the bottom line, the basis of this understanding would be "love." It will be a coming together of science and religion in the holographic heart. If you were to ask a man or woman of the future, "What is religion?", they would look at you dumbfounded and say, "Why everything!" There wouldn't be the separation of religion and education, religion and science, or—you name it. Religion wouldn't be something you just did on Sunday because you go to church. Nor would it be blindly clinging to tradition in the name of trying to keep core values alive. It would be unnatural, absurd and impractical for religion, science, math and education not to join together for the betterment of all.

L ove is a powerful force that unites. Love doesn't discriminate, separate, judge, blame or compare. It just loves. Jot down your insights if you'd like.

_____

_____

_____

_____

Exercise

Life isn't about winning or losing. It truly is about how you play the game. Do you play from your heart? "Either you are loving people or you are not loving people—in the heart or out of the heart."

How can you possibly have all of the hope you need from just the head? The head will often set up road blocks. It can be self-negating, self-deprecating and self-judging. True hope springs from the well of the heart.

Hope is always knowing you can grab a HeartMath tool when you are faced with a challenge. Become so familiar with the tools that you know which ones work best for you in different situations. Let's review some of the tools on which you can always rely:

FREEZE-FRAME
Turn off the head processors, take a time-out from stressful feelings and gain clarity or solutions from the heart.

Appreciation
There's always something to appreciate in any situation. Remember, things could always be worse.

Compassion
Have compassion for yourself and others. Everyone is doing the best they can based on their life experiences. Everyone is learning and growing, and so are you.

Love

This is a powerful frequency that will cut through density and give you a more hopeful perspective.

If you are currently facing a difficult challenge or simply want more fulfillment, select a power tool and get a more hopeful perspective. Jot down your insights.

Follow Up Exercise—Bonus Insights

Remember, you can wake up every day to a day of adventure and new growth. Today, make an extra effort to feel the hope that resides within your heart. Jot down your observations before you retire tonight.

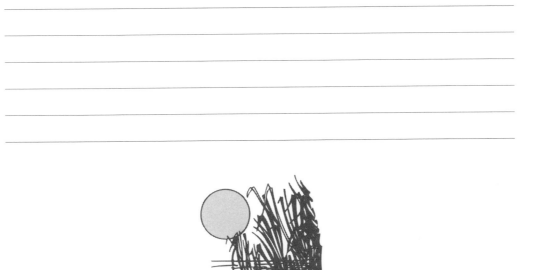

My trade and art is to live.

— *Montaigne*

Today's Reading

Continuing in *The Hidden Power of the Heart,* Chapter 25, "Fulfillment," we are reminded that sincere application of the power tools can bring more fulfillment.

> Practice having more efficiency with your vital energy. Practice seeing the difference between your head and your heart. Practice using the power tools in the traffic jams of life. This common-sense practice leads to self-management and self-empowerment. Then your fulfillment finds you. If you made a sincere effort to follow your heart directives every day, you'd magnetize transformation and all the fun "add-ons" in life.

> Add-ons are those extras in life that make it fun. They are the unexpected benefits that life brings you—in ways better than you would have imagined. They are what your deepest heart would enjoy. Add-ons accumulate in proportion to your ability to go to your core heart and make peace with yourself and life. Then life will make peace with you. By going for a more sincere, deeper love and care for every person, you magnetize the conveniences and add-ons from life.

The more you are in your heart, the more fun and fulfillment you will magnetize. Basically, you are one big magnet because of the electromagnetic field you generate. Your thoughts and feelings are the frequencies that comprise your electromagnetic field. Since like attracts like, it would be prudent to monitor your frequencies. Why not magnetize the fun stuff?

Jot down your insights about today's reading.

_____

_____

_____

_____

_____

Exercise

Life is a fun adventure when lived from the heart. A hopeful self is a mature and responsible adult and a spontaneous childlike spirit. By practicing energy efficiency we sustain hope. We are living the dimensional shift from head to heart.

Living life without heart contact keeps us stuck and depletes our vital energy. It's difficult to have hope when you're drained and exhausted. The heart, on the other hand, not only renews your spirit, it regenerates your system. If there are times when you might feel a little low or less hopeful, begin to care. Care is love in action. In the first place, it gets you out of yourself and removes you from that downward spiral. Secondly, as you know by now, it truly does feel good. And thirdly, it does regenerate your system.

We can always benefit from boosting our care up another notch. What can you do to add more care to your life by caring for others? Your care can give someone hope. Ask your heart for guidance.

Areas for More Care

_____

_____

_____

_____

Heart Intuition Response

_____

_____

_____

_____

_____

_____

Follow Up Exercise—Bonus Insights

Remember, life is an efficiency game. Invest your energy wisely—add to your energy bank account by living life from the heart. That way it's a lot easier to maintain a consistent energy level and maintain a hopeful perspective. Observe your energy expenditures today to see if you are earning any dividends. Jot down your observations before going to sleep tonight.

_____

_____

_____

_____

_____

_____

Life is short and we never have too much time for gladdening
the hearts of those who are traveling the dark journey with us.
Oh be swift to love, make haste to be kind.

— *Henri-Frederic Amiel*

DAY 4

Today's Reading

Concluding in *The Hidden Power of the Heart*, Chapter 25, "Fulfillment," Sara Paddison explains that the hope for humanity is in loving people.

As you practice loving each person you meet, you will perceive at deeper levels that Earth is all one family, a global family living in one back yard. The first step of the mathematical equation for fulfillment, one that anyone can do and understand, is to just love the people. The more people in this stressful world that can build this foundation and take Step 1, the better chance humanity has.

Our forefathers founded our nation on certain truths they considered to be self-evident: That all men are created equal, that they are endowed by their Creator with certain inalienable rights. That among these are life, liberty and the pursuit of happiness. Only a foundation of loving the people can bring this to fulfillment. "World Understanding" is the hope of the future—the hope of your next moment. It is the hope of Spirit. It doesn't matter if you believe in anything, if you don't think there is life after death, or if your views about the universe are different from what I've said. The only thing that truly matters is that you love your fellow beings—the whole human race. What would be the first amendment of the constitution of the future, one that would unite religion, science, government, medicine, education? Love People! When all is said and done, what's left is the heart.

The most important thing we can do for ourselves and the planet is just love people—all people. The more people you love, the more hope there will be—for love gives birth to hope.

What Sara has said is simple and yes, it has been said by others, but it still warrants deep consideration. Jot down your insights if you'd like.

_____

_____

_____

Exercise

Are there days when you still have trouble loving all the people? What is preventing you from giving this gift to everyone you meet? Ask your heart for understanding and how you can be more loving. Sometimes we have difficulty loving the ones we are closest with—our spouse, children, parents, etc. Perhaps it's because we have expectations and agendas for them and when they don't meet them, we sometimes withdraw our love. Our feelings get hurt, we become disappointed, etc. These might be times when we have allowed our overcare to interfere with our ability to love and allow, just the way that you would want to be treated.

Then there are occasions when we cut off our love from people who think or act differently from us. That's the head separating, judging and comparing, rather than the heart which would appreciate the differences. Negative reactions don't offer much hope to others and become a no-win situation. You're paying taxes by not being in your heart and you're also depriving others of the gift of your love.

So, do a Heart Lock-In. Just relax and ask your heart what might be left that is blocking you from loving all the people all the time. Ask for understanding to help you sincerely love people. The blocks can range from mind-sets, misperceptions, past hurts, fear of vulnerability, etc. Compassion and under-standing for yourself can help you move beyond them and into love. Jot down your insights.

Blocks to Love

_____

_____

_____

_____

_____

Heart Intuition Response

_____

_____

_____

_____

_____

Follow Up Exercise—Bonus Insights

Today is a good day to sincerely practice loving all people—no matter who they are—regardless of whether you have a history with them or even know them at all. Just keep loving.

> To finish the moment, to find the journey's end in every step
> of the road, to live the greatest number of good hours, in wisdom.
>
> — *Emerson*

DAY (5)

Today's Reading

In *Self Empowerment*, Chapter 10, "Summary: Important Points to Remember and Practice," Doc Lew Childre emphasizes the importance of care and the value of taking a serious look at it.

Caring more sincerely will help to regenerate all people systems. It's a recipe for productive living that is yet to be taken seriously by most people. If it seems like a long-range plan, then realize there are no short-range plans to bail out planetary stress. Care oils your system and prevents spark-knocks and friction. It's the most efficient cosmetic that you may ever invest in.

Something to Ponder Today

Humanity is only at the surface level of understanding the transformative energy of care and love. It's like lifting weights. If you practice loving more, then your heart power can develop to the level of producing self-empowerment. Everything else has been tried but love, so take advantage of the opportunity to dust off the ol' heart and love more. It adds refreshment to life, and youth to age. *Just Love People More* or *"Love Ye One Another"* and *see what results from this*. These are statements of energy economy, not religious platitudes or unapproachable idealisms. They are advanced mathematical equations for planetary transformation. The proof is in doing. The results of deeper love and care will find you more quickly if you don't constantly look over your shoulder to see if the flower you planted is growing. You can change the world by managing yourself and building your capacity to Love.

Y ou are a part of the "mathematical equations for planetary transformation." As you know, an equation has an equal sign and you can find yourself on either side of that equal sign, either giving or receiving love. And since all people are equal, love all people equally. Your heart knows that.

Jot down your insights about Doc's statements.

_____

_____

_____

Exercise

So how energy efficient are you throughout your day? You know the most efficient way to manage your mental and emotional energies. You have the tools—put them in your tool chest. Better yet, put them in your hope chest. You have learned a system that can bring hope, peace, fun and fulfillment to life. Realize that you have a choice in every moment to be either in your head or your heart. Why not take the more hopeful perspective? Balance, harmonize and regenerate your systems—mental, emotional, physical—from the heart. You've come this far—why not go all the way? Make it your intention to live every day from the heart. You'll be way ahead in the game of life if you do.

Our six months are drawing to an end. You have invested your precious time and energy into this program. You can continue to reap big dividends from this investment if you remember to practice the HeartMath system. We hope you do!

Jot down the most significant insights you've gained as a source of inspiration to help you remember and practice.

Inspirational Insights

_____

_____

_____

_____

_____

_____

_____

_____

_____

_____

Also ponder on what you have gained from this experience. Think of where you were when you began this program and where you are today. Notice any differences in your life, your attitudes and responses to situations that are presented to you daily, and your level of peace and fulfillment? And, of course, how could we end without saying appreciate yourself, what you have learned and the changes you have made. We appreciate you!

Ponderances

_____

_____

_____

_____

_____

_____

Follow Up Exercise—Bonus Insights

This is it. Today is your graduation day. A celebration of the heart. Share your love, care and appreciation with others as you celebrate the power of your heart! And your assignment? Love The People. Take Care.

Certificate of Completion

Please verify that you have successfully completed the HeartMath Discovery Program so that we can issue your certificate of completion. Take a few minutes, fill out the program evaluation and mail it to us. You may want to do a Heart Lock-In or a FREEZE-FRAME before answering the questions. Your evaluation will be reviewed by the Institute of HeartMath and you will then receive a certificate of completion for HeartMath Discovery Program Level One issued by the Institute of HeartMath.

Certificate holders are entitled to receive a fifty dollar discount on any HeartMath seminar conducted at IHM's training and research facility within one year of the issue date of your certificate.

We want to get to know you...

(The answers to these questions will remain confidential and will only be used to help determine how HeartMath is benefiting people and how we can better serve others.)

HeartMath Discovery Program Level One Evaluation

Name:_____

Mailing Address: _____

City:_____State:_____Zip Code:_____

Date you started program: _____ Date you completed program: _____
                            Month/Year   Month/Year

I did this program with a HeartMath study group: Yes   No

1. How would you rate the effectiveness of FREEZE-FRAME for accessing your heart intelligence and shifting perspectives?

Not effective   1   2   3   4   5   Very Effective

2. How much has your stress decreased as a result of completing the HeartMath Discovery Program?

Very little   1   2   3   4   5   Significantly

3. How much do you enjoy and benefit from doing Heart Lock-Ins?

Very little   1   2   3   4   5   Very much

4. Rate your experience of increasing your ability to love yourself and others more as a result of this program. Please circle your response.

no increase   very little increase   some increase

substantial increase   major increase

5. What noticeable improvements if any did you see in the quality of your communication with others as a result of Month Three's study on deep heart listening and speaking your truth? Please circle your response.

no improvement   very little improvement   some improvement

substantial improvement   major improvement

6. In Month Three, Week Three, Intui-Technology, you were asked to consult with your heart and make a list of your real priorities. What were they?

A. _____

B. _____

C. _____

D. _____

E. _____

7. In Month Four, Week Two, you studied Self-Care. Please list three things you determined as important for your self care.

A. _____

B. _____

C. _____

8. What are the three most significant, inspirational insights you've gained from this program that will now be important in helping you remember to practice what you have learned?

A. _____

B. _____
_____
_____
_____

C. _____
_____
_____
_____

9. Briefly describe what you gained from your practice of more consciously applying appreciation in your life.

_____
_____
_____
_____
_____
_____
_____

10. Briefly describe intuition as you now understand it.

_____
_____
_____
_____
_____
_____
_____

11. Briefly describe "higher and lower heart frequencies" as you now understand them.

_____

_____

_____

_____

_____

_____

12. Let's say you had an argument with someone. You found yourself replaying the incident, thinking about what you could have done differently, what they said and so on. What tool/tools would you use to bring yourself back to balance in the heart and why?

_____

_____

_____

_____

_____

13. You find yourself with someone who is worrying about a situation that has no immediate solution. You see that they are in overcare. Briefly describe what you might say to them in an effort to help them get back to true, balanced care.

_____

_____

_____

_____

_____

14. In Month Six you learned about DNA Blueprints, Holographic Reality and co-creating your own reality with the power of the heart. Looking at your life before you started the program and now that you have completed the program, briefly describe your holographic reality before and after the HeartMath Discovery Program.

Before starting the program: _____

_____

_____

_____

After completing the program: _____

_____

_____

_____

15. What are the three most significant concepts or tools you gained from completing the HeartMath Discovery Program?

A. _____

_____

_____

B. _____

_____

_____

C. _____

_____

_____

16. How would you rate the HeartMath Discovery Program?

Poor   1   2   3   4   5   Excellent

17. How would you rate the HeartMath Discovery Program book and daily lessons?

Poor   1   2   3   4   5   Excellent

18. How would you rate the HeartMath Discovery Program audio tapes?

Poor   1   2   3   4   5   Excellent

19. What if any improvements would you recommend for the HeartMath Discovery Program? Please describe.

_____

_____

_____

_____

_____

_____

_____

20. What additional comments about the HeartMath Discovery Program do you have?

_____

_____

_____

_____

_____

_____

_____

_____

_____

The following questions are optional. The information you provide will be helpful to the Institute of HeartMath and Planetary in our efforts to better understand the people who are our friends and customers and so we can be of more help to others in the future.

1. How did you first hear about HeartMath?

_____

_____

_____

_____

2. Gender:

Female   Male

3. Ethnic Background:

Caucasian   African American   Asian American

Hispanic   Other

4. Into which age category do you fall?

18-21   21-30   31-40   41-50

51-60   61-70   71+

5. What is your current relationship status?

Married   Single   Separated

Divorced   Significant other

6. Do you have children?

Yes   No   If so, how many? _____

7. Into which of the following categories does your estimated household income fall?

$20,000-$30,000 $31,000-$40,000 $41,000-$50,000

$51,000-$60,000 $61,000-$70,000 $71,000-$80,000

$81,000-$90,000 $100,000-$125,000 $126,000-$150,000

$150,000+

8. What was the last year of school you had an opportunity to complete?

High school   Two Year College   Four Year College

Masters   Doctorate   Additional Degrees

Other

9. How would you describe your current occupation?

Homemaker

Clerical

Professional (Legal, medical, etc.)

Middle Management

Blue Collar

Skilled Trades

Educator

Executive Management

Small-business owner

Service-oriented

Retired

Other (please specify) _____

10. What other learning programs, seminars, tapes, etc. have you used to improve yourself mentally, emotionally or physically? Please list.

_____

_____

_____

_____

Thanks. Please return to:

        Planetary, LLC

        Attention: Howard Martin

        P.O. Box 66

        Boulder Creek, CA 95006

Next Steps

Congratulations on completing the HeartMath Discovery Program Level One. You've done good work and have greatly expanded your understanding of the power and intelligence of the heart.

The most important next step you can take is to continue to actualize what you have learned. Use the tools with sincerity and consistency. They will continue to unfold new gifts.

We'd also like you to further your study of the HeartMath System. There are two primary ways to do this. First, you can obtain the HeartMath Discovery Program Level Two from Planetary—Publishers of the HeartMath System. This program will give you six more months of daily lessons with accompanying tapes that will deepen your understanding and application of heart intelligence. You can also contact Planetary for a complete catalog of other HeartMath System products. (See page 392)

Secondly, attend a HeartMath seminar. HeartMath seminars are held ongoing at the Institute of HeartMath's training and research facility in Boulder Creek, California as well as in selected cities around the world. Attending a HeartMath seminar is an experience unlike any other and would be one of the greatest gifts you could give yourself. HeartMath offers programs on personal development, business, health, women's leadership, parenting and education. You can contact HeartMath, LLC to obtain program information and a complete schedule of available seminars. (See page 391)

And lastly, you can contact the Institute of HeartMath (IHM) and participate in their volunteer and donor programs. The Institute is a nonprofit organization which conducts scientific research, capital campaigns and the administration of HeartMath Hub programs. The gifts and skills that you can provide will make a valuable contribution to furthering IHM's research initiatives and help to inform others about the benefits the HeartMath System provides for improving the quality of life world-wide. (See page 390)

The Institute of HeartMath

You can contact the Institute of HeartMath (IHM) to start or participate in small study groups (Hub groups) in your area. IHM is a nonprofit organization which conducts scientific research, capital campaigns and the administration of HeartMath Hub programs.

IHM, founded in 1991, specializes in leading-edge research showing the relationship between the heart, mental/emotional balance, cardiovascular function, and hormonal and immune system health. IHM's research has been published in many scientific journals, including *The American Journal of Cardiology* and the *Journal of Stress Medicine*.

For more information on our research, case studies, Hub groups or volunteer programs:
- Call 408-338-8500
- Visit our web site:
  http://www.heartmath.org
- Write:
  Institute of HeartMath
  PO Box 1463
  Boulder Creek, CA 95006

The HeartMath Experience . . . Retreats and Training Programs

Individuals from all walks of life interested in personal growth and professional advancement are integrating HeartMath into their lives. These popular training programs are conducted in a variety of social contexts including health care organizations, education, parenting and child development, Fortune 500 companies, personal growth organizations and government agencies.

HeartMath training programs are either held at the IHM training and research facility in Boulder Creek, California or at our customers' sites around the world.

For more information on trainings and seminars:
- Call 1-800-450-9111
- Visit our web site:
  http://www.heartmath.com
- Write:
  HeartMath, LLC
  14700 West Park Avenue
  Boulder Creek, CA 95006

Continue Exploring the HeartMath System

The HeartMath System, developed by Doc Childre, provides simple, proven techniques to help people manage mental and emotional responses to life through the natural common-sense intelligence of their own hearts. Explore and experience more of the HeartMath System with books, music, audio tapes and learning programs. These items, created with care, are rich in content, original thinking and exciting potentials!

To order or request a free catalog:
- Call 1-800-372-3100
- Visit our web site:
  http://www.planetarypub.com
- Write:
  Planetary Publications
  PO Box 66
  Boulder Creek, CA 95006

HeartMath Books and Learning Programs
Continue to discover the power within your own heart!

Books by Doc Lew Childre:
FREEZE-FRAME: Fast Action Stress Relief
CUT-THRU: Achieve Total Security and Maximum Energy
Self Empowerment: The Heart Approach to Stress Management
Teaching Children to Love: 80 Games and Fun Activities
A Parenting Manual: Heart Hope for the Family

Other Books:
The Hidden Power of the Heart: Achieving Balance and Fulfillment in a Stressful World, by Sara Paddison
IHM Research Overview, by Rollin McCraty
Meditating with Children, by Deborah Rozman, PhD

Books on Tape:
FREEZE-FRAME
CUT-THRU

Activity Tapes for Kids:
Buddy Bubbles (Ages 2-8) by Deborah Rozman, PhD and Doc Lew Childre
Heart Signals (Ages 8-14) by Doc Lew Childre and Howard Martin

Scientifically Designed Music by Doc Lew Childre:
Heart Zones: Music Proven to Boost Vitality (Cassette or CD)
Speed of Balance: A Musical Adventure for Emotional & Mental Regeneration (Cassette or CD)

Personal Learning Programs:
(Includes learning guide with books and/or tapes)

Freeze-Frame Inner Fitness System
Freeze-Frame Learning Program w/book or audiobook
Cut-Thru Learning Program w/ book or audiobook
Kids' Power Pak
HeartMath Discovery Program
Exploration of the Heart
The HeartMath Collection

To order or request a free catalog:
- Call 1-800-372-3100
- Visit our web site:
  http://www.planetarypub.com
- Write:
  Planetary Publications
  PO Box 66
  Boulder Creek, CA 95006